# Gladiators

*For all of my family, friends, and colleagues who've provided encouragement and support for this project. Special thanks to Don Gill and his photographic expertise.*

# Gladiators

## Deadly Arena Sports of Ancient Rome

Christopher Epplett

Skyhorse Publishing

# Contents

# List of Plates

# Select Glossary

*Aedile (pl. aediles)* – Roman official whose chief duties included supervision of public games, as well as the maintenance of streets and public buildings.

*Censor (pl. censores)* – Roman official whose chief responsibilities were to conduct a periodic census of the Roman population and to oversee the membership of the Senate.

*Cochlea (pl. cochleae)* – Apparatus consisting of panels fitted to a central rotating pole which was periodically used in animal spectacles, particularly during the later Empire.

*Consul (pl. consules)* – Chief magistrate of the Roman state during the Republic. Like other Republican magistracies, continued in existence under the Empire.

*Damnatio ad Bestias* – 'Condemnation to the beasts'. Common form of capital punishment in Rome.

*Damnatio ad Ludos* – 'Condemnation to the games'. Another form of punishment under Roman law. Unlike *damnatio ad bestias*, however, those condemned to fight as gladiators or *venatores* by this sentence at least had a fighting chance to earn their freedom someday.

*Editor (pl. editores)* – The official or private citizen who staged a given spectacle.

*Familia (pl. familiae)* – Group of arena performers overseen by a *lanista* which could be hired out for various spectacles. Prominent officials (including the emperor himself) or wealthy citizens commonly owned such groups for use in the events they staged.

*Infamia* – Loss of status and citizen rights suffered by gladiators and other arena performers.

*Lanista (pl. lanistae)* – Term commonly used for trainers of gladiators and/ or managers of arena training schools.

*Ludus (pl. ludi)* – Term used, first of all, for the state festivals in Rome (e.g., *Ludi Romani* / the Roman Games). Term also used to denote arena training schools such as the *Ludus Magnus*, the chief gladiatorial training venue in the city of Rome.

*Munus (pl. munera)* – Common term used for an arena spectacle.

*Noxius (pl. noxii)* – Term commonly used for the condemned criminals forced to participate in arena spectacles.

*Naumachia (pl. naumachiae)* – A marine spectacle involving a staged naval combat.

*Palus (pl. pali)* – Term originally denoted the wooden stakes which gladiators commonly used when practicing their weapon strokes. By extension, also came to denote the different ranks of gladiators within a *familia* (e.g., the highest rank was known as *primus palus* ('first stake')).

*Praetor (pl. praetores)* – Second highest magistracy in the Roman state under the Republic, primarily concerned with legal affairs.

*Summa/Secunda Rudis* ('first/ second stick') – Term used respectively for the senior and junior referees in a given gladiatorial *munus*. Arose from the long sticks which these officials carried in order to separate or otherwise discipline combatants.

*Tiro (pl. tirones)* – Term commonly used to denote a novice gladiator.

*Tribune* – Magistrate whose chief responsibility was to protect the interests and rights of the common people in Rome.

*Venatio (pl. venationes)* – Common term for animal spectacles in Rome, including both combat between men and animals and combat between animals alone.

*Vivarium (pl. vivaria)* – Generic term used for the enclosures in which various animals were kept.

# Introduction

Numerous works have been written upon the combat sports and spectacles of ancient Rome, events that are among the most famous manifestations of Roman culture. One might wonder, then, as to the need for another book on this topic. My intention is to write a survey of the Roman arena that I hope will be of interest to both a general and a scholarly audience. The two types of arena spectacles that will comprise the main focus of this book are gladiatorial events and staged beast hunts, commonly known as *venationes*. One very popular Roman sport which will not be discussed in any great detail is chariot racing, an event which, given its importance and popularity in Roman culture, merits its own detailed treatment. What sets my work on the Roman arena apart from those of many other scholars is, first of all, the attention I devote to the *venationes*. Many surveys of Roman arena spectacles focus primarily upon gladiatorial events and pay substantially less attention to the beast hunts, despite the fact that the latter spectacles were very popular in their own right, and were staged over a longer period. I will also discuss in some detail the all-important infrastructure behind the scenes that ensured the successful staging of untold numbers of both gladiatorial and animal spectacles throughout Roman territory over the course of centuries.

Fortunately, a wide variety of evidence is available to reconstruct the history of such events. First are the preserved writings of numerous Greek and Roman authors. Most such works do not take the spectacles as their focus of interest, but describe them in passing from time to time. The historians Livy and Tacitus, for example, who wrote annalistic histories of Republican and imperial Rome respectively, describe in the course of their works the noteworthy public events staged by various magistrates and emperors. Similarly, the voluminous correspondence of Cicero, one of the most important figures of the late Republic, occasionally touches upon contemporary spectacles in Rome or other topics pertaining to them.

One of our most important literary sources for the history of the Roman games is a small book of poems, *De Spectaculis* ('On the Spectacles') written by the poet Martial in the later first century AD. The subject of the poems is the dedication of the Colosseum, the most famous amphitheatre in the Roman Empire, in 79 AD, and the spectacles staged there by the emperors Titus and Domitian. Martial's work not only provides information on specific events staged in the course of these events, be they gladiatorial combat, *venationes*, or criminal executions, but also provides a vivid glimpse of the spectator reaction to them. As such, *De Spectaculis* is one of our most prominent primary sources demonstrating the importance of the arena and its associated spectacles in Roman society.

Literary works must always be used with some degree of caution, however, primarily because of potential bias or inaccuracy on the part of the author. An instructive example of just such a work is the so-called *Scriptores Historiae Augustae* (or SHA), a collection of biographies of Roman emperors from the second and third centuries. Among issues surrounding this work are the fabricated documents and persons inserted in the text by the author, which necessitate a cautious separation of fact from fiction by scholars.

Fortunately, another type of written evidence, epigraphy, is not as prone to problems of bias or inaccuracy. Inscriptions such as funerary epitaphs, for example, are normally contemporary with the events or persons to which they refer, unlike historical works that are commonly written decades or even centuries after the events they describe. In addition, inscriptions, in describing specific events or the careers of individuals, often provide specific details on various aspects of Roman spectacles that are comparatively overlooked in broader literary accounts. We shall see that epigraphy, for example, is particularly useful in reconstructing the infrastructure of the Roman games, something which writers like Livy tend not to discuss in any detail.

Other major sources of evidence when it comes to Roman arena spectacles are the surviving art and archaeological remains from that period. Among the most impressive examples of such physical evidence are the ruins of amphitheatres scattered throughout the territory of the former Roman

Empire. Such monuments, on a more general level, not only attest to the widespread popularity of Roman spectacles, but also, through their surviving architectural layouts, provide important evidence on more particular topics, such as the arrangement of spectator seating and the provisions for animal cages and other equipment in arena substructures.

The most important artistic evidence for the Roman spectacles comes to us from media such as relief sculpture and mosaics. In many cases, the events commemorated for posterity in such artwork are otherwise unattested, and these depictions therefore provide us with further important evidence of the spread and popularity of Roman spectacles. The inclusion of such visual details as the clothing and equipment of the performers is also of utmost importance in reconstructing the particulars of these events, providing us with information not found in written sources. Numerous hunting scenes from Roman mosaics also afford us a great deal of information on the infrastructure behind arena events, in particular the necessary capture and transport of wild animals prior to a given *venatio*. The most famous example is the massive 'Great Hunt' mosaic from a fourth century Roman villa in Sicily which depicts, albeit in a sometimes stylized fashion, the capture of animals from throughout Roman territory and their shipment to the port of Ostia.

Such are the many different types of evidence we can use to reconstruct the history and importance of arena spectacles in Roman society. A major part of my work will consist of tracing the development of gladiatorial events and *venationes* in Rome – from their inception during the Republic to their heyday in the high Empire. In the midst of this discussion, of course, a number of questions must be addressed. Why were the Roman games, which seem so reprehensible to many in the modern world, so popular among Roman spectators? Why did Roman magistrates and emperors go to the trouble of staging such expensive spectacles? What was in it for them? The social and propaganda roles of the Roman arena, as we shall see, were most important.

No account of Roman arena spectacles would be complete without a discussion of the veritable army of performers and specialists behind the scenes who ensured the successful production of countless spectacles over the course of centuries. Foremost among them, of course, are the trained gladiators and beastfighters who actually fought and died in the arena. As previously mentioned, however, such spectacles could not have been staged in the first place without the efforts of myriad support staff, ranging from the personnel of the training schools to the hunters who captured and shipped exotic animals from the frontiers of the Roman Empire.

My work concludes with an examination of the arena spectacles of the late Empire, and their gradual disappearance at a time when the state no longer had the requisite resources for such events. It is commonly claimed that the conversion of the Empire to Christianity in the fourth century spelled the end of gladiatorial contests, in particular, but as we shall see, the factors behind their disappearance, and that of the *venationes*, were not quite so straightforward as commonly assumed.

*Chapter One*

# Origins of Roman Arena Sports

A lthough the two most stereotypical Roman spectacles, gladiatorial contests and beast hunts (*venationes*) ultimately came to be staged in close association with one another, they each originated under decidedly separate circumstances. Due to the lack of relevant evidence, certain proposed aspects of their early development must remain conjectural, but enough does remain to suggest strongly that gladiatorial combat had a pronounced influence upon the later development of Roman animal spectacles.

Gladiatorial combats, or more broadly, publicly staged combats between armed fighters, were not a Roman invention – they appear to have originated elsewhere in Italy. Unfortunately, the evidence we possess on this point is contradictory: some suggests that such events originated among the Etruscans, the dominant civilization in northern and central Italy prior to the rise of Rome, while other evidence suggests that they may have arisen further south, in Campania. Evidence suggesting an Etruscan origin includes the ancient testimony of writers such as Nicolaus of Damascus in the early first century AD. He specifically states that the Etruscans bestowed the practice of gladiatorial combat upon the Romans. Also the term *lanista*, used in Latin to denote a trainer of gladiators, was originally an Etruscan word, at least according to the seventh century *Etymologiae* of Isidore of Seville.[1] Definite archaeological evidence for such a practice among the Etruscans, however, is lacking.

By contrast, we do possess some archaeological evidence for the emergence of gladiatorial combat in Campania, most notably tomb paintings from the late fourth century BC which depict, among other events, bloody duels between men armed with shields and spears. The later writers Livy and Silius Italicus claim that such contests were staged as entertainment at the banquets of the Campanian elite during this period.[2] Given such evidence, the majority of modern scholars favour a Campanian, as opposed to an Etruscan, origin for gladiatorial combat, despite the explicitly contrary testimony of Nicolaus of Damascus. In reference to the latter source, we shall see when we turn our attention to the origin of the *venationes* that it was not at all uncommon for ancient writers, in describing events occurring centuries before their own time, to ascribe an erroneous origin to customs such as gladiatorial combat.

The depiction of gladiatorial combats in Campanian tombs suggests that such events were among those staged in a funerary context so as to honour the deceased, and this assumption appears to be borne out by the first recorded gladiatorial exhibition in Rome. In 264 BC, Marcus and Decimus Brutus staged a combat between three pairs of gladiators in the Forum Boarium to honour their recently deceased father, Decimus Junius Brutus Pera.[3] The combatants honoured the deceased, in particular, through their display of courage and fighting skill, as well as the blood they spilled in his name. Significantly, the term used in Latin for such events was *munus* (*munera* in the plural) whose base meaning is 'duty' or 'obligation'. We can see, therefore, in the very terminology used for gladiatorial events, the sense of obligation which underlay them, whether it involved filial duty to a deceased relative, as in the case of the first recorded event, or the expectation on the part of the Roman populace that aspiring magistrates would stage such events to earn their political support, as we shall see in the case of the *munera* staged in the later Republic.

Following the spectacle of 264 BC, gladiatorial combat became an accepted component of the funerals of the elite in Rome. In fact, over the next few centuries, the scale of such events grew steadily, along with their popularity. In 216 BC, for example, the sons of Marcus Aemilius Lepidus staged combats in his honour featuring twenty-two pairs of gladiators fighting over a three-day period. The larger venue of the Forum Romanum was chosen for this as well as many subsequent *munera*, so as to provide more room for combatants and spectators alike. This extra space was certainly necessary: even a small sampling of such events over the next few decades will show how dramatically gladiatorial contests continued to grow. In 200 BC, the funeral games of Marcus Valerius Laevinus featured twenty-five pairs of gladiators, while only seventeen years later, sixty pairs of gladiators were requisitioned for the funeral of Publius Licinius.[4] Records of specific gladiatorial events for the subsequent century are not particularly abundant, in large part because of the loss of Livy's history for the period in question, but there is no doubt that they continued to grow steadily in both scale and popularity. In the *Hecyra*, produced in 165 BC, the Roman playwright Terence complained that contemporary drama placed a poor second to gladiatorial spectacles in terms of popularity.[5]

The link between gladiatorial *munera* and the honouring of a deceased Roman noble became ever more tenuous as these events grew in scale and popularity. Ambitious members of the Roman aristocracy, seeing the widespread popularity of gladiatorial events among the Roman populace, realized that they could greatly further their own popularity, as well as their political prospects, by staging such events. The one hindrance to staging gladiatorial exhibitions as a means of personal advancement, at least initially, was having enough deceased relatives to provide a pretext for their production. Therefore, as time went on, gladiatorial events gradually became dissociated from their funereal origins, so that the *editores* (those staging the spectacles) would have much greater freedom to present them whenever they saw fit. Nonetheless, even in the late Republic, it was sometimes considered politically expedient to stage *munera* under the pretense of filial piety, rather than as a blatant attempt to garner personal popularity. The most famous example of this political calculation occurred in 65 BC when Julius Caesar, as *aedile*, staged funerary games in honour of his deceased father including 320 pairs of gladiators. Caesar's father, it should be noted, had died over two decades previously, so it is certainly questionable whether any in the audience were taken in by this alleged show of filial piety. Given the popularity of gladiatorial *munera* by this time, however, it is doubtful whether many cared why Caesar had staged the event in question.[6]

The dramatic growth in scale of gladiatorial events in the final two centuries BC, as will be seen, had a significant impact upon contemporary *venationes*. The earliest animal displays in Rome, however, originally arose out of the widespread tradition of various rulers collecting, and often hunting, large numbers of beasts such as lions in order to demonstrate both their mastery over nature and their general worthiness to rule their respective states. In the Near East, this tradition can be traced back as early as the Bronze Age, in states such as Egypt, as well as the later Assyrian and Persian Empires. The large animal preserves, or *paradeisoi*, maintained by the Persian state made such an impression upon Alexander the Great and his army as they marched east in the fourth century BC that the Hellenistic states which arose in the wake of his conquests, such as Ptolemaic Egypt, came to develop their own animal preserves as a royal status symbol.[7]

It was these Hellenistic game parks, in turn, which prompted the development of Roman animal enclosures (*vivaria*) in the later Republic. As Rome began to encroach more and more upon the territories of the Hellenistic states in the second and first centuries BC, her troops encountered a number of these game parks in the course of their conquests. A number of the same members of the senatorial elite who led Rome's armies during this period, impressed by the enclosures they came across, later used their wealth to establish similar *vivaria* on the grounds of their estates. The aristocrat Lucullus, for example, (famous for his eastern campaigns against king Mithridates VI of Pontus in the early first century BC), later used his vast wealth to establish lavish animal enclosures and fish ponds on the grounds of his estates.[8] By this time, members of the elite like Lucullus had access to a relatively wide variety and number of animals with which to stock their game preserves, thanks to Roman conquests in areas like North Africa and Asia Minor.[9]

Like their game parks, the processions of exotic animals periodically staged by various Hellenistic monarchs, and in particular the Ptolemies, certainly had an influence upon Roman practice. The most famous such event was that staged by Ptolemy II in 275/74 BC, featuring hundreds of animals including antelopes, lions, cheetahs, Indian elephants, a rhinoceros, and a giraffe. Such was the size of this procession, in fact, that it was said to have taken an entire day to pass through the streets of Alexandria. One important aspect of this event, one that was not lost upon subsequent Roman *editores*, was that the animals included in a particular display could be carefully chosen so as to present propaganda claims to the assembled spectators. Ptolemy II advertised the extent of his domains to his subjects by including animals in his procession from different areas of his empire, as well as regions outside of it over which he wished, however tenuously, to claim ownership.[10]

The earliest recorded exotic animal displays in Rome took place in a somewhat different context from that of Ptolemy II: the elephants exhibited to the Roman populace in 275 and again in 250 BC had not been collected for a peacetime exhibition, but instead were spoils of war, captured from the forces of Pyrrhus and the Carthaginians respectively.[11] Nonetheless, like the beasts in Alexandria, they too advertised the power of the state that put them on display. The war elephants exhibited by the victorious Roman generals, Dentatus and Metellus, on these two occasions fit within the parameters of the parade of enemy prisoners which formed the centrepiece of the traditional Roman triumph.

In the decades following Metellus' triumph in 250 BC, exotic animal displays, in venues such as the Circus Maximus, appear to have become ever more popular spectator events in Rome. The plays of Plautus (c. 254–184 BC) suggest, in particular, that exhibitions of ostriches and other African animals had become a relatively common sight by the late third century BC. These early displays all appear to have been nonviolent; the earliest *venatio* or beast hunt, in fact, is said by Livy to have been staged by Marcus Fulvius Nobilior in 186 BC to celebrate his recent military victories against the Aetolian League in Greece.[12]

It is perhaps not surprising, given the general indebtedness of Roman culture to that of the Greeks and, more particularly, the evident influence of Hellenistic animal displays upon their Roman counterparts, that at least one ancient source claimed that the Roman *venationes* were similarly inspired by Greek precedent. A letter of the sixth century Ostrogothic king, Theodoric, claims that the Athenians invented this particular form of entertainment:

'Such a show, ennobled by its building, but most base in its performance, was invented in honour of the goddess Scythian Diana, who rejoiced in the spilling of blood. O the error, the wretched deceit, to desire to worship her who was placated by human death! The prayers of countrymen, made in woods and groves, and dedicated to hunting, first, and by a lying fantasy, formed this three-fold goddess: they asserted that she was the Moon in heaven, the Mistress [Diana] in the woods, Proserpine among the shades...This cruel game, this bloody pleasure, this – so to speak – human bestiality was first introduced into their civic cult by the Athenians. Divine justice allowed it, so that the invention of a false religion's vanity might be degraded by a public show.'[13]

There is, however, no other available evidence that corroborates Theodoric's claim concerning the origins of the *venationes*, written almost a millennium after the first such event was staged by Nobilior. We know, certainly, that exhibitions of trained animals like bears and lions had taken place in city-states such as Athens as early as the fourth century BC, but these spectacles do not appear to have been at all similar to the later Roman beast hunts.[14]

Roman *venationes*, rather, appear to have evolved out of earlier nonviolent animal displays. One might certainly ask what prompted Nobilior in the early second century BC to introduce a violent element for the first time into what had previously been nonviolent events. One possibility, at least in theory, is that elements of contemporary hunting were added to animal displays in order to create a more exciting spectacle. The problem with this theory, however, is that hunting does not appear to have originally been a particularly esteemed activity among the Roman elite, as compared to the aristocracy of other states like Macedonia. In fact, it was the conqueror of Macedonia, Aemilius Paullus, who was the first Roman aristocrat credited with a keen interest in hunting.[15] Since Paullus' career post-dated the spectacle of Nobilior, it does not appear likely, therefore, that the hunting practices of the Roman elite were an important influence in the decision to stage the first *venatio* in Rome.

Another possibility is that Roman beast hunts arose out of preexisting traditions in Italy of slaughtering animals as part of a public spectacle. The most famous archaeological evidence for such a practice comes from the Etruscan Tomb of the Augurs, dating to the late sixth century BC, which depicts a hooded man in combat with what appears to be a dog. A now destroyed Oscan tomb painting from the fourth century BC also is said to have depicted a group of men fighting against a lion.[16] Taken together, this admittedly limited evidence suggests that both the Etruscans and Samnites may have staged some sort of animal combats, at least on occasion. Animal slaughter was also part of archaic Roman religious rituals such as the *ludi Florales*, in which deer and hares were hunted in the Circus Maximus. It is certainly questionable, however, how much influence these earlier events may have had upon later Roman *venationes*, given the apparent difference in scale and variety of animals between them. At most, events like the *ludi Florales* may have helped to acclimatize urban spectators to the slaughter of animals in venues like the Circus Maximus.[17]

The main factor, seemingly, behind the introduction of violence into Roman animal spectacles was the influence exerted upon them by contemporary gladiatorial events. We have already noted in passing the dramatic growth in the latter, beginning in the late third century BC, which, according to Kyle, was initially prompted by the disastrous Roman defeat at the Battle of Cannae in 216 BC. The enormity of this debacle was such a shock to the Roman populace that magistrates staging gladiatorial *munera* thereafter sought to reassure spectators by forcing an increasing number of prisoners-of-war to participate in them; on a symbolic level, at least, the enforced slaughter of Rome's enemies in the arena provided some retribution for the thousands of legionaries killed at Cannae.[18]

Regardless of the psychological effects of the gladiatorial *munera* staged in the aftermath of Cannae, it is obvious that Roman spectators thoroughly enjoyed the increasing scale and bloodshed of such events. The popular demand for gladiatorial entertainment became so great, as we shall see, that Roman magistrates and political leaders staged larger and larger spectacles throughout the remainder of the Republic in order to keep their audiences satisfied. Given the growing popularity of violent gladiatorial spectacles, it is not surprising that contemporary animal spectacles were adapted to suit this Roman fondness for violent entertainment. By the time Nobilior staged the first recorded *venatio* in 186 BC, thirty years after Cannae, gladiatorial spectacles involving dozens of participants were already commonplace in Rome. Nonviolent animal displays no doubt appeared comparatively dull by comparison, which is evidently why Nobilior decided to introduce a violent element (combat between lions and leopards) into his own animal spectacle.[19] The subsequent growth in scale of the *venationes*, which paralleled that of contemporary gladiatorial events, certainly indicates that Nobilior correctly assessed the tastes of the Roman populace.

Such was the popularity of his *venatio*, in fact, that the Senate, evidently concerned with one of its members elevating himself above his peers through such means, introduced a ban on the importation of African felines in 186 BC, the very year of Nobilior's spectacle. The significance of this ban is that, in all likelihood, North Africa was the primary source of the lions and leopards used for the event in question. Despite this ban, however, a number of other prominent political leaders evidently staged (or attempted to stage) even more elaborate *venationes* soon thereafter, presumably by importing wild animals from other regions currently under Roman control, such as Asia Minor. In the cutthroat struggle for political power between members of the Roman elite, Nobilior's rivals could not allow his elevation in the public eye through such a lavish display to go unchallenged. The Senate was so concerned about this development that in 179 BC, only seven years after Nobilior's *venatio*, it decreed that no one could spend more on games than he had. The Senate's attempts to curb the production of ever more lavish animal spectacles, however, were not overly successful. The ban on the importation of African felines, for example, was overturned by one of the Roman tribunes, Gaius Aufidius, in 170 BC.[20] The fact that a tribune, who traditionally defended the interests of the Roman people, attacked this particular legislation is probably yet another indication of the popularity *venationes* had achieved within the Roman populace by that date.

Such was the popularity of both gladiatorial and animal events at this juncture that the Roman populace ultimately was not satisfied with occasional spectacles staged as part of a military triumph, or by pious relatives wishing to honour a deceased relative. We have already seen that ambitious members of the Roman aristocracy would exploit the popularity of arena events for the purposes of their own political advancement. By the late Republic, certainly, it was expected by the Roman public as a matter of course that their magistrates, or prospective magistrates, would stage *munera* prior to an election or during their terms of office.

The *aediles* comprised a Roman magistracy often associated with the production of arena spectacles. One reason for the involvement of these particular magistrates in the *munera* was their previous role in organizing the much older *ludi*, or state religious festivals. Originally, it appears many gladiatorial and animal events were staged in close association with such *ludi*, being carried out after the sacred portions of such festivals had been completed. In many cases, as we shall see, the *munera* were staged in the same *venues* as the contemporary *ludi*. The *aediles* were provided with funds from the state treasury, or *aerarium*, to facilitate the staging of such events; as gladiatorial and animal spectacles became more and more popular, however, politically ambitious *aediles* would often supplement these state funds with their own personal wealth in order to produce as impressive a *munus* as possible, and thereby increase their standing with Roman voters.[21]

Gaps in the historical record for the period under discussion preclude knowledge of all of the *munera* staged during the later Republic. Nonetheless, to judge from the testimony of the Roman playwright Plautus, the *aediles* were producing various animal spectacles on at least a somewhat regular basis by the late third century BC: in particular, one of the characters in the *Poenulus* refers in passing to the *aediles* bringing animals to Rome for such events, in a manner which suggests the involvement of these magistrates in the *munera* was a common occurrence, even at this relatively early date. Certainly, many of the surviving records of Republican spectacles make specific mention of the *aediles* who organized them. In 169 BC, for example, the curule *aediles* Scipio Nasica and Lentulus are recorded as having staged an animal spectacle in the Circus Maximus, while in the late 90s BC, the *aedile* Marcus Livius Drusus, a man noted for his political ambition, staged a *munus* said to be particularly extravagant.[22]

An anecdote from roughly the same period further illustrates the political importance such events had achieved by the late Republic. According to Plutarch's biography of Sulla, one of the foremost Roman political figures in the early first century BC, the latter claimed to have lost his first bid for the praetorship, the second-highest magistracy in the Roman state, because he had tried to skip serving a term as *aedile* beforehand. The Roman public, not wishing to be cheated of a potential *munus* staged by Sulla as *aedile*, elected his opponent praetor instead. Plutarch does not regard this as the real reason why Sulla lost this particular election: nonetheless, the fact that such an explanation was regarded as plausible certainly suggests that the staging of *munera* was indispensable to an aspiring political leader's career in Rome at that time.[23]

The Roman magistrates staging such spectacles during the last two centuries of the Republic were clearly at pains to increase both the size and variety of events to maintain spectator interest. One particular innovation introduced at a relatively early date was the public execution of criminals by wild beasts. In 167 BC, Aemilius Paullus condemned deserters from the Roman army to be trampled to death by elephants, as part of the lavish festivities he sponsored to celebrate his recent victory over Macedonia. Some twenty years later, his son, Scipio Aemilianus, followed this precedent in his own games, staged to celebrate his victory over Carthage in the Third Punic War. Although such a spectacle may appear truly horrific from a modern perspective, Roman audiences had no such qualms about violent executions. Execution by various means, including crucifixion and burning at the stake, had long been an established punishment for serious offences under the Roman legal system. Staging such executions as spectacle not only allowed *editores* to provide relatively cheap entertainment, it also assured the assembled audience that Roman justice was being properly carried out. Subsequently, as we shall see, such staged executions became an integral aspect of the Roman arena and its ideology.[24]

The expansion of Roman territory in the second century BC was certainly an important factor in allowing Roman spectacle organizers to provide a greater number and variety of exotic animals for their audiences, as reflected in the relevant ancient sources. According to Pliny the Elder, for example, the first combat of a large group of lions in Rome was staged in 104 BC, while the first fight involving elephants occurred five years later. The first combat between elephants and bulls appears to have been staged in 78 BC. By the mid-first century BC, *venationes* involving over a hundred animals were evidently not uncommon. Such events, of course, were only a foreshadowing of the even more elaborate spectacles staged by Pompey and Caesar only a few years later.[25]

It is abundantly clear from the dramatic growth in scale of both gladiatorial and animal spectacles in the later Republic that Roman spectators, overall, had no moral objections to the slaughter they witnessed on the arena floor. As we shall discuss in detail in a subsequent chapter, the low social status enjoyed by human performers ensured that they would earn little sympathy from the spectators at a given event. The *munera*, however, were not just popular because they presented an exciting and guilt-free spectacle for the audience: arena spectacles were thought by many ancient writers to present tangible benefits to the assembled spectators. In the case of gladiatorial events, one such benefit was the fighting skills displayed on the arena floor. Not only could these combats serve as a constant reminder of Rome's martial past, which had won her an empire, but they could also serve as inspiration for contemporary Roman soldiers. In addition, the years of training and fighting undertaken by gladiators could provide an even more tangible benefit to Roman troops: in 105 BC, gladiatorial training methods were introduced into the Roman army to increase the already considerable fighting effectiveness of its soldiers.[26]

Some ancient commentators also noted the potential moral benefits of gladiatorial spectacles. Perhaps the most famous presentation of this viewpoint comes from the Stoic writer Seneca, who was active in the mid-first century AD. Like a number of other upper class commentators on the games, Seneca took issue with the unruly behaviour of the crowds that could be prompted by the spectacles they witnessed. Nonetheless, in his opinion, gladiators could provide an example of behaviour worthy of emulation, in particular the attitude that death was nothing to be feared. The examples which Seneca provided of gladiators who had sought death to escape their miserable lot in life, such as the man who had deliberately snapped his neck in a cart's wheel on the way to a *munus*, showed that nobility of spirit was not dependent upon one's social status: '... men will make greater demands upon themselves, if they see that death can be despised even by the most despised class of men.'[27]

A similar attitude was held with regard to the *venationes* and their participants. There was little sympathy for the animals slaughtered in the arena; it is important to note that there was nothing remotely similar to the modern animal-rights movement in ancient Greece and Rome. The Stoic view of nature, which was prevalent during this period, stressed the alleged gulf in reasoning between men and wild animals. Spectators sharing this doctrine could therefore witness the slaughter of what they saw as unreasoning beasts on the arena floor with a clear conscience. In fact, the beast hunts were commonly viewed as a demonstration of the superiority of skill and reasoning, as exemplified by the *venatores* (arena hunters), over brute force.[28]

One aspect of such *munera* often neglected to varying degrees in modern studies of the Roman spectacles is the organizational arrangements behind the scenes which ensured, *inter alia*, that the requisite animals and gladiators were successfully procured for a given show. As we shall see, an elaborate and highly organized infrastructure fulfilled this purpose under the Empire. The spectacles staged during the Republic, however, had no such organization supporting them; instead, the necessary arrangements for such events were decidedly more ad hoc in nature.

One of the most important sources of gladiators, particularly in the Republican period, were prisoners-of-war, who provided a particularly inexpensive supply of labour for the arena: the very first gladiatorial *munus* of 264 BC, in fact, featured such participants. The steady expansion in the size and scale of gladiatorial *munera* over the second century BC was certainly facilitated by the thousands of military captives brought back to Italy in the aftermath of successful campaigns against such states as Carthage and Macedonia during this period. It is no coincidence that victorious generals like Paullus or their relatives, who had ready access to these prisoners, staged many of the recorded gladiatorial spectacles of the mid-to-late Republic.

Similarly, as already noted, the expansion of Roman territory into areas such as North Africa and the eastern Mediterranean during this period also gave the Romans greater access to the requisite animals for contemporary animal spectacles, in particular exotic specimens like lions, elephants, and leopards. Unfortunately, in most cases little, if anything, is known of the specific means by which the animals appearing in various events were captured and brought to Rome. The record of Metellus' exhibition of captured war-elephants in 250 BC, however, suggests how rudimentary the transport arrangements for animals could be at this early date: Metellus, in fact, was forced to build a temporary pontoon bridge so that his elephants could safely cross over the Strait of Messina between Sicily and mainland Italy.[29] As we shall see, this is in decided contrast to later animal events, when spectacle organizers could have specialized animal transport at their disposal.

Not all arena performers during the Republic – human or animal – were procured by military victories. As Roman territory expanded throughout the Mediterranean basin during this period, Italian merchants and traders were not slow to exploit new overseas markets. Amongst the many commodities they shipped back to Italy were slaves, who, as we shall see, were condemned to the arena on occasion, and exotic animals. It is conceivable, in fact, that at least some of the Italian merchants massacred in the Numidian city of Cirta in 106 BC were involved in the lucrative business of shipping exotic animals from North Africa to Italy.[30]

Certainly, the animal trade between North Africa and Rome was well established by this date. Over the course of the second century BC, so many animals were imported from this region for various spectacles that the term *Africanae* could be used as a euphemism for arena beasts, in particular felines like lions or leopards. Even before Nobilior's *venatio* of 186 BC, which, as we have seen, appears to have featured African animals, the Roman playwright Plautus could make a joking reference to *mures Africanos* ('African mice') being brought to Rome by the *aediles* for the spectacles.[31] Similarly, Livy records that sixty-three *Africanae* (most likely lions), along with forty bears and an unspecified number of elephants, appeared in a spectacle staged in 169 BC.[32]

One possible specific example of the business interests involved in the animal trade during this period concerns the family of the Aufidii. As we have already seen, it was one member of this family, the tribune Gnaeus Aufidius, who was responsible for overturning the Senate's ban on the importation of African animals to Rome in 170 BC. Certainly, given the apparent popularity of animal spectacles at the time, there was some political calculation on the part of Aufidius when he took this action. There is evidence to suggest, however, that Aufidius may also have been at least partly motivated by profit considerations. In the late Republic and Empire, the Aufidii are known to have possessed considerable business interests in North Africa, including the shipment of grain, and possibly exotic animals, to Italy. If at least some of these business interests were already present in the early second century BC, then it is certainly possible that Gnaeus Aufidius was interested in both his own political advancement and his family's wealth when he struck down the senatorial ban.[33]

Roman *editores* in the later Republic could also use their political influence to procure the requisite paraphernalia for a given spectacle from their clients overseas. It has been suggested, for example, that Scipio Nasica, one of the *curule aediles* responsible for staging an animal spectacle in 169 BC, used his family's pre-existing ties with Numidian royalty to obtain at least some of the

African fauna which featured in the event. Later, the Roman populace expected that Sulla would exploit his friendship with King Bocchus of Mauretania to procure magnificent Libyan animals for a *venatio* in Rome.[34] It should be noted, of course, that spectacle organizers did not just obtain exotic animals through such channels. In a number of recorded *munera*, for example, Roman *editores* also obtained native African hunters from their foreign contacts. Presumably, using hunters with prior experience in fighting various exotic animals, rather than Italian hunters unfamiliar with animals such as lions, would ensure a more entertaining spectacle for the audience in Rome.[35]

One of the most important examples of Roman magistrates in the late Republic using (or attempting to use) their political contacts to ensure a successful spectacle comes from the correspondence of Cicero, one of the foremost political figures in Rome during this period. In this particular instance, a certain Marcus Caelius Rufus, running for the aedileship in 51 BC, wrote a series of letters to Cicero in preparation for the *venatio* that he was expected to stage if elected. The reason why Caelius wrote to Cicero was that the latter was currently the Roman governor of Cilicia, in modern-day Turkey, a region that in antiquity possessed a relatively large population of wild animals like leopards that could be used in arena spectacles.

Beginning in June of 51 BC, Caelius wrote a series of letters to Cicero requesting leopards for his anticipated *munus* in Rome, letters that became increasingly strident as the animals failed to materialize. Two letters sent to Cicero in the autumn of 51 BC are particularly instructive:

'... Curio treats me generously, and by his bounty has put a burden on my back; for had he not made me a present of the wild beasts which had been shipped to him from Africa for his games, my games might have been altogether dispensed with; as it is, since give them I must, I should be glad if you would take the trouble–I have been perpetually asking you this favour–to let me have something in the way of beasts from where you are.[36]

In almost all my letters to you I have mentioned the panthers. That Patiscus has sent Curio ten panthers and that you should have failed to send ever so many more, will reflect no credit upon you ... If you only remember to do so ... you will accomplish all you [!] want.'[37]

The Curio mentioned in both of these letters is a certain Gaius Curio, who was collecting his own animals for the tribunician games of 50 BC, and had apparently promised some of his surplus animals to Caelius. Evidently, the latter expected the same generous gift of Cilician fauna from Cicero. The Patiscus mentioned in the second letter is an even more interesting figure, in terms of the infrastructure behind the Roman *munera*. Not only had he been involved in capturing animals for Curio, but we also learn from a subsequent letter, written by Cicero in the spring of 50 BC, that Patiscus had subsequently travelled to Cilicia to capture leopards.[38] As mentioned earlier, very little is known about the infrastructure which supported the *munera*, particularly in the Republican period, and Patiscus is one of the few individuals known by name who evidently made a living, along with the hunters undoubtedly in his employ, supplying animals to various Roman clients for their spectacles. Given the growth in the *venationes* over the final two centuries of the Republic, there must have been many other contemporary groups of anonymous hunters throughout Roman territory who made their living in a similar fashion.

Such was the demand for exotic animals at this time that Caelius, as it turns out, was not the only Roman magistrate pestering Cicero for leopards during his governorship of Cilicia. A certain Octavius, who was also running for *aedile* in 51 BC (and would end up being Caelius' colleague as *aedile* the following year), also wrote to Cicero requesting these animals for his own planned spectacle. It is clear from Cicero's own correspondence that, unsurprisingly, he viewed such repeated requests for exotic animals as a profound annoyance.[39]

The infrastructure behind Republican *munera*, as we have already seen to some extent, was decidedly ad hoc in nature, as compared to the elaborate organization dedicated to later imperial spectacles. Nonetheless, as the frequency and scale of arena spectacles increased in the later Republic, some elements of organization did gradually emerge. In describing the gladiatorial spectacle staged by Scipio Africanus in 206 BC, Livy mentions that the *lanistae*, or managers, did not procure the gladiators for this particular spectacle from the usual sources (slaves and free men who sold themselves to the arena). This particular passage, taken at face value, certainly suggests that there was a regularized trade in gladiators even at this relatively early date. It should be noted, however, that Livy, writing approximately 200 years after the event in question, might be guilty of anachronism, in projecting the gladiatorial organization of his own day upon an earlier period.[40]

Whether or not this particular anecdote is anachronistic, other evidence clearly indicates that the training of, and trade in gladiators became much more professionalized and organized over the course of the second century BC. By the end of the century, for example, we have specific mention of *ludi*, the term commonly used to denote gladiatorial training schools, as well as *doctores*, or trainers, affiliated with the gladiators. According to Valerius Maximus, in 105 BC, *doctores* from the *ludus* of Gaius Aurelius Scaurus provided weapons training for Roman legionaries, the first instance of such collaboration between gladiators and the military in Roman history.[41] As we shall see in a subsequent chapter, *doctores* were just one group of specialized personnel affiliated with the developed organization of the Roman *munera* under the Empire. If they were in existence by the end of the second century BC, we might infer that other specialist officials associated with the games were as well.

The aforementioned anecdote of Valerius Maximus, referring to the *doctores* and training school of Scaurus, also implies the contemporary existence of gladiatorial *familiae*, groups of gladiators and their requisite training and support personnel owned by wealthy Romans. As will be seen, much more is known about the *familiae* and their organization under the Empire, but it is clear nonetheless that such groups began to proliferate in the later Republic as contemporary *munera* continued to increase in size and scope. Under such circumstances, it was much easier for aspiring *editores* to either own their own troupes of gladiators, or hire such groups from one of their colleagues, rather than having to scour Roman territory to round up enough performers for a given spectacle.

The most famous of these gladiatorial *familiae* in the late Republic, arguably, was that owned by a certain Lentulus Batiatus. In 73 BC, about seventy members of this *familia*, under the leadership of a certain Spartacus, escaped from Batiatus' *ludus* in Capua. Like many of the gladiators employed by the Romans during the Republican period, Spartacus was a prisoner of war, evidently captured during fighting in northern Greece. The military experience and training possessed by Spartacus and many of his followers proved to be an extreme headache for the Roman government, because soon after their escape from the *ludus*, they were able to raise and train an army of some 70,000 disaffected slaves from the area around Capua. The forces of Spartacus, in fact, were able to inflict a number of humiliating defeats upon Roman forces, and march the length and breadth of Italy, before finally being defeated by the praetor Crassus in 71 BC. In the aftermath of this battle, 6,000 of Spartacus' troops are said to have been crucified along the Appian Way, the main road leading south from Rome to Capua, to discourage such revolts against Roman authority in future; Spartacus himself had died fighting in the final battle against Crassus, and was therefore spared this indignity.[42]

Just as the infrastructure behind the Roman games gradually evolved over time as they expanded in scope, so too did the venues in which they took place. The earliest gladiatorial and animal spectacles were staged in venues originally constructed for other purposes, but over the last two centuries of the Republic, the Romans moved towards building or adapting structures specifically for the *munera*. The first recorded gladiatorial spectacle of 264 BC was staged in the level, open space of the Forum Boarium, the cattle market of ancient Rome, but as these events came to include more and more gladiators, they were moved to the much larger Forum Romanum in the heart of the city. The main amenity for spectators at this location was the *maenianum*, a wooden viewing balcony extending out from the upper floors of the buildings that surrounded the open centre of the Forum Romanum on three sides. The exact date when the *maeniana* were first constructed is not certain, but they appear to have been in place by 184 BC at the latest.[43]

The earliest exotic animal spectacles and *venationes* were staged in the Circus Maximus, the chariot-racing venue in the heart of Rome which, according to Roman tradition, had first been laid out even prior to the fall of the monarchy in 509 BC. By the first century AD, it contained seating for as many as 250,000 spectators. Such a massive facility, with a track measuring approximately 620m by 120m, was ideally suited to whatever type of animal displays Roman magistrates might wish to stage. Even prior to the emergence of the *venationes*, archaic religious rituals, such as the burning of foxes during the *Ludi Cereales*, or the hunting of deer and hares during the *Ludi Florales*, were staged in the Circus Maximus.[44]

As mentioned earlier, the plays of Plautus provide ample evidence that various African animals, presumably obtained as a result of Rome's recent victory over Carthage in the Second Punic War, were displayed in the Circus Maximus. The following exchange from his *Persa*, produced around 195 BC, is particularly instructive:

'Toxilus: Do carry this out carefully. Fly running. (*Vola curriculo.*)
Paegnium: That's what an ostrich does in the circus. (*Istuc marinus passer per circum solet.*)'[45]

To judge from the passage in question, even at such an early date, the exhibition of ostriches in the Circus Maximus, in particular, had become so common as to be almost proverbial.

As in the case of the Forum Romanum, alterations were made to the Circus Maximus to accommodate the new type of spectacle that was staged there. In the case of exotic animal displays, particularly those featuring potentially dangerous animals like lions, arrangements had to be made to store the beasts prior to their appearance and to protect the assembled spectators. The earliest of these alterations took place in 174 BC, when the censors of that year had iron animal cages built in the Circus Maximus. Incidentally, this particular construction project indicates that animal displays were still going strong in Rome at the time, despite the previously discussed senatorial ban on the importation of African animals that was still in effect. A little over a century later, as we shall see, both Pompey and Julius Caesar installed different types of barriers around the track of the Circus Maximus to protect spectators from the hundreds of animals they had each collected for their respective events.

The stereotypical venue for Roman *munera* was, of course, the amphitheatre, the most famous example of which is the Colosseum in Rome. The earliest preserved stone amphitheatre, however, constructed in approximately 70 BC, comes not from Rome, but from Pompeii in Campania. Many earlier scholars took this fact as further evidence that gladiatorial combat originated in southern Italy, the idea being that the Romans borrowed not only the spectacle itself, but also the venue best suited to accommodate it, from the Campanians. On the face of it, however, it does appear somewhat odd, if the Romans did indeed borrow the architectural layout of the amphitheatre from the Campanians, that the earliest known amphitheatre in the region was constructed almost 200 years after the first recorded gladiatorial spectacle in Rome (264 BC).

It has recently been argued that amphitheatres spread from Rome to Campania, rather than vice versa. First, it should be noted that the amphitheatre in Pompeii was built in the aftermath of a bitter civil war in Italy between forces loyal to Sulla and those loyal to his former political rival, Marius. After his victory in this conflict, Sulla established colonies of his veterans throughout Italy, primarily intended to ensure the future loyalty of communities like Pompeii that had not previously supported Sulla. The dedicatory inscription of the amphitheatre in Pompeii specifically states, in fact, that it was erected for the pleasure of the Sullan colonists: no mention is made of the native inhabitants of the city.[46]

Although no physical traces remain in Rome of buildings that might have provided a prototype for the amphitheatre in Pompeii, the relevant literary sources certainly suggest the Romans were experimenting with such structures no later than the early second century BC. No permanent spectator venues were built in Rome prior to the Theatre of Pompey in 55 BC, in large part because of a longstanding senatorial ban on the building of such structures during the Republic. It is nonetheless clear, however, that the Roman magistrates staging various *ludi* and *munera* before that date built a number of temporary structures to accommodate both spectators and performers. In 56 BC, for example, the *aedile* Scaurus built a magnificent wooden theatre, in which, *inter alia*, he exhibited the leopards and other animals he had collected for his games. A few years later, in 52 BC, the tribune Curio was credited with building an elaborate theatre-amphitheatre: the innovation of this particular structure lay in the fact that its two semicircular theatre halves could be rotated on an axis and connected to form an amphitheatre.[47]

It is important to note that the oval shape of early amphitheatres did not arise by chance, but in large part appears to have been determined by the shape of the Forum Romanum, the location where many gladiatorial *munera* of the late Republic were staged. An oval-shaped structure, in fact, provided the ideal area within the trapezoidal centre of the forum for spectators and performers alike. As noted in a recent study, the arena of the amphitheatre at Pompeii, if transposed upon the Forum Romanum, would not only fit neatly within the available space, but would also allow surrounding seating for some 10–15,000 spectators.[48] Given the evidence, it does indeed seem likely that the stone amphitheatre at Pompeii, as well as subsequent amphitheatres built throughout Roman territory, took their inspiration from the now vanished spectacle venues of Republican Rome.

The amphitheatre at Pompeii was just one manifestation of the spread of the Roman *munera* outside Rome itself. By the first century BC, in fact, such events were not only found in various towns throughout peninsular Italy, but had also begun to spread throughout the wider Mediterranean basin. One of the earliest manifestations of the latter phenomenon is the gladiatorial event in Cartagena, Spain, which the Roman general Scipio Africanus staged in 206 BC, during the Second Punic War, to commemorate his father and uncle, who had been killed earlier in the conflict. One interesting aspect of this particular spectacle is that the participants were all volunteers from illustrious local families. The members of the local elite who participated in this *munus* undoubtedly did so to ingratiate themselves with their new Roman masters. Nonetheless, the subsequent history of the Iberian Peninsula clearly indicates the popularity of both gladiatorial and animal spectacles: perhaps somewhat ironically, given that he had staged an uprising against Roman authority, the followers of the Lusitanian leader Viriathus staged a *munus* after his death in 140 BC featuring 200 pairs of gladiators.[49]

As we shall discuss in more detail in a subsequent chapter, such events also became quite popular in the Greek-speaking territories of the eastern Mediterranean under Roman rule. The earliest recorded example of such an event in the Greek East, however, did not occur because of direct Roman rule, but of expanding Roman influence in the region during the second century BC. The Seleucid monarch Antiochus IV (175–164 BC), who had spent some years in his younger life as a political hostage in Rome, was, perhaps not surprisingly, enamoured of Roman spectacles. In particular, Livy notes that the king frequently purchased gladiators from Rome and staged *munera* for his subjects in the Seleucid Empire: although they were initially frightened by these unfamiliar spectacles, eventually, through repetition, they grew to enjoy them.[50]

The most famous event staged during the reign of Antiochus IV, and one which nicely encapsulates the merging of Greek and Roman entertainment traditions, was the massive festival staged by the king in Antioch, the capital of the Seleucid Empire, in 166 BC. It is first worth noting that, according to the contemporary Greek historian Polybius, Antiochus staged this event in a direct attempt to surpass the spectacle recently staged by the Roman general Aemilius Paullus to celebrate his victory over Macedonia. With the Roman defeat and annexation of Macedonia, which surely must have come as something of a shock to the other Hellenistic states, Antiochus perhaps felt such a lavish spectacle was necessary to reassure both his own subjects and those of other states (i.e. Rome) of his power and wealth. While the king's festival included elements seen in earlier Hellenistic royal spectacles, like the procession of soldiers, religious images, and animals through the streets of Daphne (a suburb of Antioch), one unique element was the thirty days of gladiatorial spectacles and *venationes* which were staged after the procession.[51]

Interestingly enough, while Polybius censures certain aspects of the festival, like Antiochus' behaviour at banquets, he merely notes the Roman-style events without comment. Polybius' own personal acceptance of Roman *munera* is not hard to explain: like Antiochus, he had been brought to Italy as a Roman hostage, and had thereafter become acclimatized to Roman culture. The fact that the king could stage thirty days of Roman spectacles without any apparent outrage or displeasure on the part of his subjects, however, once again indicates that, at least in certain areas of the Greek East, such events had come to be accepted by the mid-second century BC.

No discussion of Republican *munera* would be complete without an examination of the similarly lavish spectacles staged by Pompey and Julius Caesar. These particular events are not only illustrative of the general trends in the development of gladiatorial and animal spectacles discussed earlier, but also provide an important precedent for the massive *munera* staged by subsequent Roman emperors. As the two most powerful political leaders in contemporary Rome, both Caesar and Pompey possessed resources approaching those of the later emperors, and were therefore able to stage *munera* far exceeding in scale those of earlier Roman magistrates.

Pompey and Caesar ultimately rose to become the two most powerful men in Rome because of the increasing political disorder that racked the Republic in its final decades. One of the ways the Roman government attempted, albeit unsuccessfully, to curb this disorder and, more particularly, prevent the emergence of leaders and demagogues more powerful than the state was through the institution of laws regulating the staging of *munera* in association with the holding of political office. In the 60s BC, legislation was introduced which specifically forbade the exhibition of gladiators by magistrates during their term of office, or the staging of such spectacles by prospective candidates within two years of running for office. The only exceptions were *munera* specifically stipulated in wills as a funerary ceremony. The purpose of this particular clause, of course, was to prevent any unscrupulous demagogues from rising to political prominence because of the public acclaim traditionally associated with such events. One is reminded of the legislation against the importation of African animals the Senate had passed shortly after Nobilior's spectacle of 186 BC.[52]

As might be expected in the chaotic political climate of the late Republic, however, ambitious politicians did not take long to try circumventing such legislation. In a speech delivered in 56 BC, Cicero attacked one of his political rivals, Vatinius, for staging a gladiatorial *munus* while running for political office. The alleged excuses used by Vatinius, that his spectacle only involved *venatores*, or that it only included a single gladiator (as opposed to 'gladiators'), certainly suggest the ridiculous lengths men such as Vatinius were willing to go in order to obtain all-important public support through the staging of spectacles.[53]

Given his current position as one of the triumvirs of the Roman state, Pompey did not have to worry about such legal niceties when planning his own *munera*. Pompey was also able to call upon his numerous overseas political contacts, acquired during years of campaigning throughout Roman territory, to help provide the requisite animals and performers for his spectacles. Two of his most important clients in this regard were likely King Hiempsal of Numidia, whom Pompey had restored to the throne in 81 BC, and Ptolemy Auletes, whom he similarly restored to the throne of Egypt in 55 BC. Because of such assistance, Pompey was able to stage a massive *venatio* in Rome the same year, which featured 500 or 600 lions, 410 leopards, twenty elephants, and other animals including apes and a rhinoceros. In order to protect spectators from such a large number of animals, in particular the elephants, Pompey had an iron railing built between the seats and the arena of the Circus Maximus, where the spectacle took place.[54]

The general purpose of Pompey's spectacle, of course, was to increase his already considerable political standing with the Roman audience. More particularly, however, Pompey wished to advertise the expansion of Roman influence into new territories under his auspices. One of the main client states of Rome at this time, as already alluded to, was Ptolemaic Egypt. Even prior to Pompey's own *venatio*, his former lieutenant Scaurus had included in his own spectacle crocodiles and the first ever hippopotamus seen in Rome, as a direct reference to Roman influence in Egypt. Similarly, the apes and the rhinoceros exhibited by Pompey advertised alleged Roman control in Africa and the East.[55] It is important to note, of course, that the territorial conquests alleged by such exotic animal displays did not always correspond to reality: we shall encounter further examples of such exaggerated propaganda claims when we turn to imperial animal spectacles.

A final animal evidently included in Pompey's spectacle as a symbol of Roman power was a Gallic lynx. The most obvious explanation for this rather anomalous animal was that Caesar had sent it to Pompey. In 55 BC, the latter was still completing the conquest of Gaul, and since Pompey was allied with Caesar at this point, he would presumably not have had any qualms about advertising his ally's military accomplishments as well as his own.[56]

Unfortunately for Pompey, despite all the effort and expense he had undertaken to make his *munus* as impressive as possible, all did not go as planned, and his spectacle was remembered more for the displeasure it caused in the audience than for any positive impression it made upon the assembled spectators. The event that gave rise to so much angst was a combat staged in the Circus Maximus between the elephants and javelin-wielding Gaetulians from North Africa. When the wounded elephants fell to their knees, it evidently appeared that many of the spectators felt they were begging for mercy. As mentioned previously, the Romans (and the Greeks for that matter) regarded most animals as unreasoning beasts, but such was not the case with elephants: many felt a higher regard for these particular animals because of their obvious intelligence. When Pompey's elephants were apparently reduced to begging for mercy, therefore, many spectators saw this as an act of cruelty, rather than entertainment. Cicero, who was present at the event in question, concisely summarizes the displeasure felt by the audience on this occasion:

'The last day [of Pompey's spectacle] was for the elephants. The groundlings showed much astonishment thereat, but no enjoyment. There was even an impulse of compassion, a feeling that the monsters had something human about them.'[57]

It should be stressed, however, that this particular occasion was virtually the only recorded instance in the history of Roman spectacles when the audience showed any compassion for arena animals: in the vast majority of cases, spectators felt no qualms about the suffering and death of animals staged for their entertainment.

Ultimately, Caesar put on displays that surpassed even the lavish spectacles of his political rival, Pompey. Certainly, he realized the propaganda importance of such events from the outset of his political career. As we have already noted, the series of events staged by Caesar as *aedile* in 65 BC, including gladiatorial combat and a *venatio* involving condemned criminals fighting against wild beasts, bore only the most tenuous of links to their supposed inspiration, Caesar's long-dead father: the real justification for these spectacles, in Caesar's mind, was to gain as much popularity with the Roman electorate as possible. It is important to note that Caesar sought public acclaim on this occasion not only through the sheer size of the events he sponsored, but also through their novelty. The criminals participating in his *venatio*, for example, were all armed with costly silver weaponry. Even more importantly, the close association of animal and gladiatorial spectacles in the course of Caesar's *munera* formed something of a precedent for later imperial spectacles.[58] As we shall see, under the Empire, such events were commonly staged together as part of a typical day's entertainment at the arena.

Caesar spared no effort or expense in ensuring that the *munera* he staged were among the most magnificent in Rome, no small factor in his rise to become the most powerful, and popular, political leader in Rome. The large gladiatorial troupe which he, like Batiatus before him, maintained in Capua (the *Iuliani*), allowed Caesar to exhibit such a large number of gladiators during his aedileship in 65 BC: in fact, the only reason more were not brought to Rome for this particular spectacle was that the Senate, fearing the political popularity an ambitious *editor* like Caesar could achieve through such means, had limited the number of gladiators which any citizen could keep in the city to 320 pairs.[59]

Like other contemporary magistrates, Caesar also appears to have had his own personnel scouring Roman territory overseas for animals that could be brought to Rome for his spectacles – a slaughter of a number of Caesar's slaves, freedmen, and exotic animals recorded by Suetonius, which likely occurred in North Africa during the civil war against Pompey and his supporters, appears to have taken place while the former were engaged in this activity.[60] Fortunately for Caesar, many of the debts he accumulated as a result of his lavish spectacles were paid for, at least during his earlier political career, by his erstwhile political ally Marcus Licinius Crassus, the wealthiest man in Rome. In return for a share of the political popularity Caesar gained through his *munera*, Crassus was perfectly willing to fund their production, at least in part.[61]

By the time of Caesar's most famous spectacle in 46 BC, however, he had secured his position as the most powerful man in Rome, and no longer had need of financial assistance from his political allies. The sheer amount of wealth and resources at Caesar's disposal ensured that the various events he staged as part of his quadruple triumph in that year far exceeded past Republican spectacles, including those of his defeated rival Pompey. Amongst the myriad events included in Caesar's triumphal celebration were gladiatorial spectacles, athletic contests, *venationes*, and the first recorded *naumachia* (staged naval combat) in Rome.

Another interesting precedent set at this time was the participation (or attempted participation) of members of the Roman elite in Caesar's spectacles. The historian Dio records that a senator by the name of Fulvius Supinus wished to contend in the dictator's gladiatorial *munus*, but was denied permission. Suetonius, however, records that on this occasion Caesar had no issue with an equestrian or former senator participating in the spectacles. Subsequently, the Senate (perhaps in 38 BC?) appears to have formally banned members of the senatorial class from participating in arena spectacles.[62]

A considerable proportion of the expense involved in the spectacles of 46 BC came from preparing the various venues that staged them. Like Pompey before him, Caesar made modifications to the Circus Maximus to stage safely a combat involving forty elephants, approximately 500 infantry, and a number of cavalry. The 3-metre wide moat dug between the arena and the seats ensured that none of the enraged elephants could break into the crowd during the combat. It is also possible that Caesar enlarged the area of the Circus Maximus' arena on this occasion to provide more room for the elephants to manoeuvre.[63]

The most extensive modifications for Caesar's quadruple triumph, however, were made to the Forum Romanum. Caesar is credited with building a 'hunting theatre' in the middle of the forum that incorporated an awning for the shade and comfort of the assembled spectators. The spectacles which took place in the 'hunting theatre', ostensibly staged in honour of Caesar's daughter Julia who had died almost a decade earlier, comprised both beast hunts and gladiatorial events, the latter of which included both men fighting on foot and in mounted combat. This was the first occasion on which *venationes* were staged in the Forum Romanum, and in preparation for these particular events, elaborate substructures were also built under the forum. These substructures consisted of a central gallery some 3.5m below ground level, intersected at right angles by four smaller corridors spaced 15m apart. Twelve regularly spaced shafts, in turn, connected these underground passages to the surface. The remains of a wooden winch discovered in situ suggest that these vertical shafts served as elevators to transport animals and equipment from the staging area under the forum to the floor of the arena above. As we shall see, these substructures appear to have provided a precedent for similar basements found in later amphitheatres like the Colosseum.[64]

Another original aspect of Caesar's quadruple triumph, which formed a precedent for later practice, was the previously mentioned *naumachia* staged in an artificial basin, most likely in the Campus Martius, excavated by Caesar's engineers. In one sense, this event, ostensibly meant to represent a historical naval battle between the Tyrians and Egyptians, was an extension of the mass combats of gladiators that Caesar had already incorporated into some of his earlier spectacles. The sheer scale of this *naumachia* once again illustrated the wealth and munificence of Caesar: if ancient testimony is to be believed, some 2000 combatants and 4000 rowers participated in the staged naval battle. One important difference between this *naumachia* and the mass combats staged in venues like the Circus Maximus, however, was that while the latter events featured trained gladiators, the participants in the *naumachia* were prisoners-of-war, readily available after Caesar's recent victories.[65] The naval battle, then, clearly demonstrated the military prowess of Caesar and his armies to the assembled spectators.

Like Pompey before him, Caesar also demonstrated the extension of Roman power under his leadership through the animals he displayed to the Roman populace. The most obvious example is the giraffe brought to Rome in 46 BC to advertise Caesar's successes in Egypt, the first such animal ever seen in the city. Caesar, however, also alluded to his past victories through the choice of events he chose to incorporate into his quadruple triumph. One of Caesar's most important victories in the civil war against Pompey was the battle of Pharsalus, fought in the region of Thessaly in central Greece in 48 BC. It is seemingly no coincidence, then, that one of the events he introduced to Rome two years later was Thessalian bull-jumping, in which trained riders would jump onto bulls' backs in mid-gallop and attempt to wrestle them to the ground by their horns. The native Thessalians who participated in this event presumably were offered out of gratitude either for the privileges granted to the region by Caesar after his victory, or had simply been requisitioned by the latter.[66]

By the end of the Republic, as we have seen, the basic tenets of Roman arena sports were in place. Although gladiatorial events and animal spectacles arose under different circumstances, they came to be more and more closely associated over time, a development ultimately formalized under the Empire. Similarly, the propaganda elements that featured in the spectacles of Republican leaders like Pompey and Caesar were also an integral component of many subsequent imperial spectacles. Ultimately, however, the monopolization of arena spectacles under the emperors, as well as the development of a highly efficient infrastructure, allowed the heirs of Caesar to stage *munera* that far surpassed those of the Republic.

## Chapter Two

# Spectacles of the High Empire in Rome

As we saw in the previous chapter, arena spectacles had become a potent means of propaganda by the end of the Roman Republic. Certainly, the lavish events staged by Caesar played no small role in solidifying his own popularity among the populace of Rome. Not surprisingly, many subsequent emperors, beginning with Augustus, realizing how such events could increase their own political standing, spared no expense in their production. In this chapter, we shall discuss the imperial spectacles produced in Rome during the first two centuries of the Empire, as well as the efforts made during this period to bring such events under stricter imperial control. We shall also address the growing popularity of arena spectacles throughout the Roman provinces during this period, as seen in the surviving record of numerous *munera* outside of the imperial capital.

One of the difficulties encountered in studying the elaborate spectacles of this period is the almost unbelievable numbers of participants and/or fatalities sometimes alleged for such events. Could the Romans, for example, really have killed 9000 animals in *venationes* staged to celebrate the opening of the Colosseum in 79 AD? The historian Dio, writing in the third century AD, certainly viewed such figures with scepticism.

'... anyone who cared to record their number would find his task a burden without being able, in all probability, to present the truth; for all such matters are regularly exaggerated in a spirit of boastfulness.'[1]

Although he specifically refers here to the actual number of gladiators and animals involved in the spectacles of Caesar in 46 BC, Dio's words are nonetheless applicable to the figures given for later spectacles as well. The preserved figures for the massive imperial spectacles of Rome, in particular, should be approached with some caution: it has been suggested, for example, that the number of slain animals alleged for such events as the inaugural games of the Colosseum may represent the total number of beasts gathered for such an occasion, rather than the number actually killed. If, indeed, we consider such figures as rough estimates of the number of participants involved in a given spectacle, rather than an exact tally of fatalities or the like, we can still gain an impression of the changing scale of imperial *munera* over time.[2]

The first Roman emperor, Augustus,[3] played a pivotal role in the production and further organization of arena spectacles in Rome. It would indeed be more surprising if such an astute political leader had not exploited such popular events to the full. In his *Res Gestae*, or record of his accomplishments as Roman emperor, Augustus commemorates for posterity the lavish *munera* staged during his reign:

> Three times in my own name I gave a show of gladiators, and five times in the name of my sons or grandsons; in these shows there fought about ten thousand men ... in my own name, or that of my sons or grandsons, on twenty-six occasions I gave to the people, in the circus, in the forum, or in the amphitheatre, hunts of African wild beasts in which about three thousand five hundred beasts were slain.[4]

One of the most important aspects of this passage is the allusion to the monopoly on arena spectacles in Rome exercised by Augustus and subsequent emperors. Having fought his way to the apex of the Roman state, Augustus was subsequently at pains to ensure that no new candidates could emerge to challenge his rule in Rome. Therefore, the emperor limited those who were eligible to stage *munera* in Rome, and reserved the largest spectacles, as well as the resultant public acclaim, for himself or other members of the imperial family. In the 20s BC, Augustus limited the praetors to staging only two *munera* per year, with no more than 120 gladiators in each event, and his successor, Tiberius, subsequently put further restrictions on the production of spectacles in Rome by *editores* outside of the imperial family. The next important stage in this process was reached in the late first century under the emperor Domitian, when only the emperor himself or one of his chosen officials was legally allowed to stage *munera* in Rome.[5]

It was also under Augustus that important steps were made in the regularization of arena spectacles. As we saw in the previous chapter, the earliest *munera* in Rome were generally staged as part of certain traditional Roman *ludi*, or on special occasions, such as the triumphal celebrations of Roman generals. Beginning in the late Republic, however, such events began to be included in even more festivals: in 42 BC, for example, gladiatorial and animal spectacles replaced chariot races at the *Ludi Cereales*. Under Augustus, this proliferation of *munera* continued, as they began to be staged as part of additional state celebrations, such as the Saturnalia. By the end of the Julio-Claudian period, Augustus' successors had followed this trend by decreeing that ten days at the end of each December were to be specifically set aside for gladiatorial and animal spectacles.[6]

The organization of a given day's entertainment also appears to have been largely standardized by the end of Augustus' reign. As previously discussed, Caesar created a precedent by staging *venationes* in close association with gladiatorial events in the course of his spectacles in Rome. It was under Augustus, however, that the staging of animal and gladiatorial events on the same day first became commonplace. Such an arrangement, whereby animal events were staged in the morning of a given day's entertainment, followed by gladiatorial combat in the afternoon, subsequently became standard practice for arena spectacles throughout the Empire.[7]

Although Augustus' own *Res Gestae* does not provide a great deal of information on specific *munera* staged during his reign, other ancient testimony does provide such details. Since Augustus, as the first Roman emperor, served as a role model for his successors in the area of public entertainment, as well as so many other facets of rule, a more detailed discussion of the arena spectacles staged during his reign is certainly warranted. The following discussion of such events, while by no means exhaustive, nonetheless illustrates the continued growth in the size and scale of arena spectacles during his reign.

The earliest significant spectator event staged by Augustus took place in the late 30s BC, shortly before he was able to secure sole rule over the Roman Empire. In this instance, the event in question was not a *venatio* or a gladiatorial combat, but a criminal execution. Nonetheless, it certainly bears closer examination: public executions became a popular component of arena spectacles under the Empire, and the event in question certainly provided a precedent for the ever more elaborate execution spectacles staged by Augustus' successors. The focal point of this particular event was a Sicilian bandit named Selurus, who had terrorized the region around Mount Etna for years prior to his arrest. The severity of his crimes evidently dictated that he be executed in a particularly elaborate and humiliating fashion. Rather than simply being crucified or thrown to wild animals in the arena (standard punishments for capital offences under Roman law), Selurus was executed in a much more dramatic and inventive fashion. First, the bandit was placed atop a wooden apparatus representing Mount Etna; at some point, the apparatus collapsed, plunging Selurus into the wild animal cages positioned beneath, and thereby sealing his fate. Augustus had only regained control of Sicily from his rival Sextus Pompey a few years prior to this spectacle, and it was certainly a boon to his propaganda to be able to present himself as a guarantor of law and order on the island through such an event.[8]

Other elaborate events staged by Augustus at a relatively early stage in his political career include those held in 29 BC to celebrate the dedication of the recently completed Temple of the Divine Caesar; the gladiatorial *munus* and *venatio* staged as part of these celebrations were the first given in the emperor's own name. On this particular occasion, the gladiatorial *munus* featured not only gladiators matched against each other in single combat, but also a mass combat between Dacian and Suevi prisoners-of-war, captured as a result of recent Roman campaigns along the Rhine and Danube frontiers. The final notable feature of this gladiatorial spectacle was that a Roman senator, Quintus Vitellius, participated in the event. Evidently, the presumed earlier ban against members of the senatorial elite participating in such events had either fallen by the wayside, or Augustus, who certainly had the power to do so, had chosen to ignore it on this occasion.[9]

Augustus was one Roman emperor, in particular, who appears to have encouraged Romans of good family to participate in various public spectacles. The *ludus Troia*, a martial equestrian display performed by young men of the Roman aristocracy, was performed on a number of occasions during Augustus' reign, including as part of the festivities surrounding the dedication of Caesar's temple in 29 BC. The emperor evidently believed that such martial contests ideally would improve the fighting spirit and morale of the young aristocrats involved, and thereby inculcate them with the requisite *virtus* for high administrative or military posts under his administration. During Augustus' reign, noble Roman youths who belonged to the aristocratic association of *iuvenes* ['young men'] in Rome, fought in such events as part of the *ludi iuvenum* (or *Iuvenalia*), games which appear to have been first instituted as a formal event by Augustus. It is important to note that the young men who volunteered to participate in these spectacles, with the evident encouragement of the Emperor, do not appear to have incurred the level of *infamia*, or disdain, normally associated with professional gladiators and beast fighters in Roman society.[10]

It is apparent, nonetheless, that not all members of the Roman government were as taken with the idea of youthful members of the aristocracy fighting or otherwise performing in public as their emperor. In 22 BC, another senatorial decree was instituted which not only reestablished the earlier strictures against senators performing in public, but also forbade members of the equestrian class from participating in theatrical performances or *gladiatoria opera*, a term which presumably incorporated *venationes* as well. Another interesting aspect of this ban was the inclusion of women for the first time. One possible motivation for the decree of 22 BC, in fact, may have been the games staged by Augustus' heir Marcellus the previous year, in which not only an equestrian, but a woman of noble rank are said to have participated (albeit on the stage, not in the arena). Evidently, many in Rome's governing classes considered such a performance to be distasteful. As we shall see, however, the decree of 22 BC certainly did not end aristocratic or female participation in arena events.[11]

Another notable gladiatorial *munus* of 29 BC was that staged by Statilius Taurus, one of Augustus' foremost generals at the time. The esteem enjoyed by Taurus in the eyes of the Emperor is clearly indicated by the fact that he was not only allowed to stage this *munus*, but also to build a new stone amphitheatre for the event, the first in Rome, from his own resources. Augustus, indeed, encouraged his most trusted subordinates to build new monumental structures in Rome as part of the emperor's grand design to beautify the capital. Subsequently, of course, many other *munera* were staged in the same facility, such as a number of the *venationes* referred to by Augustus in the *Res Gestae*. Unfortunately, no trace of Taurus' amphitheatre remains today, as it was one of many buildings destroyed in the Great Fire of Rome in 64 AD.[12]

Another example of the *munera* which Augustus periodically allowed to be staged by his subordinates were the gladiatorial combats and *venationes* staged by Lucius Domitius Ahenobarbus, a member of the extended imperial family. It is not exactly clear when the events in question took place, although they were most likely staged during Domitius' praetorship in 19 BC and/or his consulship three years later. To judge from Suetonius' description of the *venationes*, they were quite large in scope: Domitius is said to have not only staged a beast hunt in the Circus Maximus, but in other areas of Rome as well. Unfortunately, we have no information on what other venues might have been custom-built for these other *venationes*. Suetonius does not give us any information as to the size of Domitius' gladiatorial *munus*, but he claims that it was so savage that Augustus ultimately was forced to curtail it by an edict. Clearly, Augustus' generosity in allowing his underlings to stage spectacles in Rome only extended so far, particularly when they threatened to damage the reputation of the emperor himself.[13]

More specific information survives concerning the spectacles that Augustus staged to celebrate the dedication of the Theatre of Marcellus, his recently deceased nephew, in 11 BC. One sign of the importance that the emperor attached to these events is the size of the *venatio* which took place on this occasion: 600 *Africanae* (most likely lions or other felines) are said to have been slain, the highest recorded number of animal fatalities for any beast hunt staged during Augustus' reign.[14]

It was not these animals, however, which appear to have elicited the most interest among contemporary spectators or later historians. Subsequent accounts of the events associated with the dedication of the Theatre of Marcellus make specific mention of the tiger in a cage formally exhibited to the Roman populace on this occasion. Like his predecessors Pompey and Julius Caesar, Augustus realized the potential propaganda value of exotic animals, and the tiger exhibited in 11 BC was not chosen simply for its relative novelty. The reign of Augustus saw increasing Roman trade with, and interest in the Indian subcontinent, and the tiger, native to this region, was an ideal advertisement for this Roman policy. Although we cannot know for certain, this particular animal was probably one of the tigers presented to Augustus as a gift some years earlier by visiting Indian emissaries on the island of Samos.[15]

The tiger exhibited by Augustus in 11 BC was certainly not the only such exotic animal that the Emperor employed for propaganda purposes during his reign. In his biography of Augustus, Suetonius notes that, in addition to tigers, the emperor exhibited other exotic animals, such as a rhinoceros and a snake allegedly fifty cubits (approximately eighty-five feet) in length, to the Roman populace on special occasions. Just as the tiger advertised current Roman interest in India, the rhinoceros, and perhaps the snake (if it was an African python), symbolized the contemporary desire to expand Roman trade and influence on the African continent beyond the territory that Rome already held along its northern coast.[16]

One final exotic animal should be mentioned in the context of Augustus' territorial propaganda – the crocodile. On a number of occasions during his reign, the Emperor either exhibited such animals to the Roman populace, or staged *venationes* in which they were slaughtered. Rather than merely alluding to Africa as a whole, crocodiles, in particular, symbolized the province of Egypt, which Augustus had brought under Roman control after his victory over Marc Antony and Cleopatra. The clearest evidence for this connection is a coin minted by Augustus shortly after the annexation of this territory: its obverse depicts a crocodile with the legend *Aegypto Capta* [Captured Egypt]'. As we shall see in our subsequent discussion, Augustus' successors continued to employ crocodiles as well as other exotic animals for propaganda purposes.

Among the most impressive spectacles staged by Augustus were those associated with the Temple of Mars Ultor in 2 BC. The numerous events staged to celebrate this occasion included two *venationes* and a gladiatorial *munus*. The latter event was staged in the Saepta Julia, the large voting precinct built by Augustus' right-hand man Agrippa in 26 BC. Subsequently, the Saepta was one of the venues in Rome used for various *munera* by the Julio-Claudian emperors, particularly as its original purpose became less and less important in the increasingly autocratic Roman state. The two *venationes* staged in 2 BC were put on respectively in the Circus Maximus and the Circus Flaminius, the latter being one of the smaller chariot-racing venues in Rome. The first event saw the slaughter of 260 lions, while the second saw the death of twenty-six crocodiles.[17]

The most impressive event associated with the dedication of the Temple of Mars Ultor, however, was likely a massive *naumachia* which, according to the *Res Gestae*, featured over thirty vessels and approximately 3000 combatants. The artificial lake, or *stagnum*, built for this event was larger in area than the Circus Maximus, a clear indication of the resources that the emperor had at his disposal for such spectacles. The battle of Salamis between the Greek and Persian fleets in 480 BC was the inspiration for this particular *naumachia*. It is certainly possible that Salamis was chosen as the inspiration for this particular event because of the superficial similarities between this particular battle and Augustus' victory over the combined fleets of Antony and Cleopatra at Actium in 31 BC. A parallel could certainly be drawn between the victory over the alleged eastern despot Cleopatra at Actium and that won centuries earlier by the Greeks at Salamis against another eastern potentate, Xerxes. This suggested connection between the two battles may also be strengthened by the possibility that the *stagnum* which Augustus had built in preparation for his *naumachia* was located on property in Rome which had once belonged to Antony. By the time this particular event was staged in 2 BC, almost thirty years after Actium, the emperor calling attention to a victory won, in part, over a fellow Roman leader would not have caused the potential awkwardness it might have a few decades earlier.[18]

Another notable spectacle should be mentioned in our survey of Augustus' reign, that staged by his grandson Germanicus in 6 AD. According to the later writer Pliny the Elder, the most memorable aspect of this event was the elephants who, much to the spectators' delight, performed such tricks as simulating gladiatorial combat, dancing in unison, and even (so Pliny claims) walking on tightropes. Although, as we have seen, *venationes* became the most popular animal event in Rome by the late Republic, spectacles like that of Germanicus illustrate that nonviolent displays of animals did not die out entirely, even under the Empire. Although elephants were not the only attested animals to participate in such events, they appear to have been particularly popular with spectators, no doubt in part because of the special affinity Romans felt towards these animals.

In the later years of Augustus' reign, the continuing problem of upper-class participation in public spectacles once again arose. The decree of 22 BC, which had effectively banned male and female members of the Roman elite from such activities, had begun to be ignored soon after its promulgation: the previously mentioned spectacles staged by Domitius, in fact, had included equestrians and women of high status performing on the stage as mimes. In 11 AD, in an attempt to address the flaws in its previous legislation, the Senate issued a new decree on this issue. Henceforth, members of the equestrian class were allowed to participate in gladiatorial spectacles (and presumably the *venationes* as well). Freeborn men and women under the ages of twenty-five and twenty respectively, however, were banned from participation in public spectacles. The fact that such a clause had been added to the decree suggests that young men and women attempting to participate in such events had indeed been a problem.[19]

Augustan spectacles like those highlighted in our previous discussion provided a clear model for subsequent rulers of the Julio-Claudian dynasty, which lasted until the suicide of Nero in 68 AD. The relatives and heirs of Augustus who ruled the Roman Empire during this period, seeing the popularity that Augustus had enjoyed through his sponsorship of such events, took pains to emulate the standards he had set for them. The Roman populace expected nothing less at this point. It was not enough, however, simply to equal the achievements of Augustus in this regard. Just as Republican magistrates had striven to surpass the previous spectacles of their political rivals to secure even greater public support, so too did the majority of Augustus' successors attempt to surpass the precedent he had set, and thereby win for themselves greater acclaim from the populace in Rome.

One way in which subsequent Roman emperors attempted to improve the spectacles staged under their auspices, in particular the *venationes*, was through the collection of ever-greater numbers and varieties of animals for particular events. As we saw in our previous discussion of Republican spectacles, attempting to add variety through such means was, in and of itself, nothing new in Rome. The collection of ever-greater numbers and varieties of animals, however, took on an added significance under the absolutist rule of the Roman Empire.

The animals presented by an emperor to the Roman populace, in addition to symbolizing recent conquests or territorial interests, could also, in a much broader sense, symbolize the emperor's control over nature.

The collection and slaughter of animals to demonstrate such mastery was certainly not a practice unique to Roman emperors, but was a feature of numerous autocratic states throughout history. In most other states, however, the rulers themselves hunted and killed animals to demonstrate their mastery before a relatively small group of the aristocratic elite. The kings of ancient Assyria, to name one such example, would kill lions and other beasts in carefully controlled hunts staged before a select group of spectators. In Rome, however, aside from a few exceptions we shall have occasion to discuss, the emperors did not kill the animals themselves, but had the slaughter carried out by arena performers under their auspices, before thousands of spectators drawn from all ranks of Roman society. The difference between the hunting spectacles of Rome and those of other states no doubt arose, in large part, from the profound influence that the gladiatorial combats of the arena had upon the development of the *venationes*. Despite this difference, however, the message presented by hunting spectacles in Rome and other cultures was quite similar: nature itself was subject to a given ruler's power.[20]

In a pre-industrial society like that of Rome, which depended so much upon agricultural production for its prosperity, the slaughter in the arena of wild animals, which might otherwise prove a danger to crops or farmers, could even be presented as a public service for the emperor's subjects. Once again, this particular justification for hunting spectacles was not limited to Rome, but could be found in numerous other societies as well. One long-standing justification for aristocratic fox hunting in England, for example, was that it eradicated vermin which might otherwise prey upon rural livestock. In a Roman context, one of the most succinct expressions of such a justification for animal slaughter is found in a poem, probably dating to the reign of Nero, from the *Anthologia Graeca*:

'Ye furthest Nasamonian wilds of Libya, no longer, your expanse vexed by the hordes of wild beasts of the continent, shall ye ring in echo, even beyond the sands of the Nomads, to the voice of lions roaring in the desert, since Caesar the son has trapped the countless tribe and brought it face to face with his fighters. Now the heights once full of the lairs of prowling beasts are pasturage for the cattle of men.'[21]

In a region like North Africa, which was not only one of the most important centres of agricultural production in the Roman Empire, but also an area where *venationes* were particularly popular, the perceived connection between arena spectacles and agricultural prosperity was particularly compelling.

One emperor, however, who did not exploit the propaganda potential of arena spectacles to enhance his personal popularity, and who therefore presents something of an exception to the overall growth of such events following the death of Augustus, was his immediate successor Tiberius. Although he was in most respects a competent administrator, and indeed left the Empire with a budget surplus of over two billion sesterces upon his death in 37 AD, Tiberius, who presented a somewhat dour contrast to his predecessor, was not interested in slavishly courting the affection of the masses as Augustus had done. One of the reasons why the finances of the Empire were in such a strong condition at the time of Tiberius' death was that he had saved so much money over the twenty-three years of his reign by staging or funding arena spectacles on only an irregular basis at best. The biographer Suetonius, in fact, claimed that the emperor gave no public shows at all during his long reign, although if one considers the events funded by Tiberius but formally staged in the name of one of his relatives or subordinates, this statement is not technically correct.[22]

One of the few specific spectacles recorded for Tiberius' reign, a gladiatorial combat staged by his son Drusus in 15 AD, provides a good illustration of the different attitudes towards the arena on the part of Tiberius and his predecessor Augustus. First, the seemingly excessive pleasure that Drusus took in bloodshed is said to have not only alarmed the spectators present at the event, but also earned a rebuke from his father. The complete absence of Tiberius from the event was also noted by the Roman populace: according to the later historian Tacitus, who wrote a highly critical account of Tiberius' reign, this was either because of the Emperor's dislike of large crowds, or his fear of being unfavourably compared with the more gregarious Augustus were he to attend such an event. Another historian, Dio, adds the further detail that two members of the equestrian class volunteered to fight each other as part of Drusus' spectacle. When the death of one of these combatants was reported to Tiberius, he forbid the survivor from ever fighting as a gladiator again. Only a few years later, in 19 AD, the Senate, no doubt at the instigation of the emperor, once more adopted a hardline stance towards elite participation in public spectacles by instituting a new decree which included a ban on any men or women of senatorial or equestrian rank appearing on the stage or in the arena. It should be noted, however, that this decree, like its predecessors, subsequently came to be disregarded, at least on occasion: both Caligula and Nero forced members of the elite, both male and female, to participate in spectacles staged during their respective reigns.[23]

Tiberius' parsimony when it came to public spectacles played a role in one of the most famous disasters of his reign, the collapse of a wooden amphitheatre in the town of Fidenae, just north of Rome, in 27 AD. The fullest account of this disaster comes from Tacitus, who relates that an unscrupulous entrepreneur by the name of Atilius, evidently prompted by the longing of the masses for arena events, had a large wooden amphitheatre built in Fidenae to host a gladiatorial spectacle. Unfortunately, the construction of this particular edifice was so shoddy that when thousands of entertainment-starved Romans poured into the amphitheatre for the promised event, it promptly collapsed. According to Tacitus, 50,000 spectators were either killed or wounded because of this disaster. The casualty figures given by Tacitus may well be an exaggeration. Nonetheless, because of this debacle, Atilius himself was banished, and the emperor decreed, first, that better standards were to be observed in the building of amphitheatres in future and, secondly, that no one with a fortune less than 400,000 sesterces could produce a gladiatorial spectacle – presumably, this was to avoid the kind of construction shortcuts Atillius had employed to save money.[24]

At the time of Tiberius' death a decade later, there was a great deal of public rejoicing on the streets of Rome. The people wanted a new ruler, one who would provide them with the public entertainments to which they felt entitled. Possibly no other emperor in Roman history ascended to the throne amid more public jubilation or optimism than Tiberius' successor Gaius, better known to posterity by his nickname of Caligula. One of the reasons for this support was the sympathy felt towards Caligula because of his family's travails during Tiberius' reign. His father, the popular Germanicus, had died under suspicious circumstances early in Tiberius' reign, and a majority of his family had subsequently been imprisoned and died because of the Emperor's suspicions. Somewhat paradoxically, however, the elderly

Tiberius had adopted the young Caligula and taken him as his protégé late in his reign, thereby paving the latter's path to the throne. Unlike his predecessor, Caligula demanded public adulation, and he spared no expense in providing lavish entertainments for the Roman populace.

Such was Caligula's devotion to various entertainments that, according to the later historian Dio, '... [he] ... was ruled by the charioteers and gladiators, and was the slave of the actors and others connected with the stage.'[25]

Caligula is even said to have indulged his passions by appearing as different types of performers, including as a gladiator, a foreshadowing of the later emperor Commodus. Incredible as it may seem, such were the vast sums Caligula spent on various spectacles and entertainers, as well as the lavish gifts of money to his subjects at the start of his reign, that he used up the sizable budget surplus left to him by Tiberius before the third year of his reign. He was thereafter forced to employ unscrupulous means to procure the requisite funds for further entertainments.[26]

Among his main expenditures on public spectacles were new entertainment facilities that were constructed, or at least had their construction begun, during Caligula's reign. Although the Emperor used a number of existing venues for the *munera*, such as the Saepta Julia and the amphitheatre of Taurus, he also wished to construct new, purpose-built facilities which he thought better suited to the lavish spectacles staged within them. Perhaps the best-known example of the latter is the so-called Circus of Gaius and Nero built on the Vatican Hill; as the name suggests, not only Caligula, but also Nero, indulged his passion for chariot-racing at this venue. According to Dio, Caligula, however, also demolished a number of buildings and erected temporary wooden stands for one of his spectacles, all because of his alleged dislike for the amphitheatre of Taurus. Suetonius also relates that the emperor began the construction of a new amphitheatre by the *Saepta Julia* that was subsequently abandoned by his successor Claudius. The exact relationship, if any, between these two projects is unclear, although one suggestion is that the razing of buildings mentioned by Dio provided the necessary land for the later amphitheatre mentioned by Suetonius.[27]

One means by which Caligula, faced with such expenditures, attempted to raise revenues involved the auctioning of gladiators to prospective *editores*. Some of those who bid on the gladiators, according to Dio, did so of their own free will in order to win favour, not only through filling the coffers of the imperial treasury, but also through using these performers to stage future spectacles which the Emperor himself might attend. Some of those who bid and put on spectacles, however, were forced to do so by Caligula. The Emperor reintroduced the custom, for example, whereby two praetors were expected to stage a *munus* for the populace each year as part of their official duties, and so forced the latter to participate in these gladiatorial auctions. This particular custom was not observed during the reign of Tiberius, perhaps because of the emperor's ambivalence towards public spectacles. For Caligula, however, the restoration of this practice, besides building his reputation as a restorer of Roman tradition, also offered a far more tangible benefit: forcing praetors to once again produce spectacles for the Roman populace, and do so at least in part from their own resources, provided some relief for the imperial treasury.[28]

Only a few months into his reign, Caligula provided a number of elaborate spectacles to the Roman populace for the dedication of the Temple of the Deified Augustus. The events in question included a *ludus Troia* performed by young members of the nobility, as well as two days of chariot racing and a *venatio*. The latter spectacle is said to have included the death of 400 bears, as well as the same number of *Africanae*, a much larger number than any attested slaughter of animals during Tiberius' reign. The number of chariot races held on each day (twenty and twenty-four respectively) not only surpassed anything seen during Tiberius' reign, but anything witnessed previously in the history of Roman chariot racing. It has been suggested that the animal combats took place between the races to provide some diversion for the audience. Such a practice was not unheard of on other occasions when chariot races and *venationes* were staged in close association with one another.[29]

Later in the year there occurred one of the more famous spectacle-related incidents of Caligula's reign, and one of the first manifestations of the madness that allegedly afflicted the emperor after his recovery from a serious illness. According to Dio, an equestrian by the name of Atanius Secundus, wishing to gain the Emperor's subsequent favour, had pledged during Caligula's illness to fight as a gladiator should he recover. Unfortunately, when the emperor did indeed recover, far from rewarding Secundus for his devotion, he forced him to fulfill his vow and fight in the arena. Dio suggests that, as a result, Secundus was killed, although Suetonius, in seemingly referring to the same episode, claims that Secundus was ultimately able to fight his way successfully out of his predicament.[30]

In 38 AD, Caligula staged further spectacles for the Roman populace, which were noted by Suetonius and Dio, our primary sources for his reign, not only for their extravagance, but also for the eccentric and cruel actions taken by the emperor during the events in question. First, Caligula allegedly forced a number of Roman citizens to fight in the arena as gladiators: according to Dio, it was not just the twenty-six members of the equestrian class killed on this occasion that prompted public displeasure, but also the Emperor's lust for the bloodshed. Despite previous legislation, it appears that the problem of upper class Romans fighting below their station in the arena was still present at this time, since Dio states that some of the equestrians killed in 38 AD had previously engaged in other, non-lethal, gladiatorial bouts. Later in the same year, Caligula is said to have forced another equestrian to fight in the arena, ostensibly for insulting the emperor's mother, Agrippina.[31]

In 39 AD, Caligula staged a particularly elaborate series of spectacles to commemorate the birthday of his recently deceased sister Drusilla. In addition to a public banquet and a display of pancratiasts (the pankration was the most brutal of the Greek combat sports, similar in some respects to present-day mixed martial arts), Caligula also staged chariot races as well as two days of *venationes*. The latter were even larger in scale than those he had put on two years previously: on the first day, 500 bears are said to have perished, while an equal number of *Africanae* died on the second day. Once again, these combats may have been staged for variety's sake in the interlude between chariot races.[32]

Despite such lavish entertainments, however, and other acts of generosity like the provision of public banquets, Caligula failed, in the long run, to achieve the public adoration he sought. Instead, his cruel and fickle behaviour ultimately disillusioned more and more of his subjects, certainly contributing to the conspiracy that ended the Emperor's life in 41 AD. One of the more famous instances of his cruelty, reported by the ancient sources, was the occasion when, in order to save money on the cattle normally used to feed the wild animals appearing in the arena, Caligula fed condemned criminals to them instead. On other instances, evidently out of spite, the Emperor would retract the awning (*vela*) which normally shaded spectators on particularly hot days, and exhibit subpar gladiators and wild beasts, much to the audience's displeasure.[33]

The emperor who succeeded Caligula in 41 AD, his uncle Claudius, although not without his own behavioral quirks, nonetheless provided a welcome change to most of the Roman populace, and proved to be particularly popular among the lower classes. Part of this popularity was due to the public works the Emperor commissioned during his reign, such as new harbour works at the Roman port of Ostia, but public approval was also due to the various costly spectacles Claudius staged during his reign. Suetonius, in briefly noting the many *munera* produced during this period, actually coined a new adverb, *plurifariam* ('of varied types'), to suggest their variety.[34]

Like his nephew, Claudius realized that the Roman people demanded entertainment, and he was more than happy to follow Caligula's lead in this respect without, however, deliberately antagonizing the audience as his predecessor had done. One of the earliest recorded spectator events of Claudius' reign, in fact, featuring chariot racing as well as *venationes* with 300 bears and 300 *Africanae*, was quite similar to events staged earlier by Caligula in 37 and 39 AD. Like his predecessor, Claudius also alternated beast hunts with chariot races so as to provide some variety for spectators.[35]

In the first year of his reign, the Emperor also removed the obligation of the praetors to produce *munera* on an annual basis, which had been re-imposed upon them by Caligula. Although this particular measure was no doubt popular among the magistrates affected, it did not, in the long term, lead to a reduction in the number of arena spectacles staged in Rome. In 47 AD, Claudius decreed that another group of magistrates, the quaestors, would no longer be responsible for the maintenance of roads. Instead, they would henceforth be expected to produce ten days of *munera* every December. As with a number of other steps taken during Claudius' reign, this particular measure provided a precedent for later imperial policy, and in fact remained in effect, through various vicissitudes, until the fourth century.[36]

Dio relates that the Emperor's fondness for arena spectacle, in particular gladiatorial *munera*, was thought to be excessive by some. This criticism was partly due to the fact that Claudius used such events as a means to punish and remove what he saw as less desirable elements of society. One of the major problems during the preceding reigns of Tiberius and Caligula had been the proliferation of *maiestas*, or treason trials. In the expectation of financial reward and/or gaining the emperor's favour, there was no shortage of men willing to inform upon others, and in some cases employ fabricated evidence. A particular target of Claudius were slaves or freedmen who had informed upon their masters: many such men, according to Dio, were condemned to the arena where they were killed by wild beasts or other gladiators. The Emperor was thought by some to take an unseemly amount of pleasure in the blood spilled on such occasions.[37]

In other respects, however, Claudius took pains to endear himself to arena spectators. One important step undertaken by the emperor, out of deference to the senatorial class in Rome, was to assign specific, front-row seating to them at public spectacles. This measure, which further ensured that Roman senators would not have to sit among their social lessers at such events, formed a precedent for the seating arrangements at subsequent Roman spectacles. The Emperor, however, did not neglect the other segments of the Roman populace: according to Dio, he received special praise for his willingness to mingle with the common people in the audience at the staging of *munera*.[38]

Another group to whom the Emperor showed special deference was the Praetorian Guard. Claudius, in fact, owed his elevation to members of the guard, who had allegedly discovered him hiding in a closet in the aftermath of Caligula's assassination. In order to consolidate their support, Claudius subsequently distributed a large cash donative to the Praetorian Guard, thereby setting a precedent for future emperors. In 43 AD, as a further honour, the Emperor staged a gladiatorial *munus* in the praetorian camp on the anniversary of his accession to the throne, appearing himself in military costume as an evident show of solidarity. Finally, at some point during Claudius' reign (the exact date is not attested), members of the Praetorian Guard participated in a *venatio* wherein they killed *Africanae* from horseback.[39]

This display was just one of the events staged during the reign of Claudius that were noteworthy for their novelty and/or size. Another such spectacle was an exhibition of Thessalian bull-jumping, a type of event which evidently had not been seen in Rome since the days of Julius Caesar. Another event which was somewhat reminiscent of Caesar's earlier spectacles, in particular the mass combat which had been staged in the Circus Maximus in 46 BC, was the simulated storming of a town put on in the Campus Martius by Claudius. While Caesar's event was not intended to symbolize any historical battle, Claudius' spectacle represented the recent conquest of Britain, and may even have included prisoners of war captured during that campaign. Having come to the throne in such an unorthodox fashion, the Emperor had felt that a successful military venture would be the ideal way to demonstrate his worthiness to rule and thereby secure support for his rule. In 43 AD, in fulfillment of this design, a Roman expeditionary force had crossed the English Channel and conquered southern Britain, a victory Claudius celebrated with a triumph and associated spectacles back in Rome. One of the significant features of the battle staged in the Campus Martius was the fact that Claudius presided over it in military costume. Although, in reality, the Emperor had not participated in the fighting of the campaign, it was important nonetheless, for propaganda purposes, to stress to the Roman populace that it had succeeded under Claudius' military auspices.[40]

Undoubtedly, the most famous spectacle of Claudius' reign was the massive *naumachia* staged on the Fucine Lake east of Rome. The Emperor, as another public service, wished to drain the lake because of its perceived role as a source of malaria. Before doing so, however, he wished to take advantage of the natural setting for another public spectacle, the largest recorded *naumachia* in Roman history. Like the previously discussed battle in the Campus Martius, the naval battle on the Fucine Lake took an ostensibly historical inspiration (a clash between the fleets of Rhodes and Sicily), although one not as near and dear to Claudius' heart. Unsurprisingly, given the size of this event, a number of ancient historians describe it in their works, although their accounts are not always consistent with one another. Taken as a whole, however, these accounts suggest that the *naumachia* may have involved as many as 19,000 condemned criminals, fighting from as many as fifty vessels of varying types on each side. In addition, members of the Praetorian Guard – stationed on rafts with artillery – surrounded the fray, so that no vessel filled with the condemned might try to escape.[41]

Apart from its sheer size, this particular spectacle was also famous to posterity for the exchange between the Emperor and the combatants that took place prior to its commencement. Dio and Suetonius both present very similar accounts of this incident, namely that the condemned performers, evidently in hope of being pardoned for their crimes, cried out, 'Hail emperor, we [or 'they'] who are about to die, salute you.' Subsequently, upon not receiving any sort of pardon, the performers displayed a certain reluctance to begin the sea battle, which understandably annoyed Claudius. There is, unfortunately, some confusion in the ancient sources as to the prisoners' ultimate fate once the *naumachia* finally began: Dio states that the criminals were forced to fight until all were destroyed, while Tacitus suggests that, after a bloody and hard-fought spectacle, the survivors earned a reprieve (at least on this occasion).[42]

Like his predecessor, Claudius ultimately was assassinated, not however because members of the Praetorian Guard plotted against him, but because of domestic intrigue. The chief architects of Claudius' death in 54 AD were his wife (and niece) Agrippina the Younger, and her son, Nero, whom she wished to succeed to the throne instead of Claudius' own son, Britannicus. Upon the Emperor's death, mother and son were not slow to consolidate their power.

In many respects, Nero was reminiscent of Caligula. Apart from the fact that they both took the throne at a relatively young age, both emperors were also inordinately fond of the spectacles and other amusements, and spent vast sums of money upon them. Both Nero and Caligula also considered themselves talented performers in their own right, and were not hesitant to flaunt their supposed skill in front of their subjects. In addition, Nero, like Caligula, not being entirely satisfied with the existing spectacle venues at the start of his reign, built a new amphitheatre in Rome.

Early in his reign, Nero made some important, albeit shortlived changes to the organization of *munera* in both Rome and the provinces. In 55 AD, the Emperor exempted the quaestors from the production of arena spectacles, an obligation imposed upon them less than a decade earlier by Claudius. Two years later, Nero issued an edict that barred provincial governors from producing any sort of *munus*. The historian Tacitus, commenting upon the latter measure, presents it as a virtuous act on the part of the emperor, one that spared various communities from the exorbitant financial demands of governors staging such events. Nero's earlier ban on quaestorian spectacles, sparing the officials in question from such an expensive undertaking, may be viewed in a similar light. Both of these laws, however, also presented at least one important benefit to the Emperor: by substantially reducing the number of officials who could stage *munera* in Rome and the provinces, the emperor could further monopolize the public acclaim surrounding such events for himself.[43]

The first series of spectacles Nero staged during his reign, in 55 AD, was, not surprisingly, reminiscent of those staged earlier under Claudius. Members of the Emperor's bodyguard, for example, are said to have slain 400 bears and 300 lions, a similar quarry to that found in earlier *munera*. Dio also relates that, on this occasion, mounted men rode alongside bulls and brought them down. Dio nowhere uses the term 'Thessalian' to describe this particular event, but it does nonetheless seem to bear a resemblance to the Thessalian bull-jumping exhibited in Rome by Nero's adoptive father. On the other hand, however, the same spectacle also saw thirty members of the equestrian class fight as gladiators, a practice not observed during Claudius' reign. Unfortunately, it is not clear from Dio's relatively brief account whether or not these men were compelled to fight by the Emperor, or if they were ordered to fight to the death.[44]

An even more elaborate series of events was staged by Nero in the wooden amphitheatre he had built in the Campus Martius in 57 AD. Our best description of this magnificent new venue comes from the poet Calpurnius Siculus, who appears to have been a contemporary of Nero. To judge from Calpurnius' description, no expense was spared in the construction of this impressive new facility:

'I saw a theatre that rose skyward on interwoven beams and almost looked down on the summit of the Capitoline...Just as the valley here expands into a wide circuit, and, winding at the side, with sloping forest background all around, stretches its concave curve amid the unbroken chain of hills, so there the sweep of the amphitheatre encircles the level ground, and the oval in the middle is bound by twin piles of building. Why should I now relate to you things which I myself could scarcely see in their several details? So dazzling was the glitter everywhere ...'[45]

The accounts of Dio and Suetonius, although they overlap to some degree, focus upon different aspects of the show Nero staged in his new amphitheatre in 57 AD. Taken together, they illustrate what a unique spectacle this must have represented to the assembled audience. First, the Emperor flooded the amphitheatre (or part of it) to present a *naumachia*, ostensibly representing a naval battle between the Persians and Athenians. The fish and marine animals released into the water enhanced the realism of this particular event. No sooner had the sea battle ended than the water was drained away, and single and mass combats were staged between performers on the arena floor. On this particular occasion, the performers were not run-of-the-mill gladiators, but – according to Suetonius – 600 equestrians and 400 senators whom Nero had compelled to participate in his spectacle. We have already seen that the participation of the elite in arena spectacles was nothing new: what was a novelty was such a large group of nobles forced to participate in mass combat (*gregatim*). Subsequently, these same men were forced to participate in the *venatio* Nero also staged as part of the proceedings. Suetonius stresses that no one died in these contests, which indicates that they were more in the vein of weapon exhibitions or the like, rather than regular arena combat. He also adds the detail that some of those compelled to participate were wealthy and possessed spotless reputations, which seems to suggest that by this point, only those members of the nobility who had monetary difficulties, and/or were of questionable character, would normally be considered as potentially suitable for the arena.[46]

The aforementioned poem of Calpurnius Siculus also makes mention of an elaborate *venatio* staged in Nero's wooden amphitheatre, featuring such animals as zebus, hippopotami, elk, and the now extinct auroch. It is not clear whether this particular event was part of the larger extravaganza staged in 57 AD. Calpurnius' text, since it gives an excellent impression of the profound effect a lavish imperial spectacle might have had upon a regular citizen of the Empire, is worth citing at some length:

'Look, the partition-belt begemmed and the gilded arcade vie in brilliancy; and withal just where the end of the arena presents the seats closest to the marble wall, wondrous ivory is inlaid on connected beams and unites into a cylinder which, gliding smoothly on well-shaped axle, could by a sudden turn balk any claws set upon it and shake off the beasts. Bright too is the gleam from the nets of gold wire which project into the arena hung on solid tusks … Beasts of every kind I saw; here I saw snow-white hares and horned boars, here I saw the elk, rare even in the forests which produce it. Bulls too I saw, either those of heightened nape, with an unsightly hump rising from the shoulder-blades, or those with shaggy mane tossed across the neck, with rugged beard covering the chin, and quivering bristles upon their stiff dewlaps. Nor was it my lot only to see monsters of the forest: sea calves also I beheld with bears pitted against them and the unshapely herd by the name of horses, bred in that river whose waters, with spring-like renewal, irrigate the crops upon its banks. Oh, how we quaked, whenever we saw the arena part asunder and its soil upturned and beasts plunged out from the chasm cleft in the earth; yet often from those same rifts the golden arbutus sprang amid a sudden fountain spray (of saffron).'[47]

The rotating ivory cylinders on top of the podium wall of the arena, as well as the gold netting mentioned by Calpurnius, actually served a practical purpose, as he alludes to in the poem. Many of the exotic animals collected by the Romans for their spectacles, such as tigers, could leap very high into the air, higher, in fact, than the podium walls of existing theatres or amphitheatres. If additional safety measures were not implemented, there was a significant chance of such animals leaping into the crowd and attacking spectators, detracting from the intended entertainment value of these events. Safety measures such as netting and rollers fixed on top of podium walls were common throughout the Empire: what set such measures apart in Nero's amphitheatre, of course, was the costly materials with which they were constructed.

Other features of Nero's amphitheatre were also reminiscent of those found at other venues. To judge from Calpurnius' description, for example, the former was equipped with some sort of lift system in its basement, to allow animals as well as stadium props like trees to be brought rapidly to the arena floor. It also appears that, like some later amphitheatres, Nero's venue had some sort of basin set into the arena floor that could be flooded. If the entire arena were flooded, of course, there would have been no way to keep animals and various stage props at the same time in the amphitheatre's basement.[48]

The Emperor's use of members of the nobility was not limited to the elaborate spectacle of 57 AD, but is also attested at other points during his reign. In 59 AD, as part of the spectacles Nero staged to commemorate his recently deceased mother, he had men and women of both the senatorial and equestrian classes perform publicly in a number of capacities, including as gladiators and beast fighters. He did so, according to the historian Tacitus, to make his own performing in public seem less shameful. Some members of the nobility who participated were forced to do so by the Emperor, while others, who had evidently fallen upon hard times financially, were more than willing to accept the lavish bribes offered for their participation. As late as 63 AD, Nero was still able to find both men and women of the nobility to participate in his *munera*.[49]

Members of the nobility were also forced to participate in one of the more singular participatory spectacles of Nero's reign, one described with disgust by the later historians Tacitus and Dio. In 64 AD, Nero, in close collaboration with his praetorian prefect Tigellinus, used the *stagnum* of Agrippa created during Augustus' reign as the venue for a series of events including gladiatorial combats, a *naumachia*, and *venationes*. The *stagnum* (or at least a portion of it) appears to have been alternately drained or flooded depending upon which event was taking place. According to Tacitus, Nero had collected a wide variety of both terrestrial and marine animals in preparation for these events. The 'highlight' of the occasion occurred when Nero and Tigellinus staged an elaborate banquet on barges floating in the lake, complete with brothels for the convenience of the Emperor's guests. The women collected in these brothels, including members of the nobility, were forced to submit themselves to whichever guests demanded their services.[50]

A final series of spectacles from this period that must be mentioned are those following the Great Fire of Rome in 64 AD, one of the more infamous events of Nero's reign. In the wake of this calamity, which destroyed much of the city, the Emperor offered aid to the survivors and enacted a number of beneficial measures, such as safer building standards for Rome. Nonetheless, many in Rome were unimpressed with Nero's munificence, and went so far as to accuse him of setting the fire in the first place in order to clear ground for his magnificent new palace, the Domus Aurea, which he built in the heart of the city following the fire. To deflect such widespread public criticism, the Emperor decided he needed a scapegoat for the fire. He chose the Christians. Untold numbers were rounded up in the city and subjected to dire public executions that, according to Tacitus, were staged both on the grounds of Nero's estate and in the Circus of Gaius and Nero. These executions featured some of the condemned wrapped in animal skins being mauled to death by dogs, as well as others being crucified by day and subsequently set alight as a source of illumination by night. Such excessive cruelty on the part of Nero, however, did nothing but prompt pity for his victims.[51]

The immolation of condemned criminals appears to have been a favoured method of execution during the reign of Nero. Tigellinus, for example, was said to have crucified and set alight his detractors in a manner similar to which Nero dealt with some of his Christian victims. An even more elaborate immolation, however, one involving a mythical re-enactment, was also staged during the reign of Nero, although the exact date is uncertain.[52] On this occasion, a certain condemned criminal by the name of Meniscus was dressed up as Hercules in front of an audience and burnt alive. As is the case with many such executions recorded in our sources, it is not clear what crime he committed to earn such an awful punishment. The poem commemorating the event, however, mentions that Meniscus, like Hercules, stole apples from the Garden of the Hesperides, which has led to the suggestion that the former's crime was perhaps trespassing onto the grounds of Nero's Domus Aurea: certainly, with poetic licence, the divine Garden of the Hesperides could be likened to an imperial estate.[53]

The controversy surrounding the Great Fire of Rome and its aftermath was just one of the factors in the Emperor's increasing unpopularity, an unpopularity that ultimately resulted in his removal from the throne and suicide in 68 AD. In the struggle for power which ensued, the so-called Year of the Four Emperors, not many *munera* are recorded in the ancient sources: the candidates for the throne, understandably, devoted the majority of their attention to political and military affairs, rather than public entertainment. The emperor Vespasian, who emerged victorious from the civil war in 69 AD, is said to have staged several *venationes* during his decade of rule, but evidently not many gladiatorial bouts, due to his dislike of the latter type of spectacle.[54]

Far more important than the spectacles staged during Vespasian's reign was the magnificent new amphitheatre begun under his rule, the Colosseum. The emperor, as the founder of a new imperial dynasty (the Flavians) following a bitter civil war, was at pains to rally the Roman populace behind him and his heirs, and in this respect, the building of the Colosseum was a brilliant propaganda success. First, the site of the Colosseum was carefully chosen to draw a contrast between the hated Nero and Vespasian. The amphitheatre was built where an artificial lake had once been located on the grounds of Nero's Domus Aurea, land that had been dedicated to the emperor's own amusement. By contrast, of course, the Colosseum was built for the benefit and enjoyment of the Roman people. Additionally, the head of the colossal statue of Nero which had been erected beside his lake (and which gave the later Colosseum its name), was altered to that of the much more pleasing sun god, Sol. Also, as we know from the Colosseum's dedicatory inscription, the funds for building this structure came from the considerable booty which the Roman army under Vespasian and his son Titus had recently captured while crushing the revolt in Judaea which had broken out late in Nero's reign. Therefore, the Colosseum also stood as a permanent reminder of the military victories of the Flavian dynasty.[55]

The Colosseum, representing the pinnacle of amphitheatre design, was a truly worthy entertainment venue for the capital of the Roman Empire. The building as a whole measured some 188m by 156m, and is estimated to have held as many as 50,000 spectators. One particular design feature instituted for their comfort was the *velum*, a linen awning that could be extended over the seating sections to provide protection from the elements. The complicated rigging for the *velum*, ultimately attached to the top tier of the amphitheatre by a series of wooden masts, resembled nothing so much as the rigging of a ship, and it is no surprise that a detachment of sailors from the naval port of Misenum were entrusted with furling and unfurling it as need demanded. The stone façade of the amphitheatre, crafted from travertine stone, was decorated with Greek and Roman architectural orders, bronze statues and shields in the 240 arches of the facade, and a triumphal arch on the first level, marking access to the imperial box within. Finally, in its developed form, the basement of the Colosseum contained almost 200 animal cages, as well as a complicated system of lifts and ramps whereby both beasts and spectacle props (eg. artificial trees) could be raised to the level of the arena in a matter of minutes. The scale and design of this amphitheatre, unsurprisingly, was copied to varying degrees by a number of larger cities throughout the Empire in an attempt to place themselves on an equal footing with the imperial capital (at least in terms of entertainment amenities), El Djem in North Africa being just one notable example.[56]

Vespasian, unfortunately, did not live to see his magnificent monument completed. It was left to his son and heir Titus to inaugurate the Colosseum with a magnificent series of spectacles lasting a hundred days in 80 AD. Unsurprisingly, a number of ancient authors commemorate these events in their works. Perhaps the most impressive is the book of poems, *On the Spectacles*, written by the contemporary poet Martial to immortalize the occasion. 9,000 animals are said to have been killed in the various *venationes* which took place at this time and, if Suetonius is to be believed, 5,000 of these were killed in a single day. As stated earlier, figures such as these are commonly assumed to be inflated. Nonetheless, the figures given for the inaugural games of the Colosseum represent the second highest attested total in Roman history of animals slain in the arena, which in and of itself gives us a notion of just how comparatively large in scale these events were. Another notable feature of these *venationes*, according to Dio, was the fact that not just male *venatores* were involved in killing these animals, but female performers as well.[57]

Ancient testimony also maintains that a number of aquatic spectacles were staged in the Colosseum at the time of its inauguration. As already noted, the finished basement of the Colosseum contained animal cages, spectacle props, and a lift system, which would have made a flooding of the arena floor impossible. The consensus among scholars, however, is that the basement in its final form was not constructed until the reign of Domitian (81–96 AD), which would have made possible the aquatic spectacle recorded for the Colosseum's inauguration. It is unclear, however, whether the entire arena was flooded, or only a basin built into the arena floor: examples of the latter are periodically found in later amphitheatres outside of Rome.[58]

The first aquatic event was a recreation of a naval battle between the Corcyrans and Corinthians. Presumably, this particular display involved some of the gladiators who, according to Dio, fought both on land and on water as part of the inaugural spectacles. A second marine event in the Colosseum, also attested by Dio, appears to have involved horses and bulls performing some sort of nonviolent dressage routine in the water. As Coleman notes, the water on this occasion must have been quite shallow, or else the animals involved would have just swum around or trod water, rather than perform any sort of manoeuvres.[59]

Two other aquatic events which appear to have been staged in the Colosseum, and which drew their inspiration from Greek mythology, were a group of 'Nereids' (water nymphs) cavorting, and 'Leander' swimming to meet his beloved, Hero. In the original myth, Leander drowned while on his way to one of these trysts. It has been suggested, therefore, that the man who played the role of Leander in the latter spectacle, like performers in other known mythical re-enactments, was a condemned criminal, and that the original intention of this event was for him to drown like his mythical namesake. If so, the somewhat enigmatic reference in the contemporary poet Martial's account of this spectacle, that 'Leander' was ultimately spared by 'Caesar's wave (*Caesaris unda*)', may mean that, perhaps at popular request, Titus ultimately decided to spare him.[60]

The aquatic spectacles staged at the Colosseum's inaugural games were not limited to that venue. A number of ancient authors record, in varying degrees of detail, the three days of events Titus also staged on the *stagnum* of Augustus. The poet Martial gives the fullest and most picturesque description:

'It had been the labour of Augustus to pit fleets against one another here and rouse the waves with naval trumpet. What fraction of our emperor's achievement does this amount to? Thetis and Galatea have seen strange beasts among the waves; Triton has seen chariots churning up the water like dust, and thought it was his master's horses galloping by; and while Nereus was organizing fierce battles for the hostile fleets, he shuddered to go on foot over the limpid water. Whatever can be seen in the Circus and the Amphitheatre the diverse wave has provided at a blast of Caesar's trumpet. Boasting about Fucinus and Nero's pools should stop: posterity must acknowledge this *naumachia*, and this one only.'[61]

As Martial suggests, the events staged at the *stagnum* included gladiatorial combat, chariot racing, a *venatio*, and a *naumachia* representing the famous conflict between Athens and Syracuse during the Peloponnesian War. Taken as a whole, the different accounts of these spectacles suggest a wooden platform was built over part of the *stagnum* on which the gladiators, *venatores*, and animals fought. The *venatio*, in particular, must have been massive in scale, since Suetonius suggests that this is the occasion on which 5,000 animals were killed in a single day. The herding of various animals from the platform into the water during this combat probably explains the reference in Martial's poem to the sea deities Thetis and Galatea seeing 'strange beasts' in the water.[62]

The naval battle staged on the final day of events in the *stagnum* appears to have been approximately the same size as Augustus' recreation of the Battle of Salamis staged at the same venue just over eighty years earlier: both *naumachiae*, for example, featured 3000 combatants, most likely prisoners-of-war and/or condemned criminals. One interesting feature of Titus' spectacle was that, although inspired by an historical battle, its outcome did not correspond to historical reality – in this instance it was the 'Athenians' who defeated the 'Syracusans'.[63]

The ahistorical outcome of the naval battle on the *stagnum* of Augustus highlights one of the important propaganda messages that the spectacle presented to the assembled audience. On one level, of course, the lavish and costly *naumachia* represented the wealth and munificence of the emperor. Perhaps even more importantly, however, it represented his supreme power. Not only could he recreate a famous historical battle for the audience, he could also (at least in the eyes of the spectators) alter its outcome as he saw fit. Other aquatic spectacles presented by Titus broadcast the same message: forcing terrestrial animals to fight or perform dressage manoeuvres in water, for example, symbolized the emperor's almost divine power to subvert the laws of nature for the amusement of both himself and the assembled spectators.[64]

Some of the public executions presented as mythical re-enactments by Titus and his brother Domitian, as commemorated in Martial's *On the Spectacles*, served a similar function. Two such spectacles saw condemned criminals dressed up as Daedalus and Orpheus ultimately torn apart by bears in the arena. The significance of their manner of death is that it was not how either figure died in myth: Orpheus, for example, who was famed for playing music sweet enough to charm even wild beasts, was torn apart by women. Once again, however, the alleged power of the emperor was such that he could rework the famous myths of antiquity to his own liking.[65]

One particularly grisly execution recounted by Martial merits special discussion:

> 'Believe that Pasiphae was mated to the Dictaean bull: we have seen it, the old legend has won credence. And let not hoary antiquity plume itself, Caesar: whatever Fame sings of, the arena affords you.'[66]

In Greek myth, Pasiphae was the wife of King Minos of Crete, who developed an unnatural affection for his prize bull. Thanks to the aid of Minos' court inventor, Daedalus, Pasiphae was ultimately able to mate with the bull, thereby giving birth to the monstrous Minotaur nine months later. In the horrific execution recounted by Martial, a female condemned criminal in the guise of Pasiphae was mounted by a bull in the arena, which proved fatal for the woman in question. Some scholars in the past have speculated that Martial in this instance exaggerated, and that such a method of execution was implausible. Enough other evidence does exist, however, to suggest that having women mounted and/or mauled by various wild animals was a common enough method of execution. The first century Christian writer Clement of Rome, for example, records women in the guise of Dirce being executed in the arena: since a bull killed Dirce in myth, we can assume that her arena counterparts were as well. As a final example, a number of clay lamps discovered in Athens, depicting women being mounted or mauled by a wild ass, are thought to represent executions in the arena, a method of punishment also mentioned by the second century writer Apuleius in his *Metamorphoses*.[67]

In one sense, of course, the execution recounted by Martial again symbolized the power of the emperor to make the world of myth, even the most fantastic or implausible elements, come alive for spectators. On another level, however, executions such as those of 'Pasiphae' represent the Roman state's apparent desire to punish female capital offenders in a particularly harsh manner. Apparently, such women were considered doubly dangerous: their crimes, in general, not only represented an affront to Roman justice, but also the fact that traditionally subservient women in patriarchal Roman society would dare to commit such crimes presented a serious threat to Roman social order in and of itself. The especially horrific executions reserved for female criminals, then, served both to punish whatever specific crime had been committed, and to reassure spectators that the traditional gender roles of Roman society had been restored.[68]

It is important to note that not all of the attested spectacle re-enactments of the Flavian period revolved around famous Greek naval battles or episodes from Greek myth. Incidents from Roman history were also presented to the audience. On at least one such occasion during the reign of Domitian, an unfortunate criminal was forced to re-enact the exploits of the early Roman hero Scaevola. In Roman lore, Scaevola was renowned for unflinchingly burning his right arm to a crisp in order to demonstrate the bravery and tenacity of the Roman people to the Etruscan king, Lars Porsenna. Similarly, in the arena spectacle, the criminal playing the role of Scaevola was forced to burn his own arm. It is unclear in this case if the punishment was meant to be fatal, or if the loss of an arm was deemed sufficient penalty by the Roman authorities. Once again, this spectacle served the function of reassuring the audience of the efficacy of Roman justice; it also served the added purpose, however, of glorifying an episode from Rome's own illustrious past.[69]

Domitian had much more opportunity to use the Colosseum for various spectacles than his brother Titus, who died unexpectedly in 81 AD after only two years on the throne. Suetonius notes, in fact, that throughout his fifteen-year reign, Domitian staged numerous extravagant events not only in the amphitheatre but the Circus Maximus as well.[70] One of the most memorable *munera* of Domitian's reign was the exhibition of a two-horned rhinoceros in the Colosseum. One-horned rhinoceroses had sporadically appeared in previous Roman *venationes*, but this is the first recorded appearance of the multi-horned variety in Rome. Domitian's rhinoceros, to judge from the poetry of Martial, thrilled the audience not only because of its novelty, but also because of its strength and fury:

'The rhinoceros displayed all over the arena, performed for you, Caesar, battles that he did not promise. How he lowered his head and flamed into fearful rage! How mighty a bull was he, to whom a bull was as a dummy!'[71]

The poems of Martial were not the only means by which this event was commemorated for posterity: a series of coins depicting two-horned rhinoceroses, datable to sometime between 83 and 85, evidently allude to Domitian's spectacle in the Colosseum.[72]

We have already noted the general connection between the exhibition of various exotic animals and contemporary Roman territorial claims. In the case of the rhinoceros displayed by Domitian, however, we may be able to draw a more detailed connection between this particular animal and current Roman exploration in eastern Africa. The investigation of this region appears to have begun in earnest during the reign of Nero, when a detachment of the Praetorian Guard marched to the upper Nile. Among the alleged objectives of this expedition was military reconnaissance for a possible campaign in the region, as well as an attempt to discover the source of the Nile. The surviving accounts of this undertaking, however, also suggest that the Romans had a keen interest in the local flora and fauna: their scouts made note of the monkeys and parrots encountered during the journey, as well as the tracks of rhinos and elephants they found near the city of Meroe on the upper Nile.[73]

These reports of exotic fauna may have in part inspired a later expedition to Ethiopia under the command of a certain Septimius Flaccus. Flaccus and his troops are said to have marched over the course of three months from Libya to Ethiopia through the land of the Garamantes. Unfortunately, many other details of this expedition remain unknown, such as the exact identity of Flaccus, or the date of his undertaking: the scholarly consensus appears to be that the expedition was launched in the late 70s AD. One of the purposes of this march was probably to overawe the Garamantes, and thereby curb any future attacks on Roman territory. Another aim of Flaccus and his men, however, may have been to capture exotic beasts for the spectacles in Rome, most notably those associated with the opening of the Colosseum. Given the thousands of animals which are said to have been killed on that occasion, as well as the fact that wildlife rich Ethiopia was an important source of exotic beasts for Roman *venationes*, it would perhaps have been strange if Flaccus and his men did not take an active interest in the various animals they encountered on the course of their march.[74]

Flaccus' expedition, in turn, may have prompted the later exploration of a certain Julius Maternus, and the acquisition of the two-horned rhinoceros commemorated both by Martial and the coinage of Domitian. According to the geographer Ptolemy, Maternus accompanied the king of the Garamantes on a campaign against the Ethiopians, and after a march of a little more than four months, reached the territory of Agisymba, which ostensibly had a sizeable population of rhinoceroses. As in the case of Flaccus' earlier march, there are a number of questions surrounding the expedition of Maternus: was he, for example, a military commander or a civilian trader, and where exactly was Agisymba located? The exact date of Maternus' endeavour is also unclear, although it must have occurred between the expedition of Flaccus and 110 AD, thought to be the latest possible date of composition for Ptolemy's work. The possibility certainly exists, however, in part because of the specific mention of rhinoceroses in Ptolemy's account, that Maternus' expedition to central Africa took place during the reign of Domitian, and that it was he who sent the exotic two-horned rhinoceroses back to Rome to feature in the emperor's spectacle.[75]

Like earlier emperors, Domitian also staged spectacles that, through forcing the animals involved to behave contrary to their natural instincts, demonstrated his supposed power over nature. Such displays included bisons drawing chariots, as well as animals such as leopards and bears being led in procession. By far the most impressive spectacle for the audience, however, were the lions trained to allow hares to pass in and out of their open mouths unharmed. The following is just one of the six poems Martial wrote to commemorate this particular spectacle:

'We have seen the pranks, the sportive gambols of the lions, Caesar (this too the arena offers you), when the hare as often as seized returned from the gentle fang and ran at large through the open jaws. How comes it that a greedy lion can spare his captive prey? Ah, but he is said to be yours. Therefore he can.'[76]

No expense was spared for the elaborate series of spectacles Domitian staged in the fall of 89 AD to celebrate his recent victories against the Dacians on the lower Danube. Among the more notable events of this period were mass infantry and cavalry battles in the Circus Maximus, reminiscent of those staged by Caesar at his triumphal celebrations over a century earlier, as well as a *naumachia* in a new *stagnum* which Domitian had excavated for this very purpose. Since Suetonius records that the emperor also staged such an event in the Colosseum, it is possible that the naval battle in Domitian's *stagnum* took place after the amphitheatre's basement had been equipped with animal cages and the like, thereby rendering it unsuitable for further aquatic spectacles.[77]

According to a number of ancient sources, the most notable innovation of Domitian's triumphal celebrations, as well as other spectacles staged during his reign, were the unique performers he sometimes enlisted for such events. On at least one occasion, in fact, the emperor staged combats of women and dwarves for the audience. The contemporary poet Statius gives the most vivid description of such an event:

> The sex untrained and ignorant of weaponry takes stand and dares engage in manly combat. One would think them troops of Thermodon in battle heat by Tanais or wild Phasis. Here comes a bold string of midgets. Nature is cramped for them, finished in a trice, she tied them once for all into knotted balls. They deal wounds and mingle fists, and threaten one another with death–by what hands!'[78]

One of the questions pertaining to such events concerns the amount of training the participants received beforehand. Obviously, one of the main attractions for spectators on these occasions was the novelty of seeing women and dwarves fight as gladiators. Yet was this novelty enough to maintain audience interest, particularly if, as suggested by our ancient sources, combats of women and dwarves were staged on several occasions during Domitian's reign? In the passage cited above, Statius suggests that the women, in particular, received no training before they fought. In the same passage, however, he likens their fighting prowess to that of the mythical Amazons. Faced with this contradictory evidence, it is perhaps preferable to assume that the women and dwarves received at least some training before they fought in public. Otherwise, there would be little to maintain spectator interest once the initial novelty of seeing them perform as gladiators wore off.

Not all the members of the audience, however, were necessarily enamoured of such a spectacle. In his sixth satire, written not long after the reign of Domitian, the poet Juvenal includes in his litany of the alleged vices of the fairer sex the fact that (horror of horrors!) some of them even fight as gladiators: 'What modesty can you expect in a woman who wears a helmet, abjures her own sex, and delights in feats of strength?'[79] Presumably, however, the moral outrage professed by Juvenal over such performers was not shared by a majority of his contemporaries, or else Domitian would not have staged *munera* featuring them on more than one occasion, as appears to be the case. Nonetheless, as we shall see, the staging of similar spectacles featuring female gladiators during the reign of Septimius Severus approximately a century later does appear to have provoked considerable outrage, enough at least, for the Emperor to ban women fighting in the arena.

Such was Domitian's passion for the *munera*, and his evident desire to be seen as a munificent emperor, that he forced various officials to stage spectacles under his auspices. As Suetonius notes, Domitian not only revived the *munera* staged by the quaestors during his reign, but also made sure to attend them.[80] In addition, the Emperor decreed that priests administering the *Quinquatria*, an annual festival dedicated to Domitian's patron deity Minerva, should stage *venationes* as part of the festivities. Evidently, no expense was spared for these events: even a hostile source like Suetonius describes them as *eximias* ('outstanding').[81]

Domitian also demonstrated his generosity to the Roman populace through other means at such events. At the aforementioned quaestorian games, for example, the emperor would allow the audience to select two pairs of gladiators from his own imperial stable, who would then fight as a grand finale to the day's events. On three separate occasions, Domitian also gave a largesse of 300 sesterces to each of the assembled spectators. Finally, the Emperor is credited with staging a large public banquet as part of the annual *Septimontium* festival at least once during his reign, followed by a random distribution of prizes to the audience. Nonetheless, Domitian, when provoked, was not hesitant to exercise his infamous cruelty upon spectators who earned his displeasure: on one occasion, according to Suetonius, the Emperor had a citizen thrown to the dogs who had dared to suggest that Domitian showed undue favoritism towards the 'Thracian' gladiators.[82]

Another recorded victim of Domitian in the context of the spectacles was a former *consul*, Acilius Glabrio. At some point during his later reign, the Emperor evidently forced Glabrio to fight a lion and bears at the former's private estate. The fact that Glabrio appears to have slain the animals pitted against him with relative ease suggests that this was certainly not the first time he had participated in such a dangerous event, and that, by extension, the practice of Roman aristocrats periodically fighting in such spectacles had not died out entirely, despite previous measures against it. Nonetheless, it was evidently considered an unseemly enough activity for a member of the Roman elite by Domitian's day that he could use it as a pretext for Glabrio's subsequent execution. Although the latter was condemned for fighting as a gladiator against wild animals, it may be that the emperor's jealousy was the real cause of Glabrio's death. Domitian was inordinately proud of his hunting and archery skills, and quite possibly took a dim view of Glabrio showing him up by overcoming such dangerous animals.[83]

The considerable costs of the many spectacles and associated extravagances of Domitian's reign further contributed to the acrimonious relationship between the Emperor and the senatorial aristocracy in Rome. Like Caligula before him, Domitian was forced to employ unorthodox means to cover such expenditures: Dio, in fact, alleges that many of the prominent citizens executed or murdered during Domitian's reign were killed so that their wealth could be expropriated for the imperial treasury. Unsurprisingly, when the Emperor did fall victim to an assassination plot in 96 AD, it was members of the senatorial elite who took the most pleasure in this event.[84]

Suetonius' collection of imperial biographies, one of our main sources for the spectacles of the early Empire, unfortunately ends with the assassination of Domitian. For subsequent imperial spectacles, we have to rely, in part, upon fewer written sources, sometimes of questionable veracity. The *Scriptores Historiae Augustae* or SHA, for example, a collection of imperial biographies extending from the early second to the late third century AD, is notorious for the quantity of dubious material found within its pages. Nonetheless, the accumulated evidence does indicate that imperial spectacles continued to grow in scale following the reign of Domitian, reaching their height during the subsequent century.

The main action taken by Domitian's successor Nerva (96–98 AD), with regard to the *munera*, was to limit their production to save the imperial treasury money after the excesses of Domitian's reign.[85] The next emperor, Trajan, however, whose reign from 98 to 117 AD saw the Empire reach its maximum territorial extent, had no such problem with finances: as a result, some of the largest recorded spectacles in Roman history occurred under him.

The most important of the many military campaigns waged by Trajan were his two wars against the Dacian king Decebalus, which resulted in the annexation of Dacia (roughly corresponding to modern-day Romania). One of the main advantages of this conquest, apart from stabilizing the Roman frontier on the lower Danube, was the abundant mineral wealth of the new province, which allowed Trajan to commemorate his victories with a magnificent new forum in the heart of Rome, as well as lavish spectacles.

Dio, for example, recounts that Trajan staged gladiatorial *munera* to celebrate his first victory over Decebalus in 102 AD, although he gives no specifics as to their size or scale. Whatever events the emperor staged on this occasion, however, were dwarfed by the subsequent spectacles, including a *naumachia*, organized to celebrate Trajan's second and final victory over Decebalus in 105 AD. Over the course of 123 days, some 10,000 gladiators fought in *munera* staged by the emperor. Perhaps even more astonishing to a modern reader, however, is Dio's claim that 11,000 animals were killed in the numerous *venationes* which took place over the same period of time, an even larger number of animal fatalities than those attested for the inaugural games of the Colosseum some twenty-five years earlier. Trajan probably included numerous native Dacian animals in these events as another means to remind the assembled spectators of his recent conquest.[86]

Trajan's successor Hadrian (117–138 AD), although he staged no events as large as those associated with the Dacian triumph of 105 AD, nonetheless was very active in producing arena spectacles and other public entertainments during his reign, not only in Rome but also in other cities which he visited as emperor. According to the SHA, for example, Hadrian often staged beast hunts in the Circus Maximus featuring over a hundred lions. The same source also alleges that one of the Emperor's birthday celebrations in Rome included a *venatio* involving over 1,000 beasts. Perhaps this is the same event referred to in an inscription from nearby Ostia, which records the killing of 2689 animals at a spectacle staged by Hadrian in approximately 120 AD. The emperor is also said to have put on a *venatio* involving 1000 beasts for the Athenian populace during one of his visits to that city.[87]

One important measure passed by Hadrian with regard to the games was a law that forbade the sale of slaves to gladiatorial schools without just cause. This particular decree followed the precedent of an earlier law, likely instituted in the late first century AD, which similarly forbade slaves from being condemned to the *venationes* by their masters without due process. Hadrian's legislation, however, should not be taken as an indication he disliked gladiatorial *munera*: as alluded to previously, he was an avid enthusiast of such events. On one notable occasion, according to the SHA, the emperor sent 300 condemned criminals into the arena to fight wearing gold-embroidered cloaks he had just received as a diplomatic gift from the king of the Iberians, in order to advertise his disdain for this particular offering. According to the same source, such was Hadrian's passion for the arena that he was actually well versed in the use of gladiatorial weapons.[88]

Despite his alleged mastery of gladiatorial combat, there is no record of Hadrian ever personally descending into the arena to fight as a gladiator. At least once, however, he is said to have publicly fought wild animals as part of his birthday celebrations in Rome. According to Dio, on the occasion in question, the emperor killed a hundred lions and an equal number of lionesses.[89] Certainly, a number of sources, including the Hadrianic hunting roundels affixed to the Arch of Constantine in Rome, amply attest to Hadrian's love of hunting in the wild. Given this passion for the hunt, it is perhaps understandable that, at least once during his reign, Hadrian might wish to display his skills to the Roman public. The emperor's participation in public spectacle, however, was evidently not on such a scale as to provoke public displeasure, unlike that of the emperor Commodus later in the century.

The continuing growth in scale and slaughter of imperial *munera* over the first and early second centuries AD appears to have been accepted enthusiastically by most Romans, to judge from the extant literary evidence. Contemporary criticism of the spectacles, predominantly leveled by writers belonging to the upper classes, largely concerned their particular appeal to the lower classes, or the unruly behaviour they might provoke in the audience. Most commentators appear to have had no issue with the actual events on the arena floor: virtually no complaint is found, for example, concerning the hundreds or even thousands of animals killed in the massive *venationes* of the period. Suetonius, in fact, notes with approval the 5,000 animals allegedly slaughtered on a single day during the inaugural games of the Colosseum, as emblematic of Titus' munificence. Even the hated Domitian is praised by the same writer for the *eximias venationes* ('outstanding beast hunts') produced during his reign. By contrast, Suetonius criticizes Caligula for insulting the Roman people through exhibitions of subpar gladiators and animals. Certainly, by the reign of Hadrian, when Suetonius wrote his imperial biographies, it was expected that any self-respecting emperor would produce lavish *munera* and other spectacles for the Roman people.[90]

The reign of Hadrian's successor, Antonius Pius (138–161 AD), arguably witnessed the apex of the Roman Empire. With few exceptions, the frontiers were quiet during his rule, and the state was at the height of its prosperity. Unfortunately, our sources for Antoninus Pius' reign are not particularly abundant, but they do indicate that on at least two special occasions, the Emperor took advantage of these settled and prosperous conditions to stage magnificent spectacles for his subjects in Rome.

The first of these spectacles appears to have been staged in 148 or 149, probably to celebrate the 900th anniversary of the foundation of Rome. Coins minted at that time, depicting diverse animals including lions and elephants, and bearing the legend MUNIFICENTIA ('Munificence'), evidently were issued to celebrate this event. A passage from the SHA also appears to refer to this particular *munus*:

'He [Pius] held games at which he displayed elephants and the animals called corocottae [hyenas?] and tigers and rhinoceroses, even crocodiles and hippopotami, in short, all the animals of the whole earth; and he presented at a single performance as many as a hundred lions together with tigers.'[91]

In this instance, the Emperor was not using exotic animals to advertise a recent military conquest, but instead to show the extent of Roman territory on both land and sea under his benevolent rule.[92] A decade later, Antoninus Pius once again included exotic animals like tigers in the games staged to celebrate his twentieth anniversary on the throne.

Apart from the evidence for these two spectacles, however, not much specific information is preserved concerning arena *munera* during Antoninus Pius' reign. The SHA merely notes that the Emperor carried out repairs on the Colosseum during his reign, and instituted a limit on the amount of money spent on a gladiatorial spectacle.[93] Evidently, the exorbitant cost of staging *munera* in communities outside Rome had become ruinous for many local officials responsible for their production, and the Emperor's legislation was intended to provide some measure of relief. Antoninus Pius' successor, Marcus Aurelius (161–180 AD), as we shall shortly see, was compelled to introduce similar legislation during his reign.

The latter, of course, is famous for his philosophical proclivities, and it is not at all surprising, given such inclinations, that he was not especially fond of arena spectacles. Although Marcus Aurelius staged a number of *munera* in Rome during his reign, such as a *venatio* that featured the slaughter of a hundred lions, he himself had evidently little interest in attending them, and is said to have only done so under compulsion. Marcus Aurelius' attitude towards such events contrasts with that of Lucius Verus who, at Marcus' behest, co-ruled the Empire with him from 161 to 169 AD. The latter is said to have been so fond of gladiatorial spectacles and other forms of entertainment that he neglected administrative matters. As the SHA states, apart from his lack of cruelty, Lucius Verus was in many ways a second Nero.[94]

The most significant action undertaken by Marcus Aurelius in respect to arena spectacles was undoubtedly the law he introduced along with his son and heir Commodus in 177 AD to limit the expense of gladiatorial *munera*. As noted previously, by the second century the cost of staging such events had evidently become prohibitive for many local magistrates and officials in the cities of the Empire. Priests of the imperial cult in these communities, who were responsible for staging various public spectacles as part of their official duties, were particularly hard hit financially. In an effort to lessen expense, the new law not only placed a limit on the amount that could be charged

for different grades of gladiators, but also abolished the taxes previously
levied upon the *munera* and their production, a cost evidently passed on
from the *lanistae* to the officials organising such events.[95] Marcus Aurelius'
attitude towards arena spectacles is nicely encapsulated in the section of the
law concerning this abolition of taxes on the *munera*:

> 'And so they [Marcus Aurelius and Commodus] removed the Fiscus
> [imperial treasury] from the arena completely. For what does the
> Fiscus of Marcus Aurelius and [Commodus] need with the arena? All
> the money of these emperors is pure, not contaminated by the splash
> of human blood, not soiled with the wealth of sordid gains, and it is as
> innocently produced as it is collected.'[96]

Despite his participation in the promulgation of this law, Commodus
(180–192 AD) subsequently proved to have a much more enthusiastic
attitude towards arena spectacles. Not content, in fact, merely to be a
spectator, the Emperor himself ultimately participated in such events
to display his supposed martial prowess to the Roman people. According
to the contemporary historian Dio, who, as a member of the Senate, was
forced to witness the Emperor's exploits in the arena, many of the new taxes
introduced by Commodus during his reign were used specifically to fund
lavish *venationes* and gladiatorial spectacles.[97]

Dio provides us, in particular, with a vivid account of the fourteen
consecutive days of spectacles staged by Commodus late in his reign,
perhaps on the occasion of the *ludi Romani* in the autumn of 192 AD. The
emperor would descend into the arena in the costliest finery available to
fight as *venator* or gladiator, sometimes as both on the same day. In the latter
contests, Commodus would fight as a *secutor*, his favourite type of gladiator.
It is important to note, however, that these bouts were much more akin to
sparring matches than fatal duels, and certainly posed no danger to the
Emperor. Commodus himself was armed only with a wooden sword and
shield, and his opponents would speedily submit to him after merely being
wounded.[98]

Even more memorable were the Emperor's exploits as a *venator* in the
arena. Commodus saw himself as the new Hercules, a fact amply attested by

the coinage and sculpture of his reign, and as such, missed no opportunity to demonstrate that his hunting skills, particularly with the bow and arrow, were equal to those of his mythical role model. Among the animals slain by Commodus in public, according to ancient testimony, were many bears, lions, hippopotami, elephants, and rhinoceroses, as well as a giraffe and tiger. Dio even claims that the Emperor, once again in imitation of Hercules, slew disfigured men in the arena he had dressed up in the guise of giants from Greek myth. Once again, it is important to note that such spectacles were carefully organized to place Commodus in no real danger: the Emperor, for example, hunted bears from intersecting crosswalls above the arena floor so he could spear them in perfect safety.[99]

Arguably, the most famous hunting exploit of Commodus involved his slaughter of Mauretanian ostriches. Such was the Emperor's marksmanship with crescent-tipped arrowheads that he is said to have routinely decapitated the birds with a single shot. This was possibly the infamous occasion, as related by Dio, when Commodus attempted to threaten the assembled senators by brandishing a severed ostrich head at them from the arena floor, a ridiculous spectacle, however, which provoked more amusement than fear.[100]

The erratic behaviour of Commodus both inside and outside of the arena alienated not only members of the Senate, but also prominent officials like his praetorian prefect, Laetus, commander of the imperial guard. Ultimately, the latter was one of the ringleaders of the plot that ended with Commodus' assassination on the last day of 192. According to ancient testimony, the plot was set in motion by the discovery that the Emperor was planning to execute a number of prominent officials, including Laetus, and issue forth from the gladiatorial barracks on the first day of the new year as both *consul* and *secutor*. This latest harebrained scheme appeared to many in the Emperor's entourage as final proof of his irredeemable madness.[101]

While much of the ancient testimony concerning Commodus, in particular Dio's history, reflects the attitudes of the upper or senatorial class in Rome, another contemporary historian, Herodian, provides some insight as to what the broader Roman populace thought of their emperor's exploits in the arena. The following passage immediately follows Herodian's description of the Emperor's hunting exploits:

'So far, Commodus was still quite popular with the mob even if his conduct, apart from his courage and marksmanship, was unfitting for an emperor. But when he ran into the amphitheatre stripped and carrying his weapons for a gladiatorial fight, the people were ashamed to see a Roman emperor of noble lineage, whose father and forebears had all celebrated great triumphs, now disgracing his office with a thoroughly degrading exhibition, instead of using his weapons to fight the barbarians and prove himself worthy of the Roman empire.'[102]

We have already seen that in Roman society participation in arena spectacles was generally considered to be beneath the dignity of members of the elite, much less the emperor. Herodian's account suggests, however, that fighting against wild beasts, perhaps because it was viewed as symbolizing power over nature, was deemed preferable to fighting against the dregs of society as a gladiator. A reflection of this attitude can perhaps be seen in the coinage of the period: while such coins periodically depict various exotic animals, as well as *venationes* in the arena, not a single coin minted in Rome depicts gladiators or a gladiatorial combat.[103]

We will end our survey of imperial spectacles, for the time being, with the reign of Commodus. His death, the end of the Antonine dynasty, ultimately led to a struggle for the throne, out of which Septimius Severus emerged victorious in 193. Although Severus himself was a competent ruler, the dynasty he founded was not characterized by the type of strong rule enjoyed by Rome throughout much of the second century. Even worse, the assassination of the last Severan ruler in 235 ushered in the so-called era of the soldier-emperors, a half-century when the Empire faced a myriad of challenges, including civil war and disastrous defeats on the frontiers. The challenges faced by the Roman state at this time, unsurprisingly, contributed to changes in the nature of imperial spectacles in the later Empire, which we shall address in a subsequent chapter.

# Chapter Three

# *Munera* Outside Rome

Our discussion of arena spectacles, up to this point, has focused upon the *munera* staged by the magistrates and emperors in Rome herself. Such events, however, were equally popular in other cities and towns throughout Roman territory. A local notable or official could gain the same type of popularity through the staging of a successful *munus* in his community that the emperors in Rome earned through their own munificence, albeit to a lesser extent. In this chapter, we shall discuss these local spectacles, as well as the challenges faced by those staging them.

We have already seen that elected officials in Rome, like the *aediles*, were expected to provide *munera* to the city populace, especially prior to the establishment of the Principate, after which the production of such spectacles in the capital was largely monopolized by the imperial bureaucracy. Similarly, their counterparts in the smaller cities and towns of the Roman Empire were expected to produce spectacles for their fellow citizenry. The emperors, of course, did not view such local spectacles as a potential challenge to their authority, unlike *munera* produced by *editores* outside the imperial family in Rome itself. On average, it appears that the chief magistrates (*duoviri*) of a given community were expected to provide at their own expense about four days of spectacles per year, including not only arena events, but other entertainments like chariot racing and theatrical productions as well.[1]

One of the greatest challenges faced by local *editores*, of course, was cost. While emperors and members of the imperial family possessed almost unlimited funds with which to stage the exorbitant spectacles discussed in the last chapter, spectacle organizers in the smaller centres of the Roman Empire had a much smaller pool of funds for their own events. Add to this the related consideration that, under the terms of the previously discussed legislation introduced in the late second century to regulate the cost of gladiatorial spectacles, even the most modest category of *munus* (rated at a cost of 30,000 sesterces or less) could still cost up to £200,000 (or $US 335,000) in modern currency.[2]

Apart from the *duoviri* and their deputies, other officials commonly entrusted with the production of local spectacles were the priests of the imperial cult found in cities throughout the Empire. As part of their official duties, they too were normally required to stage *munera* in their respective communities on an annual basis. Most appear to have owned their own troupes, or *familiae*, of gladiators and *venatores*, which, of course, facilitated the production of such events. A good example of such an organization is found in an early third century dedicatory inscription from Heirapolis in Asia Minor. The text honours two chief-priests of the imperial cult in the city on behalf of the local *familia*. The latter included not only gladiators, but *venatores* and bull baiters as well. Presumably, grouping different performers together into one troupe, as in this example, rather than overseeing a different *familia* for each arena specialty, was much more convenient for spectacle organizers when it came time to organize a given event.[3]

The regular *munera* put on by the *duoviri* and priests of the imperial cult, however, were often not the only arena spectacles citizens had to look forward to in a given year. Such was the public demand for the *munera*, and the potential popularity gained by staging them, that prominent magistrates and wealthy citizens within a given community would commonly stage them even when not officially required to do so. An inscription from the town of Pozzuoli in southern Italy, for example, records that a magistrate by the name of Cassius Cerialis staged a gladiatorial spectacle there in honour of the emperor Nero, perhaps during an official visit to Pozzuoli by the latter.[4]

Such *editores* could, at least on occasion, receive funds from their respective communities in order to defray the considerable costs associated with staging an arena spectacle. Those organizers, however, who refused such financial assistance, and instead paid for *munera* entirely with their own wealth, could receive a special commendation from their fellow citizens. A late second century inscription from Tibur, for example, specifically praises an *editor* for staging both a *venatio* and a gladiatorial spectacle using solely his own money (*sua pecunia*).[5]

Another excellent example of this type of civic munificence, and the lengths to which spectacle organizers would go to satisfy public demand,

can be found in an early second century letter sent from Pliny the Younger
to his friend Maximus in Verona:

> 'You did well to put on a show of gladiators for our people of Verona,
> who have long shown their affection and admiration for you and
> have voted you many honours. Verona was also the home town of the
> excellent wife you loved so dearly, whose memory you owe some public
> building or show, and this kind of spectacle is particularly suitable for a
> funeral tribute. Moreover, the request came from so many people that
> a refusal would have been judged churlish rather than strong-minded
> on your part ... I am sorry the African panthers [leopards] you had
> bought in such quantities did not turn up on the appointed day, but
> you deserve the credit although the weather prevented their arriving in
> time; it was not your fault that you could not show them.'[6]

On this occasion, of course, the residents of Verona used the recent death of
Maximus' wife as a pretext to demand that he stage a *munus* in her honour;
this despite the fact that such events had long since moved beyond their
funereal origins. Maximus went beyond the call of duty in organizing this
spectacle, particularly in attempting to import costly African leopards for
the event. In his mind, as well as those of many other *editores*, the long-term
popularity resulting from such a lavish spectacle was worth any short-term
expense.

To judge from the available evidence, most organizers of *venationes* in
the smaller centres of the Roman Empire preferred to use readily available
local animals like boars, not only to save money, but also to avoid potential
difficulties such as those Maximus experienced with his leopards. Having
costly animals arrive late for a spectacle was, in fact, just one of the issues
that could arise when *editores* attempted to add an exotic flair to their events.
Even when such beasts arrived in plenty of time for a given spectacle, they
might fall ill and die in the interim, due to the lack of proper supervisory
staff and facilities in all but the largest cities of the Empire.

In certain instances, however, even the slaughter of relatively mundane
local animals could be a valuable public service on the part of magistrates
staging *munera*. Capturing and destroying wild beasts from the territory

surrounding the towns and cities where spectacles took place was one way to clear arable land for agricultural exploitation. This connection between the *venationes* and agricultural prosperity was perhaps most prevalent in Roman North Africa, a region not only home to numerous wild animal species featured in Roman spectacles, but also extensive cultivation of such crops as grain and olives. Certainly, as the following excerpt from the sixth century poet Luxorius illustrates, North Africans were aware of the beneficial relationship between spectacle and cultivation in the region:

'The countryside marvels at the triumphs of the amphitheatre and the forest notices that strange wild beasts are there. The many farmers look at new struggles while plowing and the sailor sees varied entertainments from the sea. The fertile land loses nothing, the plants grow in greater abundance while all the wild beasts fear their fates here.'[7]

Occasionally, local spectacles are referred to in contemporary literature such as the poetry of Luxorius or the correspondence of Pliny the Younger, but understandably, they receive far less attention in Greek and Roman literary sources than the massive shows put on by the emperors in Rome. Most of our specific information on the local *munera* in cities and towns across the Empire comes from inscriptions commissioned to commemorate these events, and the generosity of their patrons, for posterity. These inscriptions often provide detailed information on the various aspects of a given *munus*, particularly those considered to be exceptional, and it is through the relatively detailed records of local arena events found in Roman epigraphy that we can reconstruct their general character.

Such epigraphic evidence is of even greater importance when it comes to studying Roman arena spectacles in the eastern Empire. Magistrates and spectacle organizers in the Greek East, rather than incurring the cost of building an amphitheatre, would often adapt pre-existing structures, like theatres and stadia, for gladiatorial contests and *venationes*. The lack of amphitheatres in the eastern Empire led many scholars in the past to conclude that Roman arena spectacles were not nearly so popular among the Greek-speaking population as they were in Rome's western provinces. This alleged disdain was tied to the perceived cultural superiority of the

Greeks, and the belief that such civilized people would hold nothing but contempt for the bloody combats of the arena. In 1940, however, the noted French epigrapher Louis Robert published his seminal work, *Les Gladiateurs dans L'Orient Grec*, which, through a close study of surviving spectacle inscriptions from the eastern Empire, conclusively demonstrated that the Greek-speaking population was as fond of arena spectacles as their western counterparts.

Not surprisingly, cities in the Greek East with a strong Roman element appear to have been particularly fond of arena spectacles imported from Italy. A primary example of just such a community was the city of Corinth, sacked by the Romans in 146 BC, but later refounded as a Roman colony by Julius Caesar just over a hundred years later. The substantial number of Roman colonists who settled in the area thereafter clearly brought their passion for the *munera* with them; as we shall see, the theatre in Corinth, like others in the Greek East, was substantially modified to accommodate gladiatorial bouts and *venationes*.

The available evidence suggests, in fact, that the citizens of Corinth under the Empire were particularly fond of Roman beast hunts. An anonymous letter, thought to date to the late first or early second century, records the alleged abuses perpetrated by the Corinthians against the nearby city of Argos in order to support this particular passion:

'But now the Corinthians, since Argos has been assigned to their territory ... have grown insolent in ill-doing and are compelling the Argives to pay them tribute ... it is not to furnish gymnastic or musical contests that the Corinthians need so much money, but they buy bears and panthers for the hunting shows which they often exhibit in their theatres.'[8]

The likely context for this complaint is that Corinth was the centre of an imperial cult to which other regional centres like Argos were expected to contribute. Interestingly, the anonymous writer of this letter contrasts the (in his mind) lesser *venationes* with the much more traditional Greek musical and gymnastic competitions.[9]

In examining the surviving epigraphic record of *munera* staged across the Roman Empire, the modest scale and duration of most arena spectacles outside of Rome is readily apparent. An inscribed statue base from Telesia in southern Italy, dating to approximately 100 AD, gives a good impression of the typically modest *munera* staged by local notables like Lucius Fabius Severus, the dedicatee of this particular inscription:

'The council and citizens most willingly granted a statue to Titus Fabius Severus, patron of the colony, on account of his services at home and abroad, and because he, first of all producers, at his own expense, provided five Libyan beasts with a gladiatorial troupe and great pomp.'

The inscription does not specify how many gladiators fought in Severus' *munus*, but the number of attested animals (five) is decidedly modest. Nonetheless, the text is careful to note that these at least were 'Libyan beasts', most likely lions, and that Severus was the first *editor* to import such animals from Africa to Telesia. The inscription does not state how long Severus' spectacle lasted, but in cases like this, where a text fails to specify the duration of a given *munus*, we can assume that it was staged on a single day, given the relatively limited resources of most local *editores*.[10]

As in the case of Severus' spectacle in Telesia, the epigraphic records of other such events across the Empire, apart from often denoting the number of participants in a given *munus*, also emphasize any elements thought to be particularly exotic. A priest of the imperial cult from Beroe in modern-day Bulgaria, for example, was honoured for staging a *venatio* which allegedly featured every type of animal, both local and foreign. Similarly, a beast hunt put on by an unknown *editor* from Panormus in Sicily is said to have featured every type of herbivore as well as numerous eastern beasts. As a final, even more vague example, a Greek inscription from Ancyra in modern-day Turkey denotes a local *venatio* as both expensive and *paradoxon* ('contrary to expectation'): the latter term no doubt refers to the unusual assortment of animals allegedly collected for this particular event.[11]

Another noteworthy feature of Roman spectacles occasionally mentioned in the epigraphic record is the inclusion of *noxii* ('condemned criminals') in a given day's entertainment. We shall have more to say about these performers and their status in a subsequent chapter; suffice it to say for now that under the Roman legal system, those condemned for certain offences could be forced to fight as gladiators or *venatores* or, even worse, be publicly executed in the arena. Such was the popularity of these executions, as we shall see, that the *noxii* became something of a prized entertainment commodity across the Empire. Those spectacle organizers who wished to include executions of the condemned in their *munera*, as a further sign of their munificence, but did not have a sufficient supply of *noxii* at hand in their own communities, could, at least on occasion, purchase them from the imperial government. Normally, *editores* in smaller centres who included what was usually a limited number of *noxii* in their events would stage their execution between the *venationes* and gladiatorial bouts.[12]

Those organizers with the requisite funds to stage ambitious spectacles could face bureaucratic obstacles. We have already seen that emperors such as Nero and Marcus Aurelius placed various limitations on the production of *munera* across the Empire, in part, at least, to spare *editores* from the potentially ruinous costs associated with such events. The specific details of these restrictions are not always found in the extant sources: spectacle organizers appear to have been barred from including more than a certain number of gladiators and/or animals in their events. It is important to note, however, that communities across the Empire had the right to seek an exemption from such restrictions, should they wish to stage a particularly opulent spectacle. Tacitus records such an exemption granted to the city of Syracuse by the Senate during the reign of Nero, and adds that such decrees were exceedingly common (*vulgarissimum*).[13]

The need for imperial sanction to stage larger spectacles is often reflected in the epigraphic record of local *munera*, particularly from the second century onwards. The prevalence of such inscriptions from the later Empire may be more than a statistical anomaly in the extant epigraphic record. As we shall discuss in more detail in a subsequent chapter, gladiators and exotic animals appear to have been harder to come by after the first century. The government in Rome may have more strictly enforced limits on the size of spectacles produced outside Rome to ensure enough gladiators and exotic animals were available for events staged by the emperors themselves.[14]

Examples of local *editores* being forced to obtain imperial permission for lavish spectacles, as reflected in the epigraphic record, include the magistrate Titus Ancharius Priscus who, *ex indulgentia Augusti* ('with the emperor's permission'), was able to stage a gladiatorial *munus* lasting eight days in the Italian town of Pisaurum in the later second century. Similarly, the magistrate Publius Baebius Justus took advantage of this same *indulgentia* to stage four days of *venationes* in the town of Minturnae in 249 AD. As a final example, from Gortyn in the Greek-speaking eastern half of the Empire, a fourth century inscription honours the chief-priest of the local assembly for his unprecedented achievement in obtaining imperial permission to stage three days of *venationes*, during which he was allowed to slaughter as many animals as he wished, as well as four days of gladiatorial combat, in which at least four pairs of gladiators appear to have fought to the death each day. The specific mention of the granting of imperial permission in inscriptions such as these further underlines the solicitude of these men on behalf of their respective communities.[15]

Occasionally, events such as gladiatorial combat and *venationes* were staged as part of *ludi iuvenum* or *Iuvenalia* ('youth games'). We have already noted the emergence of these games in Rome under the first emperor, Augustus. It is clear from the epigraphic record, however, that the *ludi iuvenum* also spread beyond the capital, providing a means for youthful members of the local elite in various communities across the Empire to demonstrate their mettle to their fellow citizens. A late second or early third century inscription from Carsulae in central Italy, for example, commemorates the generosity of a certain Lucius Egnatius Victorinus, *editor Iuvenalium*, for the outstanding *venationes* he staged, in which local *iuvenes* appear to have taken part. Interestingly, Victorinus is also identified in the inscription as a municipal magistrate and as patron of the local imperial cult, illustrating the potentially close connection between such offices, as well as their responsibility for staging local *munera*.[16]

Another, roughly contemporary funerary inscription from Aquae Sextiae in southern France indicates the variety of duties the *iuvenes* themselves could perform. In the relevant section, the deceased dedicatee, Sextus Julius Felicissimus, lists his various accomplishments:

'... well-skilled in the teachable sport of young men [*lusus iuvenum*] in the arena, I was that handsome man who often fought the beasts, armed with different weapons, but I also lived as their doctor and a comrade of the *ursarii* [*comes ursaris*] ...'

In addition to his evident participation in local *venationes* associated with the *ludi iuvenum*, Felicissimus also suggests that he acted as veterinarian, at least on a part-time basis, for the same beasts against which he and his compatriots could fight in the arena. Doctors and veterinarians were some of the most important behind-the-scenes personnel associated with the gladiatorial contests and beast hunts of the arena. It is not surprising, therefore, that a person with the requisite skill, like Felicissimus, could perform double-duty as both veterinarian and combatant, perhaps as a cost-saving measure. More curious is Felicissimus' evident association with the *ursarii* (bear hunters). As we shall see, this term could denote either Roman soldiers who specialized in capturing bears on the frontiers, or arena performers who specialized in fighting such animals. Given the fact that Felicissimus does not appear to have served in the Roman army, the latter interpretation is perhaps more likely in this instance.[17]

Apart from epigraphic testimony, one of the most important types of evidence available for the study of Roman spectacles is contemporary art, particularly in media such as sculpture and mosaic. Numerous depictions of arena spectacles survive from throughout Roman territory, and in many cases, such artwork provides us with as much detailed information on the *munera* as contemporary inscriptions. On occasion, mosaics depicting *venationes* feature not only the names of the animals participating in a given event, but also the number of each species, denoted by the letter N (*numerus*), followed by a number, inscribed on the sides of various beasts. A third century *venatio* mosaic from Carthage, for example, depicts a bear with the inscription N XL, an ostrich with N XXV, and a wild goat with N X, indicating that on one particular day during the spectacles commemorated by the mosaic, forty bears, twenty-five ostriches, and ten wild goats fought in the arena. As we shall see in a subsequent chapter, such artwork also provides indispensable evidence for the equipment and weaponry borne by gladiators and *venatores*, as well as their tactics.[18]

One of the more important depictions of a spectacle in a smaller city of the Empire is the famous fresco of an amphitheatre riot discovered in Pompeii. The painting in question does not provide any specific details of combat in the arena, but rather provides us with a vivid illustration of the passions, sometimes verging into the destructive, which the *munera* could evoke in spectators. The fresco provides an overhead view of the amphitheatre and adjacent gladiatorial barracks in Pompeii, as well as the surrounding area. The depiction of a group of combatants on the arena floor is common; what is noteworthy in this scene is the combat between spectators spilling out onto the streets surrounding the barracks and amphitheatre.

Fortunately, in this particular instance, we also have surviving literary testimony to clarify what the fresco depicts. According to Tacitus, this spectator violence was precipitated by a *munus* staged by the ex-senator Livineius Regulus in 59 AD. On this occasion, not only Pompeians, but also a large number of spectators from the neighbouring town of Nuceria attended the spectacle. These two groups of spectators soon began attacking each other, first verbally, and then as their anger grew, physically. In the resulting melee, the Pompeians overcame the Nucerians, and a substantial number of the latter were killed or wounded. The subsequent senatorial inquiry in Rome saw Pompeii punished by being barred from hosting any sort of arena spectacles for ten years, and Regulus, the *editor* of the spectacle at the centre of the trouble, being sent into exile.[19] It is important to note that clashes like that occasioned by Regulus' *munus*, whether between spectators from rival towns, or between fans of a given performer or faction, must have been relatively common in the sporting venues of the Roman Empire, albeit not normally as violent as the debacle in Pompeii. One need only consider the brawls and disorder involving spectators of many modern sporting events.

Many of the finest depictions of arena spectacles are found on mosaics from Roman North Africa. Unlike in other areas of the Empire, where exotic animals like lions were relatively hard to come by, such animals were comparatively abundant in North Africa and, as a result, local *editores* likely found *venationes* less expensive to stage than gladiatorial spectacles. This appears to be one of, if not the main reason for their marked prevalence in the surviving mosaic depictions of *munera* staged in Rome's North African provinces. This is not to say, however, that depictions of gladiators are entirely absent from the artwork of the region.

One of the best representations of gladiators as part of a large arena spectacle, in fact, is found on a mosaic, likely dating to the later second century, from a Roman villa at the site of Zliten in modern-day Libya. Just as an inscription commemorating a given *munus* routinely lists its various constituent events, so too does the Zliten mosaic depict all of the various events making up a day (or days?) at the arena in one continuous frieze. Somewhat unusually for a North African mosaic, pride of place is given to the gladiators: multiple pairs, with differing types of equipment, are shown in various stages of combat with each other. Other aspects of the *munus* are not neglected. A number of musicians, who evidently provided a similar diversion to that of organists and recorded music at modern sporting events, are depicted on the frieze, as well as various unfortunate *noxii* being pushed towards waiting leopards and lions. A number of *venatio* scenes are also shown, including combat between animals as well as human *venatores* and other beasts. The most unusual of the depicted struggles is that between a dwarf and boar, evidently emblematic of the 'light entertainment' commonly included in many *munera* as relief from bloodier or more violent events.

To judge from the available evidence, the type of execution depicted on the Zliten mosaic, *damnatio ad bestias* (condemnation to the beasts), was the standard judicial punishment enacted by *editores* who were able to procure condemned criminals for their spectacles. The elaborate 'fatal charades' staged by the emperors in Rome were, of course, far beyond the resources of a typical spectacle organizer in the provinces. In some cases depicted in contemporary artwork the condemned was shoved towards a waiting animal by an arena attendant, a technique that could present almost as much risk to the latter as to the former. Sometimes, however, the *noxius* would be tied to a stake in the arena floor before his executioner was released, an arrangement which offered more safety to the attendants. The Zliten mosaic depicts a more elaborate form of *damnatio ad bestias*, wherein the condemned was tied to a stake on a cart which was then wheeled from behind by an arena attendant towards an expectant animal. Presumably, one of the advantages of this method, as opposed to merely staking the *noxius* to the middle of the arena floor, was that with the cart, the animal could be provoked into mauling his victim more quickly than if it were left to find the condemned criminal on its own. Regardless of the exact method employed, *damnatio ad bestias* was, in some respects, a relatively inexpensive means for a spectacle organizer to provide additional entertainment for his audience: in particular, some of the animals procured for the morning's *venationes* could presumably be reused for the midday executions.

Regarding the overall composition of the Zliten mosaic, it is obvious that the various events conflated together on the frieze could not have been staged simultaneously on the arena floor. The realistic depiction of individual scenes, however, such as the combat between different pairs of gladiators, suggests that the mosaic commemorates an actual *munus*, rather than being simply a work of imagination. To judge from the number and variety of participants in this spectacle, the *editor* who staged it (and presumably commissioned the subsequent mosaic as well) was extremely wealthy, even by the standards of the local aristocratic elite. Unfortunately, due to the lack of any other evidence, that is about all we can suggest about this particular benefactor.[20]

One of the most important and informative depictions of a local spectacle is found on another mosaic from Smirat, in modern day Tunisia, probably dating to the mid-third century AD. As in the case of most other North African arena mosaics, the *munus* depicted is a beast hunt, in this case involving four *venatores* in combat with four leopards. Several other figures feature in the scene, including the *editor* of the spectacle, Magerius, as well as his herald. For the purposes of our present discussion, the most interesting aspect is the herald's proclamation included in the mosaic:

'Proclaimed by the *curio* (herald): 'My lords, in order that the *Telegenii* should have what they deserve from your favour for [fighting] the leopard, give them 500 denarii.'[21]

The *Telegenii*, about whom we shall have more to say shortly, were the corporation that produced the *venatio* commemorated on the mosaic. Evidently, an *editor* like Magerius would pay such groups separately for each animal appearing in a given show, rather than a bulk sum for all of the beasts, presumably so that if one or more of the expected animals was unable to appear in the spectacle (perhaps because it died in captivity), he

would not be left out of pocket. This conclusion is supported by the fact that
Magerius' herald is shown holding four bags containing 1,000 denarii apiece,
as indicated by the symbols on them, one for each of the leopards. The fact
that each of the bags contains twice the amount of money requested by the
herald is further proof, of course, of Magerius' munificence.[22]

The acclamation of the crowd, also preserved on the mosaic, not only
further emphasizes the generosity of Magerius, but also highlights a few
typical features of spectacles staged in the smaller centres of the Empire,
some of which we have already encountered:

> 'They [the crowd] shouted: May future generations know of your
> *munus* because you are an example for them, may past generations
> hear about it; where has such a thing been heard of? When has such
> a thing been heard of? You have provided a *munus* as an example to
> the quaestors; you have provided a *munus* from your own resources.
> That day: Magerius gives. This is wealth. This is power. This is now.
> Night is now. By your *munus* they [the *Telegenii*] were dismissed with
> moneybags.'[23]

First of all, as in some of the spectacle inscriptions discussed earlier, the text
is at pains to emphasize that Magerius paid for the *munus* commemorated
by the mosaic out of his own pocket. More specifically, the acclamation
makes the claim that Magerius' spectacle was so lavish as to rival those of
the quaestors staged each year in Rome itself. At the same time, however, by
seemingly linking the departure of the *Telegenii* to nightfall, the text suggests
that the event in question lasted but a single day, typical, as we have seen, of
spectacles staged outside of Rome.[24]

The Magerius mosaic is just one piece of evidence illustrating the
widespread popularity of hunting corporations like the *Telegenii* in Roman
North Africa: at least ten such groups, in fact, have been identified by scholars.
*Venationes* appear to have been much more popular spectator events in the
region than gladiatorial combat, due at least in part to the ready availability
of animals like lions and leopards, and as a result, the groups which were
hired to organize such events found ready employment. Perhaps the most
vivid testimony as to the existence of these hunting-corporations is found in

yet another North African mosaic, in this case an early third century work from the town of El Djem (ancient Thysdrus) in modern-day Tunisia. The mosaic appears to depict five *venatores* from rival corporations carousing in an amphitheatre, above a group of zebus and attendants, on the night before a spectacle. The rowdy behaviour of the men seated above the arena floor is indicated not only by the text placed beside them (e.g. '*Bibere venimus* ['We've come to drink!]'), but also by the admonition of the attendants below ['*Silentiu[m] dormiant tauri*[Silence! Let the bulls sleep.]').[25]

The most notable aspects of this particular mosaic, arguably, are the various items held by the *venatores*, as well as the symbols branded into the flanks of the zebus on the arena floor. The former include a millet stalk, an ivy leaf, and a crescent-tipped staff, while the latter also include a millet stalk and ivy leaf, as well the figure of a gladiator. At first glance, the significance of such seemingly random objects might not be clear. The presence of these motifs in other Roman mosaics and pottery from North Africa, however, has led scholars to conclude that, far from being simple decorative elements, they instead represent specific hunting-corporations active in the region. The *Telegenii*, for example, are represented by the crescent-tipped staff, while the *Leontii* and *Taurisci* are represented respectively by the millet stalk and ivy leaf. In the context of the mosaic under discussion, then, the collected symbols and attributes indicate that not only the *venatores* in the scene, but also the zebus, belonged to specific hunting-corporations.[26]

The relevant artistic and epigraphic evidence from North Africa gives us a good idea of the scope and popularity of these groups and their activities. First, for example, artwork pertaining to the hunting-corporations largely dates to the third and fourth centuries AD, suggesting that *venationes* were particularly popular in Roman North Africa during that period. The relative ubiquity of the crescent-tipped staff as a motif in contemporary art also suggests, more particularly, that the *Telegenii* were the most popular corporation associated with the beast hunts of that time. As we shall discuss in more detail in a subsequent chapter, gladiatorial spectacles appear to have been in decline throughout much of the western Empire as early as the third century. It is no surprise, therefore, that as such events became less and less frequent, the already popular *venationes* in North Africa, as well as the services of the corporations producing them, were even more in demand.[27]

The accumulated evidence, in particular inscriptions mentioning various hunting-corporations, also suggests that such groups, as well as the performers affiliated with them, were active in specific regions, rather than being equally represented across Roman North Africa. The *Telegenii*, for example, appear to have been most active in the area around El Djem, while the *Leontii*'s centre of operations lay in Sousse (ancient Hadrumetum) to the north. Interestingly enough, these different groups appear to have attracted a strong regional following, similar in some ways to the circus factions of the later Empire. A number of North African vases from the later third century, decorated with scenes of animal combat in the arena, as well as acclamations like *Perexi Nika* ['Win, Perexii!'] or *Telegeni Nika* ['Win, Telegenii!], were evidently commissioned by adherents of particular corporations. In addition, extant funerary inscriptions in which the deceased are specifically identified as partisans of a given group like the *Telegenii* are also indicative of the loyal following which such corporations inspired in Roman North Africa.[28]

We have already noted the perceived beneficial link between the slaughter of wild animals in the *venationes* and the clearance of land for agriculture in the Roman Empire. This was particularly true in North Africa, which was both the breeding ground for some of the most dangerous wild animals ever witnessed in the Roman arena, and one of the most important sources of lucrative agricultural commodities such as olive oil. Not surprisingly, then, the available evidence suggests that North African hunting corporations had vested agricultural interests in addition to their arena-related activities. It is perhaps no coincidence that hunting corporations like the *Telegenii* first appear in the third and fourth centuries, precisely the period when the agricultural exploitation of Roman North Africa was at its height.[29]

Examples of evidence pertaining to the mercantile activities of specific hunting corporations in North Africa include amphorae stamped with the insignia of the *Telegenii* found at the site of Roman ports like Ostia. These indicate that this faction was involved in the lucrative shipment of olive oil from North Africa to Italy. A fragmentary fourth century mosaic from Tebessa (in modern-day Algeria), which includes among its motifs a ship carrying olive oil amphorae, as well as a crescent-tipped staff and a millet stalk, further suggests that not only the *Telegenii*, but also the *Leontii*, were involved in the olive oil trade. The latter supposition is reinforced by the epigraphic record

**Plate 1.** Coin of Domitian depicting two–horned African rhinoceros. (*Photo by the author*)

**Plate 2.** Bust of Commodus as Hercules. (*Photo Credit: Alfredo Dagli Orti / The Art Archive at Art Resource, NY*)

**Plate 3.** Amphitheatre riot in Pompeii. (*Photo Credit: Alfredo Dagli Orti / The Art Archive at Art Resource, NY*)

**Plate 4.** Portion of Zliten mosaic depicting gladiators and referee. (*Copyright: Gilles Mermet / Art Resource, NY*)

**Plate 5.** Magerius mosaic from Smirat. (*Copyright: Vanni Archive / Art Resource, NY*)

**Plate 6.** Amphitheatre mosaic from El Djem. (*Photo Credit: Erich Lessing / Art Resource, NY*)

**Plate 7.** Tomb relief from Rome. (*Photo Credit: Erich Lessing / Art Resource, NY*)

**Plate 8.** Relief depicting combat between female gladiators. (*Copyright: The Trustees of the British Museum / Art Resource, NY*)

**Plate 9.** Figurine depicting combat between *hoplomachus* and 'Thracian'. (*Photo Credit: Erich Lessing / Art Resource, NY*)

**Plate 10.** Mosaic depicting combat between two gladiators, with referee in background. (*Photo Credit: HIP / Art Resource, NY*)

**Plate 11.** Relief depicting combat between various animals and armoured *venatores*. (*Photo Credit: HIP/ Art Resource, NY*)

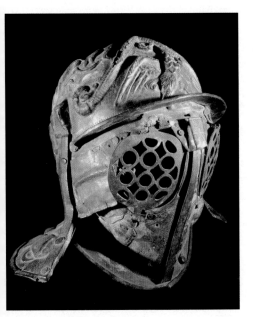

**Plate 12.** Gladiator helmets discovered in Pompeii and environs. (*A: Photo Credit: Gianni Dagli Orti/ The Art Archive at Art Resource, NY. B: Copyright: RMN–Grand Palais/Art Resource, NY*)

**Plate 13.** Detail of animal combat from Zliten mosaic. (*Copyright: Gilles Mermet/Art Resource, NY*)

**Plate 14.** Model of *Ludus Magnus* in Rome. (*Copyright: Vanni Archive/Art Resource, NY*)

**Plate 15.** Scenes of animal capture and transport from 'Great Hunt' mosaic. (*A: [elephant] Photo Credit: Erich Lessing/Art Resource, NY; B: [wagon] Photo Credit: Scala/Art Resource, NY; C: [bull] Photo Credit: Erich Lessing/Art Resource, NY*)

Plate 16.  Coins minted to celebrate Philip's Secular Games. (*Photo by author*)

Plate 17.  Diptych of Areobindus. (*Photo Credit: HIP/ Art Resource, NY*)

of a certain Publius Junius Junianus Martialanus, governor of Numidia in the early third century, which testifies not only to his agricultural estates in the province, but also his family affiliation with the *Leontii*.[30]

Although the lion's share (no pun intended!) of evidence for hunting corporations like the *Leontii* comes from North Africa, such groups are also attested elsewhere in the Empire. This is a clear indication of the general popularity of the *venationes*, particularly in the late Empire when, as we shall see, gladiatorial contests appear to have disappeared from the Roman arena. One of the apparent differences between the hunting corporations of North Africa and those found elsewhere, however, is that while the latter appear to have been largely modelled upon, or linked with contemporary gladiatorial troupes from an early date, groups like the *Telegenii* were seemingly independent entities, having no such affiliation with other arena performers. The main reasons for this disparity appear to be, first of all, that gladiatorial spectacles were never as popular in North Africa as in other regions of the Roman Empire and, as previously mentioned, the *Telegenii* and other factions only emerged in the third century, when the production of gladiatorial *munera* was already in decline.

One of the foremost examples of a private hunting corporation outside North Africa in the late Empire is that alluded to by the famous orator and rhetorician of Antioch, Libanius, in the later fourth century. In one of his extant speeches, Libanius attacks the current governor of Syria, Tisamenus, for hiring a seemingly disreputable entrepreneur from the nearby town of Beroea for an upcoming spectacle in Antioch:

'He [Tisamenus] thought up an idea that nobody else would ever have dreamed of. He invited that fellow from Beroea, along with the beasts he maintains and the men hired to fight them. And along he came, with bears and panthers and the fellows who had at times lost to them and at times beaten them, and he was cock-a-hoop at overcoming the greater city with the less.'[31]

The existence of such a hunting troupe, even in a relatively small settlement like Beroea, suggests that even in the later Empire, similar groups may have been scattered throughout Roman territory, particularly in areas like

Asia Minor where wild game was still relatively plentiful. As we shall see subsequently, the evident popularity of *venationes* in the later Empire, as attested to by contemporaries like Libanius, presumably meant that such corporations found ready employment.

One important final element in our discussion of the myriad spectacles staged outside of Rome herself is the venues in which they took place. Originally, many smaller centres, in the western Empire at least, appear to have staged *munera* in the forum, which provided a flat, open space well-suited to such events. The primary concern of *editores* under such circumstances was providing a strong, high temporary barrier around this space to prevent the participants, in particular the wild beasts, from attacking spectators. Given the leaping abilities of some animals employed in the spectacles, such a barricade would need to have been at least 5m to 6m in height. Over time, however, as the logistical and spatial limitations of the forum for the staging of *munera* became more and more apparent, most smaller towns and cities built their own modest amphitheatres so as to be able to provide larger gladiatorial bouts and *venationes* in a safer venue for the populace. This trend mirrors the process in Rome where the *munera* over time moved from venues like the Forum Romanum to purpose-built facilities like the Colosseum.[32]

On occasion, rather than build an entirely new edifice for the *munera*, communities would instead adapt pre-existing structures for the spectacles, or build multi-purpose facilities. A prime example of the latter phenomenon is the series of 'arena-theatres' or 'theatre-amphitheatres' built primarily in Gaul over the first two centuries AD. As their nicknames suggest, these structures could be used to stage both theatrical performances and various *munera*: their proximity, in many cases, to preexisting Celtic temples has led to the suggestion that they were only used on religious occasions associated with these places of worship. Other such mixed venues, however, free from any possible connection with Celtic worship, are found in the Greek East. The theatre at Stobi, built in the early second century, is emblematic of such designs. Although its *cavea* and orchestra are similar to those found in regular theatres, the complete absence of a stage left much more room for gladiatorial and animal combats – evidently more popular than traditional theatre in Stobi. Evidence of a temporary fencing system, which could be raised above the podium wall as occasion demanded, has also been found here.[33]

An even more common practice in the Greek east was to convert pre-existing theatres and stadia for Roman *munera*. Perhaps the best example of a Greek theatre adapted for Roman spectacles comes from the city of Corinth, whose citizens, as we have already seen, were avid partisans of the *munera*. The restructured theatre at Corinth appears to have been in use from the late first century BC (soon after the establishment of a Roman colony by Julius Caesar) through to the third century AD. As in other such theatres in the Greek world, the first step in converting Corinth's theatre for the *munera* involved removing the lower rows of seats (to create more space for combatants), and walling up the front of the stage and the side exits from the orchestra to create a relatively large, enclosed space for combat. The podium wall was also raised and likely surmounted by an iron grating to provide complete security for spectators.[34]

Stadia were, perhaps, the preexisting venue in the Greek world best suited for Roman events. The floor of such a venue did not normally need enlarging, since the oblong space of a stadium provided substantially more room for such spectacles than the smaller orchestra of a theatre. One should remember that the Romans themselves, prior to the building of the Colosseum, staged a number of *munera* in the Circus Maximus. One of the main concerns was spectator security. To judge from the archaeological evidence, a number of Greek stadia, including the second century Panathenaic stadium in Athens, had fencing and netting added to the tops of their podium walls to protect spectators from wild animals during the *venationes*, evidence that such events were staged in these venues.[35]

The foregoing discussion, while certainly not exhaustive, has nonetheless amply illustrated the popularity of Roman arena spectacles beyond the imperial capital. Like their counterparts in Rome, *editores* in the smaller centres of the Empire often sought to turn this popularity to their political advantage. As already touched upon, spectacle organizers, be they emperors or municipal magistrates, staged a wide variety of events, and it is the different types of events, as well as the performers who participated in them, to which our focus now turns. We shall also examine more closely the all-important interaction between *editor*, spectator, and arena combatant, which could often determine the success or failure of a given event.

*Chapter Four*

# Performer and Spectator in the Arena

By the early Empire a typical day's *munus* had come to include both gladiatorial contests and beast hunts, and, on occasion, executions of condemned criminals in the arena. Given the close association between *venationes* and gladiatorial bouts, it comes as no surprise that the participants in these events, despite their different specializations, shared a number of similarities in characteristics such as social status and organization. The arena itself, regardless of the specific event unfolding within it, also served a number of shared social and political functions for the assembled spectators, as our subsequent discussion will make clear. Certainly, the popularity of the *munera* did not lie solely in their perceived entertainment value.

However, one should not overlook the more 'mundane' attractions of arena spectacles. At a certain level, of course, spectators appreciated the simple, visceral thrill of seeing man and/or beast pitted against one another. An added enticement of these bouts, for many members of the audience, was the possibility of profiting from them. Gambling, certainly, is by no means a modern invention: just as we often bet upon such sports as horse-racing and boxing, the Romans wagered upon a wide variety of contests and sports, the latter including chariot racing and gladiatorial combat. A number of ancient sources[1] attest to the popularity of such sports betting in antiquity

Many scholars have concentrated upon the broader, deeper functions of the events in the arena, some of which we have already touched upon, including the concept of gladiators, at least in an idealized sense, serving as an example of courage in the face of death, or the display and slaughter of animals as symbolic of human mastery over the world of nature and, more particularly, the extent of Roman territorial control. In a society with a proud military tradition like Rome, as we shall see, spectators also appreciated the martial skills of both gladiators and *venatores*. One of the broader importances of the arena, however, lay in its reinforcement of Roman identity, and the social solidarity of the spectators within it.

Many scholars have rightly identified the role that the architecture of venues like the Colosseum played in reinforcing the traditional divisions within Roman society. The seats within Roman amphitheatres were not randomly assigned; rather, where you sat, or were permitted to sit, reflected your social standing. In general, the lower down you sat within the *cavea* (the seating section of an amphitheatre or theatre), the higher your status. In the Colosseum, the imperial family had its own box or section directly above the arena floor from which to witness the action. The prominence of the imperial box, surrounded by subjects from all social strata in the amphitheatre, was a microcosm of the emperor's central role within Roman society as a whole. Other elite groups that enjoyed the privilege of seating in the lower *cavea* included not only members of the senatorial class, the *crème de la crème* of the Roman aristocracy, but also members of prominent priesthoods like the Vestal Virgins. The members of the latter group were among the few women given the right to enjoy such premium seating. Above and behind the senatorial elite were the members of the equestrian class, followed by citizens of a lower social status. The very top of the *cavea* was reserved for the two most politically disenfranchised segments of Roman society – slaves and women.[2]

Another of the arena's roles, evidently, was to maintain this social order. Paradoxical as it might seem at first glance, the violence of the events on the arena floor is believed to have helped ensure the lawful behaviour of the assembled spectators in their everyday lives. The *munera*, in this context, are commonly viewed as a liminoid ritual, from the Latin word for 'threshold' (*limen*). In presenting a level of carnage and violence far exceeding the threshold tolerated in everyday society, gladiatorial contests and the like allowed spectators to vent any tension or violent urges they might possess, and in so doing ensured (or sought to ensure) that the latter would lead peaceful, law-abiding lives outside of the arena. A similar and very popular liminoid ritual in modern society, to name just one example, would be mixed martial-arts competitions. Once again, spectators experience a certain catharsis witnessing the violence in the octagon, violence the vast majority would never dream of perpetrating in their everyday lives.[3]

Another way in which the arena reinforced social identity and solidarity was through the demonstration of Roman justice, particularly in the execution of condemned criminals (*noxii*) which often accompanied gladiatorial contests and *venationes*. Such executions reassured the audience that justice was being exacted upon those convicted of serious crimes like arson and banditry. They were also a popular form of entertainment in their own right, as can be seen in the efforts of Roman emperors, particularly in the first century, to stage particularly elaborate executions as part of a larger series of spectacles.

The psychological effects underlying the popularity of such events are thought to have been twofold. First, violent arena executions appear to have exerted the same type of fascination upon spectators as other types of state-sanctioned killing have in more recent history. It is instructive to note, in terms of such parallels, that the last public hanging in England attracted tens of thousands of spectators: the perceived Roman blood-lust (or whatever one wishes to call it), so often disparaged in the modern day, is not so alien to our sensibilities as we would like to believe. Secondly, as in the case of gladiatorial contests and beast hunts, arena executions may also be seen as another form of liminoid ritual: the cruel punishments in the arena, at least on paper, allowed the assembled spectators to restrain their own violent tendencies.[4]

Not all ancient commentators, however, were convinced of the social benefits of attending a day's *munera*. It is instructive to note that relatively few criticisms of the spectacles concern the events themselves: one of the few exceptions, in fact, is the previously discussed outrage directed at Pompey for his slaughter of elephants in 55 BC. Much more prevalent is criticism of the perceived moral effects of the *munera* upon those who witnessed them. Arguably, the most famous example of this criticism, albeit a late one, comes from Augustine, writing at the end of the fourth century. Augustine relates the tale of his friend, Alypius. Dragged to a gladiatorial *munus* by his fellow students in Rome, Alypius initially had no intention of enjoying such a barbaric spectacle, but before long was overcome by the seductive violence on the arena floor:

'For so soon as he saw the blood, he at the very instant drunk down a kind of savageness; nor did he turn away his head, but fixed his eye upon it, drinking up unawares the very Furies themselves…Nor was he now the man he was when he first came thither, but become one of the throng he came unto; yea, an entire companion of theirs that brought him thither.'[5]

Augustine tells us that Alypius was eventually able to overcome his addiction to the arena, but his account nonetheless illustrates the powerful passions that could easily overwhelm spectators at a given event.[6]

Spectator behaviour could often be particularly unruly when *editores* distributed prizes to the audience at a given event, a practice most commonly attested for the emperors in Rome. The giving of such gifts was meant to illustrate further the munificence of the latter, and thereby win them even greater public acclaim. Prizes could vary widely, ranging from food and sweets to domesticated, or even, on occasion, wild animals. Most commonly, tokens would be distributed among audience members for various prizes, which could then be redeemed when the spectacle was over. According to Seneca, such occasions, not surprisingly, often provoked scuffles and other violent behaviour in the crowd, a scenario familiar to those who have witnessed the use of T-shirt cannons and the like at modern sporting events. Even more dangerous, however, were those instances when spectators descended onto the arena floor in order to claim their prizes directly. Perhaps the best-known example of such carnage occurred in the early third century, when a number of spectators were killed in the struggle to seize various items put up for grabs during one of the emperor Elagabulus' lavish spectacles.[7]

Another way in which *editores* might further increase their popularity with spectators, although perhaps not as common as those benefactions already listed, was through the distribution of free meat from the carcasses of slaughtered arena animals after a *munus*. This would have been a beneficial and presumably popular addition to the often limited diet of the urban populace. There is little evidence for this particular brand of euergetism, perhaps because of its more mundane nature, but enough does remain, nonetheless, to verify its periodic occurrence. The Christian writer Tertullian, for example, refers to this practice, and its cannibalistic overtones, as part of his broader criticism of the pagan *munera*:

'... what of ... those who dine on the flesh of wild animals from the arena, keen on the meat of boar or stag? That boar in his battle has wiped the blood off him whose blood he drew: that stag has wallowed in the blood of a gladiator. The bellies of the very bears are sought, full of raw and undigested human flesh ...'

In terms of archaeological evidence, the bones of such animals as boar, bear, leopard, and ostrich found in close proximity to the Colosseum also attest to the periodic distribution of arena meat on the part of Roman emperors.[8]

In addition to such rewards as the giving of prizes, another attractive element of arena spectacles such as staged executions, at least from the perspective of the spectators, was the amount of power the crowd could often wield on such occasions, a degree of power absent in the vast majority of their lives. In the later Empire, one of the standard forms of trial was the *cognitio* (inquiry), in which a single magistrate would hear a case and pass a sentence not subject to appeal. A number of these *cognitiones*, to judge from contemporary Christian martyrdom accounts, were held in public venues like amphitheatres, so as to allow as many citizens as possible to witness the Roman justice system at work. Although the power of the magistrates presiding over these inquiries was absolute, at least in theory, one can see how they might have been influenced in their verdicts by hundreds or thousands of spectators clamouring for a given sentence.[9]

One such example of the popular pressure exerted upon a magistrate under such circumstances comes from the martyrdom of a group of Christians in Lugdunum (modern-day Lyons) during the reign of Marcus Aurelius in the late second century. One of the condemned Christians on this occasion was a Roman citizen who, in accordance with his status, should only have been beheaded, a form of capital punishment the Roman authorities considered less humiliating. The unruly crowd of spectators, however, ultimately convinced the presiding magistrate to throw the unfortunate man to the beasts along with other non-citizen Christians, a clear contravention of Roman law; on this occasion, the judge clearly ranked pleasing the whims of the public above the niceties of Roman law.[10]

As the above anecdote suggests, *damnatio ad bestias* appears to have been by far the most popular type of capital punishment commonly meted out on the arena floor. On occasion, in fact, executions could be delayed until the requisite animals were available: another prominent Christian martyr, Polycarp, was only burned at the stake because the Roman authorities, on this particular occasion, did not want to delay his execution by waiting for lions to be brought to the city.[11]

As professionally trained gladiators became ever harder to procure and more expensive, *noxii* in general, whatever the exact method of their punishment, became an increasingly valued commodity in the arena. A late second century imperial edict suggests that the value of even the lowliest gladiator at that time was at least six-times that of a condemned criminal, clearly illustrating the financial attraction of the latter type of performer for prospective *editores*. Further imperial legislation in the following century instructed provincial governors to reserve particularly combative *noxii* for spectacles in Rome, indicating that the sale of condemned criminals for the spectacles had become so widespread, in fact, as to endanger the provisioning of the emperors' own events, something which the imperial bureaucracy naturally could not tolerate.[12]

Undoubtedly, the best known way in which spectators exercised their power in the arena was through passing judgement on whether a defeated gladiator should be slain, or spared. This, of course, is the origin of the 'thumbs up'/'thumbs down' gesture still widely used today. Interestingly enough, however, we in modern society may be using the gestures incorrectly, at least as compared to their original usage. According to the usual interpretation, Roman spectators would give a 'thumbs up' if they wanted a gladiator to be spared, while the 'thumbs down' gesture meant they wanted him killed for a lacklustre performance. Some scholars, however, have suggested that we may have the meaning of the gestures backwards, and that 'thumbs up', with the digit pointed towards the jugular, actually signified death, while 'thumbs down' actually was a vote for sparing the gladiator, with the lowered digit signifying a sheathed sword. The main reason for this uncertainty is the comparative lack of relevant evidence in the ancient sources. The poet Juvenal uses the phrase *pollice verso* ('turned thumb') to describe the gesture for sparing a gladiator, but the interpretation of this rather vague phrase depends upon whether one views the natural position of the thumb as being pointed upwards or downwards.[13]

The magistrate or *editor* in charge of the *munus* was not technically obliged to heed the spectators' wishes, regardless of which way their thumbs were pointing: the final decision on the fate of a defeated gladiator was his alone. Nonetheless, a spectacle organizer who ignored the crowd ran the risk of incurring its wrath. The arena, or the circus for that matter, was one of the few venues in Roman society where men and women from all walks of life had the opportunity to interact with the rich and powerful, even in some cases with the emperor himself, and spectators wished to exercise that privilege. Those *editores* who failed to cater to the crowd, or take an active interest in the spectacles they had organized, were certainly subject to the crowd's censure, regardless of whatever other merits they might possess: both Julius Caesar and Marcus Aurelius were criticized for their apparent lack of interest in the *munera*. Conversely, otherwise terrible emperors like Nero and Commodus, as we have seen, were popular at least within a certain segment of the population because of their devotion to the spectacles.

The sense of power and superiority enjoyed by the spectators at a given *munus* was due in no small part to the negligible status of the performers in the arena. Under Roman law, public execution was generally reserved for only the most serious of crimes, and it was this consideration, as well as the fact that such punishments were designed to be as humiliating as possible, which helped ensure members of the audience felt only scorn and derision for a given *noxius*. The thoroughgoing degradation of the condemned ensured that any harm to the social order brought about by his or her crimes was fully rectified. In addition, as previously mentioned, the most horrific methods of execution, like *damnatio ad bestias*, were reserved, at least on paper, for the lower classes. Therefore, the average spectator could feel a clear sense of superiority over any condemned criminals on the arena floor based on his or her social status, regardless of the specific crime the *noxius* had committed.[14]

Apart from condemned criminals, the other performers found in the arena were also usually of low social standing, which once again ensured, under normal circumstances, that the spectators at a given *munus* would not suffer undue concern over any tribulations the former suffered on the arena floor. Many gladiators during the Republican period, as we have already seen, were originally prisoners of war captured during Rome's wars of conquests, and successful warfare continued to provide gladiators and other arena combatants on an intermittent basis during the Empire as well. Obviously, given their origin, they could expect even less sympathy from spectators than other performers!

Another common source of gladiators and *venatores* alike was criminals condemned *ad ludos* ('to the games'). As the term suggests, individuals convicted of serious crimes, albeit crimes not serious enough to warrant execution, were often sentenced to fight in the arena. The extant sources, unfortunately, are often not explicit as to what offences merited specific sentences like condemnation to the games, but among those mentioned in connection with such performers are arson, sacrilege, and murder. There was obviously an overlap between some of the offences punishable by *damnatio ad bestias* or *damnatio ad ludos*, but the judicial niceties which determined, for example, whether a given arsonist was condemned to be torn apart by wild beasts or to fight as a gladiator are, unfortunately, lost to us. In practice, of course, *damnatio ad ludos* was preferable to *damnatio ad bestias*. The former sentence, at the very least, offered a slim prospect of eventual release, especially for those who could fight well enough to earn their freedom from the arena.[15]

A related, albeit less formal phenomenon was the practice of slave-owners punishing their own slaves by selling them to the *lanistae*, the managers of the training schools for gladiators and *venatores* about whom we shall have more to say subsequently. This practice, although seemingly common during the late Republic and early Empire, was eventually banned by the state, which did not appreciate private citizens taking the law into their own hands. Legislation introduced during the reign of the emperor Hadrian in the early second century explicitly stipulated that slaves could only be condemned *ad ludos* by a court of law, not at the whims of their masters.[16]

A final category of arena combatants comprises those who chose to fight as a gladiator or *venator* of their own free will. Such performers, of course, were far less numerous than those who were forced to fight in the arena, but they are nonetheless attested in the epigraphic record. Unfortunately, such inscriptions shed little light on why someone might volunteer to participate in such a dangerous sport: one possibility, by way of example, is that some of those who consigned themselves to the arena were driven to it by bankruptcy or financial desperation. Others may have been attracted to such a profession by the lure of celebrity. As we shall discuss in greater detail later in this chapter, successful gladiators and *venatores* could sometimes achieve a devoted following among fans of the *munera*, a fame which, in the eyes of some, outweighed the dangers of the arena.[17]

Regardless of their specific background, those who were condemned to the arena, or chose to fight in the *munera* as a career, were all branded with the same label: *infamis* ('disreputable'). The same status, incidentally, was conferred upon other professions deemed immoral by Roman authorities, including actors and prostitutes. *Infamia* was formalized by the oath that gladiators were required to take upon their entry into the training-schools, which can be reconstructed as follows from the *Satyricon* of the first century writer Petronius: 'We solemnly swear to obey [the *lanista*] in everything. To endure burning, imprisonment, flogging and even death by the sword.'[18]

It is unclear whether or not *venatores* who entered the formal training schools (*ludi*) had to take such an oath, but given the many similarities between gladiators and beast hunters in terms of their organization, it is certainly plausible. Regardless, as we shall see presently, both types of performer suffered from the same *infamia*.

As noted previously, those arena performers who fought well and survived did have the opportunity eventually to earn their freedom. On rare occasions, in fact, a particularly proficient *venator* or gladiator might earn his outright release from the arena thanks to the particularly boisterous acclamations of the crowd. In the case of other performers, surviving the arena was not quite as difficult as commonly assumed. Some scholars in the past have maintained, for example, that a gladiator stood about a fifty per cent chance of dying in any given *munus*, but a close look at the extant evidence, in particular epigraphic texts, suggests that only about ten per cent of the gladiators met their deaths in any given spectacle. Those who fought well but were defeated could usually expect to be spared by the *editor* to fight again another day. The extant evidence suggests that, under ordinary circumstances, a successful gladiator could earn a reprieve from fighting after three years, and his freedom after five. Gladiators and *venatores* who survived their careers in the arena, however, were still stigmatized with the same *infamia* they had earlier possessed. Those considered *infamis* possessed no citizen rights, and suffered under a multitude of legal restrictions, such as being barred from serving on municipal councils or juries. [19]

Not much information, unfortunately, survives concerning the careers pursued by successful gladiators and *venatores* after their retirement from the arena. Some particularly accomplished arena combatants, certainly, could continue serving as trainers and the like within their respective *familiae* after their retirement from the arena. It should also come as no surprise that ex-gladiators and *venatores* who chose to pursue careers outside of the *munera* were nonetheless employed in professions which took advantage of their fighting ability. In the turmoil of the late Republic, for example, many prominent figures are known to have hired groups of former arena combatants as bodyguards. The two most famous examples are the bitter political rivals Clodius and Milo, who both employed gangs of slaves and gladiators to, at the same time, protect themselves and intimidate their opponents. Matters came to a head in early 52 BC, when the rival groups encountered each other just south of Rome in an encounter that swiftly led to a violent confrontation. The death of the popular demagogue Clodius in the fighting ultimately had serious political repercussions, including the subsequent exile of Milo from Italy. Despite the infamy of this episode, however, retired gladiators and *venatores* continued to be employed as bodyguards by powerful and wealthy Romans well into the imperial period. [20]

Whatever the career prospects of arena performers who survived until retirement, those who fought well in the arena, as alluded to previously, could attract a considerable following among spectators. The most accomplished could even amass considerable wealth or property for their retirement, usually, it appears, because of imperial patronage: Tiberius, for example, is said to have awarded the princely sum of 100,000 sesterces to one recently retired gladiator. Such instances, of course, are the exception rather than the rule. Nonetheless, as is made clear by the relevant epigraphic testimony, many arena performers earned enough money over the course of their careers to support a wife and children. The prizes routinely given out by *editores* to those gladiators or *venatores* who fought particularly well at a given spectacle could be important sources of income. [21]

Among our best sources of information on the careers of individual gladiators are the extant tombstones erected for them after their deaths. As well as listing the name and age of the deceased, most of these epitaphs also record the discipline under which a given gladiator fought and the rank he had achieved, as well as the number of times he fought, and won, in the arena. It is no surprise, of course, that the wives and children of the deceased dedicated many of these memorials; many, however, were also erected by members of the deceased gladiator's *familia*, including former trainers and comrades-in-arms. An even more interesting dedicant, perhaps, appears in an epitaph from Tergeste (modern-day Trieste):

> 'Constantius who gave the *munus* has given this tomb to his gladiators because the *munus* was well received. To Decoratus the *retiarius*, who killed Caeruleus and died himself; as both died by the same sword, so the same pyre covers both. Decoratus, the *secutor*, after nine fights, left his wife Valeria grieving for the first time.'

As the epitaph states, the *editor* Constantius, as a final display of generosity sure to be appreciated by fellow-citizens and surviving gladiators alike, erected a funerary monument for the three dead combatants. Evidently, the cost of such an undertaking, in Constantius' estimation, was easily outweighed by the positive publicity he could reap through this gesture.[22]

Another type of epigraphic testimony, the surviving notices of specific combatants in upcoming spectacles, provides clear evidence of the celebrity some performers could earn during their careers in the arena. Such notices, of course, are very reminiscent of the star billing the most famous athletes receive in modern-day advertisements of upcoming boxing or mixed-martial arts cards, to name only two examples. Our best source for ancient advertisements of upcoming *munera* (as opposed to the commemorations of various spectacles discussed last chapter) is the city of Pompeii, where the eruption of Mount Vesuvius preserved many of these painted notices from 2,000 years ago. One of the best examples of such notices, in the context of our present discussion, is the advertisement of an upcoming spectacle featuring a *venatio* and thirty pairs of gladiators. The only named performer in the entire notice, the gladiator Ellius, is listed at the very end of the text. Whoever wrote up this advertisement, evidently having some marketing savvy, deliberately left Ellius' name until last, so that the final impression passersby who read the notice would be left with would be the participation of a famous gladiator.[23]

Another common way in which the participation of specific gladiators and *venatores* in various *munera* would be commemorated for posterity was through the inclusion of their names in depictions of the events in question. In addition to the notices of upcoming spectacles, numerous graffiti have been preserved at Pompeii depicting gladiatorial bouts in the arena, with the names of the participants written beside them. One particularly informative example is a graffito showing the combat between two gladiators, Marcus Attilius and Hilarus. In this instance, the writing beside the figures not only gives their names, but also additional details, such as the fact that Attilius was a *tiro* (a novice gladiator), and his opponent Hilarus had won twelve of his previous fourteen matches. The abbreviation 'NER' beside Hilarus, in addition, indicates that he was a member of the *Neroniani*, the imperial gladiatorial *familia* set up by the emperor Nero. Finally, the graffito also indicates, perhaps most importantly, who won the bout. The letter 'V' (for '*vicit*'/'he conquered') beside Attilius shows that he won the duel against his far more experienced rival, while the 'M' (for '*missus*'/'sent away') beside Hilarus indicates that although he was defeated, he was spared to fight again another day.[24]

Similar information is often included on arena scenes found in other media, most notably mosaics and relief sculpture. A fragmentary tomb relief from Rome, for example, dating to the late first century BC, provides a number of interesting supplementary details concerning the gladiators depicted upon it. The fragmentary inscription beside the gladiator on the far left ('IVL VVV') informs us, for example, that he not only won the bout depicted, but that he was a member of the *Iuliani*, another gladiatorial *familia* established by Julius Caesar. The fact that the gladiator beside him, Clemens, lost the match, but survived, is once again indicated by the letter 'M' ('*missus*'). Sadly, as another notation informs us, the ultimate fate of the gladiator on the far right of the scene was not as fortunate. The two letters beside his head ('MΘ'/'*missus*'-'*thanatos*') indicate that, like the central gladiator, he was spared after being defeated. The 'Θ', however, representing the Greek word for 'dead', indicates that he subsequently died of his injuries, a fate not unfamiliar to arena combatants.[25]

We have already encountered another example of a spectacle scene including the names of the participants, namely the so-called 'Magerius' mosaic from Smirat. One interesting aspect of this mosaic, which is often mirrored in other North African arena scenes, is that not only the human combatants, but also their animal opponents are named as well. While the inclusion of such names was often done merely to provide as detailed a record of a given *munus* as possible for posterity, we shall see, nonetheless, that particularly ferocious animals, just like their human counterparts, could achieve a certain measure of celebrity as well.

A final category of epigraphic text testifying to the popularity of arena performers, which should be mentioned in the context of our present discussion, is the curse tablet from Roman North Africa. Such tablets, usually made of lead, were inscribed with a magical formula meant to doom a given performer to defeat, serious injury, and/or death. Curse tablets are more commonly associated with chariot racing, a sport which certainly provoked as fierce a partisanship among its fans as any other in Roman society, but some have been found dating to the second or third century which pertain rather to the world of the arena, in particular *venatores*. The fact that, for example, only two out of the twelve arena curse tablets refer to gladiators rather than beast hunters clearly suggests that, as previously discussed, the popularity of *venationes* had eclipsed that of gladiatorial contests by that period, at least in North Africa. A typical curse tablet, in terms of the invective used against a performer, is a third century example directed against the beast hunter Maurussus, which prays that his feet be bound and that he be exhausted and unable to run, all of which would make him easy pickings for an animal like a lion or bear. Interestingly enough, one of the extant tablets is directed not just against a single *venator*, but seven: perhaps they all belonged to a single faction or corporation like the *Telegenii*.[26]

One of the curse tablets in question, dating to the second or third century, also provides us with some useful information on the niceties of combat in the *venationes*, particularly important since such details are not particularly abundant in other sources. The text in question suggests, not surprisingly, that accomplished beast hunters were expected not merely to slaughter the animals they were pitted against, but display at least a modicum of skill in doing so. In particular, the author of the tablet prays that a *venator* by the name of Gallicus prove his incompetence by being unable to kill a bull or bear with one, two, or even three blows. Evidently, accomplished beast hunters would display their skill to spectators by killing a given animal with a predetermined number of strikes. The emphasis upon the skill of the *venator* is reminiscent of modern-day bullfighting, in which the audience similarly expects the matador to kill his quarry with a degree of finesse.[27]

Some of the most detailed testimony concerning specific gladiators or *venatores* and their feats in the arena comes from Roman and Greek literature. Pride of place in this instance should be given to the work of Martial, *On the Spectacles*, which provides a vivid account of contemporary imperial *munera* in the newly-opened Colosseum. Two of the epigrams in this collection mention gladiators by name, performers who had evidently already achieved great fame because of their fighting prowess. Given the auspicious nature of the *munera* recounted by Martial, it is to be expected, of course, that only the best and most famous of combatants would enter the arena on such an occasion.

It is important to note that both of the poems in question are at pains to emphasize the generosity of the Emperor and his solicitude for the audience. In the first epigram, with half the crowd clamouring for the gladiator Myrinus, and the other half calling for another by the name of Triumphus, the Emperor displays his munificence by allowing both men to enter the arena at the same time. In the second poem, the Emperor decides a long and evenly-matched struggle between two gladiators, Priscus and Verus, by awarding them both with the prize of victory; as Martial succinctly concludes: '…this has happened under no emperor except you, Caesar: two men fought and two men won.'[28]

Among celebrity performers, however, pride of place in Martial's work is taken by the *venator* Carpophorus. Just as the imperial bureaucracy had spared no expense in importing particularly exotic animals like tigers and rhinoceroses for the *munera* in the Colosseum, so too did it arrange for a beast fighter of unsurpassed talent (at least to judge from Martial's description!) to appear as well. In his poems concerning Carpophorus, in fact, Martial claims that the beast hunter's exploits in the Colosseum easily surpassed not only those of famous Greek heroes like Meleager, Bellerophon, Jason, Theseus, and Perseus, but even those of Hercules himself, the mightiest warrior of Greek myth:

'If the ages of old, Caesar, in which a barbarous earth brought forth wild monsters, had produced Carpophorus, Marathon would not have feared her bull, nor leafy Nemea her lion, nor Arcadians the boar of Menelaus. When he armed his hands, the Hydra would have met a single death, one stroke of his would have sufficed for the entire Chimaera. He could yoke the fire-breathing bulls without the Colchian, he could conquer both the beasts of Pasiphae. If the ancient tale of the sea monster were recalled, he would release Hesione and Andromeda single-handed. Let the glory of Hercules' achievement be numbered: it is more to have subdued twice ten wild beasts at one time.'[30]

In this particular poem, which claims that Carpophorus could have killed on his own all the hideous monsters dispatched by a multitude of Greek mythical heroes in the distant past, no mention is made of the specific animals Carpophorus killed in the arena, only that he allegedly killed twenty at once (as compared to the lesser twelve labours of Hercules, spread out over a long period of time). In a second poem dedicated to Carpophorus, however, Martial claims that he killed a boar, bear, lion, and leopard in the arena. Given all of the hyperbole of Martial's poetry, of course, we cannot state with certainty what Carpophorus did in the Colosseum, only that it greatly impressed Martial as well as his fellow spectators.[31]

Centuries later, the exploits of another popular *venator*, a black Egyptian by the name of Olympius, were recorded by the poet Luxorius. One interesting aspect of the poems in question, written in sixth century Carthage, is the evidence they provide that the *venationes* continued to be popular in the region a century after the collapse of Roman authority. Secondly, Luxorius' testimony also suggests that Olympius' great fame and popularity as a *venator* overcame the negative stereotype many had of the physical appearance of native Africans:

'... animal fighter Olympius, you bear a fit name because of your bodily strength, a Hercules by virtue of your neck, shoulders, back, and limbs ... Not at all does your swarthy body harm you because of its blackness ... so does the huge elephant please because of its dusky limbs, so do black Indian incense and pepper give pleasure ...'[32]

The fame arena performers such as Olympius could achieve is further stressed in the epitaph Luxorius wrote for him after his sudden death, perhaps in the arena:

'... Alas, now this tomb contains you carried off so unexpectedly by envious death, you whom the walls and towers of Carthage could not bear when you triumphed in the arena! But you lose nothing among the shades because of this bitter death. The fame of your glory will live everlastingly after you, and Carthage will always say your name!'[33]

It is important to note that human performers like Carpophorus and Olympius were not the only arena participants who could achieve a certain celebrity among spectators. On occasion, animals that fought well in the *venationes* could evidently earn some notoriety as well. One indication of such a phenomenon is the regularity with which animal as well as human performers are labelled in artwork like mosaics pertaining to the *munera*, such as in the aforementioned Magerius mosaic. It is possible, of course, that such names were an invention of the artist. What seems more likely, however, is that animals, like human gladiators and *venatores*, often fought under various stage names, and those animals who survived multiple appearances in the arena could achieve name recognition among spectators, like their human counterparts. The suggestion that certain animals were known by name to the audience is borne out by an anecdote from the reign of Marcus Aurelius: at one of his *munera*, the spectators called for a specific lion which was renowned for its especially bloodthirsty nature, much to the disgust of the Emperor.[34]

Various methods were certainly available to help ensure that popular animals would survive combat in the arena. Martial specifically records, for example, that an animal that fought well, like its gladiatorial counterpart, could be granted a reprieve (*missio*). Another apparent method in the case of particularly popular animals was to pit them against much weaker animals in the arena. By this means, the 'celebrity beast' could display its savagery without much risk of injury or death.[35] No plan is foolproof, however, and the poet Statius, writing during the reign of Domitian, records an incident wherein a popular lion, much to the crowd's displeasure, was apparently killed quite unexpectedly by the weaker animal which had been pitted against it:

> You are slain, educated ravager of tall beasts. You were not hemmed in by a Massylian band [from North Africa] and a cunning net nor plunging over hunting spears in a fearsome leap nor deceived by a pit's hidden cavity, but vanquished by a fleeing beast ... the placid lions are angry that such an outrage has been suffered.'[36]

Female gladiators and *venatores* comprised another category of celebrity performer in the arena, one noted for its novelty. The vast majority of performers in such dangerous professions were male. Nonetheless, a number of *editores*, in an attempt to add the novelty that was one of the hallmarks of a successful *munus*, included professional female combatants, as opposed to upper-class novices, in their spectacles. Such performers are not known with certainty to have participated in imperial spectacles prior to the reign of Titus, but they were certainly one of the novelties introduced by the Flavian emperors to make the inaugural games of the Colosseum even more exciting. In one of his epigrams, Martial recounts a female hunter (*venatrix*) who, like Carpophorus, put Hercules to shame:

> 'Illustrious fame used to sing of the lion laid low in Nemea's spacious vale, Hercules' work. Let ancient testimony be silent, for after your shows, Caesar, we have now seen such things done by women's valour.'[37]

As discussed previously, Domitian also included not just women, but dwarves, in gladiatorial spectacles staged during his reign.

Female arena combatants were, however, not just limited to Rome. Our best artistic evidence for the participation of female gladiators in the *munera*, in fact, a first or second century relief sculpture, comes from the city of Halicarnassus in Asia Minor. The relief shows two named gladiators, Amazon and Achillia, confronting each other with raised shields and drawn swords. The Greek verb at the top of the scene, *apeluthesan* ('they were released'), an apparent equivalent to the Latin term *stantes missi* ('they were sent away standing') suggests that the women fought to a draw. As in the case of many other arena performers, of course, the names under which they performed were intended to recall the world of classical myth. The natural connection to the Amazons, the fierce women warriors of Greek legend, is drawn not only by the name of one of the gladiators, but also by the fact that both fought bare-breasted, as their mythical counterparts had. The name of the second combatant, Achillia, is a little stranger at first glance, being the feminized form of the name Achilles, but in this instance, of course, a clear parallel is being drawn between her and the greatest hero of the legendary Trojan War. Among his many other martial accomplishments during that conflict, Achilles fought and killed the Amazon queen, Penthesileia, which may well have provided something of an inspiration for the duel depicted on the relief.[38]

The practice of women fighting as gladiators was formally banned during the reign of Septimius Severus (193–211). The events leading to this ban are unclear, but what appears to have happened is that a group of aristocratic women fought in one of the Emperor's spectacles as gladiators, an act which, according to the contemporary Dio, led to mockery not only of the performers, but also of upper-class Roman women as a whole. To ensure such a disreputable event never happened again, Severus subsequently banned female gladiators outright, regardless of their social status. To judge from the available evidence, female gladiators do not appear to have featured in many, if any spectacles in Rome following the death of Domitian in 96 AD, so the spectators of Severus' day, far less accustomed to such performers than their counterparts a century or so earlier, may indeed have found them an outrageous proposition. As in the case of so many other previously mentioned decrees, however, there is reason to believe the Emperor's ban did not spell an end to this practice entirely. An inscription from Ostia alluding to a *munus* with female gladiators, which appears to date to the later third century, suggests that Severus' ban was ignored even in close proximity to the capital.[39]

Sex appeal is one other important aspect of arena performers' charm that should be addressed, apart from fighting prowess and novelty. Certainly, a very common motif in Roman literature is the lust of upper-class Roman women for the brutish gladiators fighting on the arena floor. Perhaps the most famous exposition of this theme is in Juvenal's sixth satire, written in the early second century. As mentioned earlier, the poem is a diatribe against the vices of women, and one of the most infamous examples of alleged depravity that Juvenal adduces is the tale of a senator's wife by the name of Hippia who left her family behind to follow her lover, an ugly gladiator named Sergius, to Egypt:

> ... his face was really disfigured: there was a furrow chafed by his helmet, an enormous lump right on his nose, and the nasty condition of a constantly weeping eye. But he was a gladiator. That's what makes them into Hyacinthuses. That's what she preferred to her sons and her fatherland, to her sister and her husband. It's the steel that they're in love with.[40]

Unfortunately, we do not have any other information with which to corroborate Juvenal's account. It may well be that he employed some poetic licence to make a stronger case overall for the alleged turpitude of women.

One of the most famous instances of such alleged infidelity in ancient Rome is said to have involved no less a figure than the empress Faustina the Younger, wife of Marcus Aurelius and mother of the future emperor Commodus. Basically, many Romans had a difficult time believing that Marcus Aurelius could be Commodus' father, given their seemingly antithetical personalities. While the former was noted for his philosophical detachment, and relative distaste for the spectacles, Commodus, as we have seen, was arguably the most passionate adherent of the Roman *munera* ever to sit on the imperial throne. Given such profound differences, many believed that the empress Faustina must have been unfaithful to her husband, and the result of one such dalliance with a gladiator was her son, Commodus. This story, however, appears to belong to the realm of scurrilous gossip rather than fact. Sons with decidedly different personalities than their fathers has been a relatively common phenomenon throughout history, and does not need explaining by marital infidelity.[41]

Other, less questionable sources of evidence from the Roman world do nonetheless amply attest to the passions inspired by arena performers among appreciative spectators. One such source is arena-related graffiti from Pompeii. In addition to the notices of upcoming spectacles discussed earlier, another category of graffiti consists of amatory pronouncements made by arena performers or their fans. Two particularly boastful gladiators in Pompeii, to judge from the available evidence, were the *retiarius* (net-fighter) Cresces and the *Thrax* ('Thracian') Celadus. In one such graffito, Cresces refers to himself as *suspirium puellarum* ('heartthrob of the girls'), while in another, Celadus, not to be outdone, calls himself 'the doctor to nighttime girls, morning girls, and all the rest'.[42]

One of the more famous archaeological finds from the ruins of Pompeii was thought by some scholars to provide even more vivid evidence of the romantic attachment between gladiators and their fans. During the excavation of the gladiatorial barracks in Pompeii, archaeologists discovered the skeleton of a young noblewoman, identifiable as such by the fine jewelry found with her remains. A common assumption was that the young lady, an embodiment of Juvenal's Hippia, was carrying on an affair with one of the gladiators in the city, and had run off to be with him (and ultimately died with him) when Mount Vesuvius erupted.[43] Attractive as this reconstruction of events might be, however, it cannot be proven. It is just as possible that the young woman merely happened to be near the gladiatorial barracks when the volcano erupted, and sought shelter there before being overcome by the ash.

Other mementos of the arena surviving from the Roman era also attest to the devotion, carnal or otherwise, which gladiators and *venatores* could inspire in their fans. One of the 'side industries' associated with the *munera* was the production of statuettes and other small items depicting performers in the arena, which could be purchased by spectators and taken home after a given *munus*. One such memento, for example, is a small bronze mirror depicting on one side a *venator* fighting a boar. A common category of such souvenirs, one that plays on the lewder associations of arena combatants, is the depiction of such performers in association with the Roman god of fertility, Priapus, and/or his most prominent attribute, an oversized phallus. An excellent example of such a memento is a small hanging bronze lamp depicting a gladiator with a gigantic phallus.[43]

Often, spectators were not just partial to individual gladiators, but to a particular type of combatant as well. Such partisanship, unsurprisingly, could extend to the emperors themselves. The emperor Caligula, for example, was an adherent of the 'Thracian' gladiators and, as previously alluded to, is said to have appeared as one in the arena. Commodus' favourite type of gladiator, according to Dio, was the *secutor* ('follower'). Beast hunters, as we shall see, fought in much less varied equipment than gladiators, and as a result, did not attract the same type of partisanship based upon their style of armament.[44]

There are, in total, some twenty different types of gladiators attested in ancient literature and art, who differed in terms of their weaponry and defensive armament. Unfortunately, due to differing levels of popularity enjoyed by the various types of gladiators, as well as gaps in the relevant ancient evidence, we have far more information on some types of gladiators than others. In some cases, for example, while we might possess the name of a particular class of gladiator, there might be no surviving depictions of it in ancient art, which makes it very difficult, of course, to reconstruct with certainty the type of equipment and weaponry borne by the gladiator in question.

As discussed in our first chapter, gladiatorial events began at Rome in the mid-third century BC, at a time when the city-state was beginning a period of dramatic expansion that would see it become, over the next couple of centuries, not just mistress of Italy, but of the entire Mediterranean. It is perhaps not surprising, during this period of frequent conflict, that the earliest attested types of gladiator in Rome took their inspiration from Rome's recent or current enemies. At a certain psychological level, of course, the spectators of these early *munera* could take some comfort or satisfaction from seeing Rome's enemies, as symbolized by the gladiators on the arena floor, being killed, just as their counterparts had been, or were about to be, crushed by Rome's armies on her frontiers.

The oldest attested gladiatorial type in Rome was the 'Samnite', named after the powerful tribal coalition of central and southern Italy which Rome fought three wars against from the mid-fourth to early third century BC. According to Livy, the 'Samnite' gladiator originated during these conflicts, namely after a major battle in 310 BC between the Samnites on one hand, and Rome and her Campanian allies on the other. Many of the Samnites who fought in the battle are said by Livy to have worn ostentatious armour, including plumed helmets, large, oblong shields, and greaves on their left legs. After the battle, which resulted in a Roman victory, her Campanian allies chose to humiliate further their defeated enemies by dressing up their gladiators in armour taken from the battlefield, thus creating the 'Samnite' gladiator. Rome ultimately followed suit, and it was 'Samnite' gladiators, in fact, who featured in the first recorded Roman gladiatorial *munus* in 264 BC. Like their namesakes, the 'Samnites' fought with swords or, less commonly, spears. Those who fought in Roman spectacles, however, were not always as heavily armed as their Campanian progenitors, sometimes, for example, fighting with smaller round shields rather than the larger oblong variety.[45]

Two other 'ethnic' gladiatorial types which emerged in Rome during the Republic were the 'Gauls' and 'Thracians'. The Romans, of course, had been very familiar with the Gauls since the sack of Rome in 390 BC, and after that particular disaster, the figure of the Gaul had become something of a bogeyman in the Roman collective consciousness. In the last two centuries of the Republic, however, the Romans began annexing Gallic territory, culminating in Julius Caesar's conquest of Gaul in the 50s BC. It was during these campaigns that captured Gallic warriors began to appear in Roman arenas as 'Gauls', armed with traditional Celtic weaponry – a flat shield and longsword, for example. Similarly, 'Thracian' gladiators also emerged in the second century BC, as Rome began expanding into the territory of Thrace (roughly speaking, modern day Bulgaria and northeastern Greece), and captured natives were forced to fight in their ethnic armament for the Roman public's amusement. The weaponry of the 'Thracian' gladiator normally included a brimmed helmet and small rectangular shield. The most distinctive items of his equipment, however, were the greaves he wore on both legs, as well as a distinctive type of curved short sword, native to the lower Danube region, know as a *sica*.[46]

By the early Empire, gladiator types based upon ethnic caricatures had largely faded in popularity: the last extant mention of 'Samnite' gladiators, for example, dates to the reign of Augustus. Undoubtedly, the main reason for this change in fashion was the fact that, by the first century AD, Rome's most active period of territorial conquest had ended, and she was no longer involved in continually fighting large coalitions like the Gauls or Samnites. As a result, gladiators representing such ethnic groups in the arena no longer resonated with spectators as they once had. While 'Thracian' gladiators remained popular until the end of gladiatorial *munera* in the Roman Empire, the other two principal ethnic types of gladiator, the 'Gaul' and the 'Samnite' evolved by the earlier Empire into newer categories of combatant identified by their distinctive equipment or combat methods rather than the ethnic group they professed to represent. The 'Samnites', for example, appear to have evolved into the *hoplomachus*, while the 'Gaul' transitioned into the *murmillo*.[47]

The *hoplomachi* ('armed fighters') and *murmillones* ('fish fighters') were both heavily armed types of gladiator. Like the 'Samnites', the *hoplomachus* wore a greave on his left leg, as well as a brimmed helmet with visor. The most distinctive piece of equipment borne by the *hoplomachus*, however, was a small, round, concave shield. His offensive weaponry normally consisted of a spear, dagger, or short sword. It is not clear why this type of gladiator was given a Greek name, but perhaps the most plausible suggestion is that the weapons carried by the *hoplomachi* were reminiscent of those borne by the hoplites of classical Greece. The *murmillones*, who possessed the most bizarre name, at first glance, of all the gladiatorial types, were so called because of the fish motifs that commonly decorated their brimmed helmets. The other defensive equipment of a *murmillo* included a large rectangular shield (*scutum*), similar to that carried by Roman legionaries, as well as short greaves. Longer leg-guards were not necessary because of the length of shield carried by the *murmillo*. Both the *hoplomachus* and *murmillo* fought without any sort of chest armour. The usual weapon carried by the latter was a short sword, or *gladius*, which, like his shield, was also reminiscent of the weaponry carried by regular Roman troops.[48]

In most cases, different types of gladiators were pitted against each other in the arena to provide an interesting contrast in both armament and fighting styles for the assembled spectators. 'Thracians' and *hoplomachi*, for example, appear to have most commonly fought against *murmillones*, but far less commonly against each other. Numerous depictions of such combats survive from the ancient world, including a first to second century terracotta sculpture depicting a duel between a *hoplomachus* on the left, easily recognizable by his small round shield, and a 'Thracian' bearing a rectangular shield on the right. One suggestion explaining the specific appeal of such contests for spectators is that the legionary style armament of the *murmillo* would form an interesting contrast with the Greek style equipment of the *hoplomachus* or the even more exotic weaponry of the 'Thracian'.[49]

Gladiatorial contests did not remain static, of course, during their long history, and one of the most notable results of this continuing evolution in the first century CE was the emergence of two more popular types of gladiators, the *secutor* and the *retiarius*, who fought against each other in the arena. The *retiarius*, who does not appear to have emerged prior to the mid-first century AD, was so named because of his *rete* (throwing net), one of his most important pieces of equipment. The other important piece of a *retiarius'* arsenal was his trident. Unlike other types of gladiator, the *retiarius* wore no armour to speak of, and therefore had to rely almost entirely upon his speed and nimbleness against more heavily encumbered opponents. His basic offensive strategy was to try to entangle his adversary in his net, leaving him vulnerable to a thrust from his trident. If all else failed, he also had a dagger with which to defend himself. The *secutor* ('follower') took his name from his standard tactic, namely stalking his opponent with shield raised around the arena floor and waiting for an opportune moment to press home his attack. In most respects, he was identical to the *murmillo*: the only distinct difference between the two types of gladiator lay in their respective helmets. Rather than wearing an ornate visored helmet like that of the *murmillo*, the *secutor* wore a smooth helmet whose only accoutrements were a simple crest and two very small eyeholes. Such a helmet may well have reminded many spectators of a fish head, adding to the 'maritime theme' already suggested by the *retiarius'* net and trident. Why Roman *editores* of the early Empire evidently decided to introduce such an element into their spectacles, however, remains a mystery.[50]

What is abundantly clear, however, is the popularity this new pairing of gladiators achieved among Roman spectators. Among the clearest indications of this popularity, naturally, are the numerous depictions of both *secutores* and *retiarii* in Roman art. Even today, arguably, the *retiarius* is the first type of gladiator that springs to mind when we think of the Roman arena, and they have commonly appeared in such Hollywood sword-and-sandals epics of the past as *Spartacus* and *Gladiator*. One of the best ancient illustrations of a combat between *retiarius* and *secutor* comes from the gladiator mosaic found in a Roman villa near Nenning, in modern-day Germany, created no earlier than the late second century AD. Unlike many depictions of gladiatorial combat, which often show the victorious and defeated gladiators at the end of a given bout, the Nenning mosaic seemingly depicts the contest between the two gladiators at its height. The *retiarius*, however, appears to have already thrown and lost his net, which would put him at a disadvantage against his opponent. The figure standing behind the two combatants is a referee, about whom we shall have more to say presently.

As stated previously, the vast majority of gladiators fought against other varieties of combatant in the arena to provide a more interesting spectacle for the audience. Two exceptions to this general rule, however, beginning in the late Republic, were the *equites* and *provocatores*, who appear to have fought only against gladiators of their own type. In the case of the *equites* ('horsemen'), the reason for this practice is not hard to discern – having one gladiator fight on foot and another on horseback would grant an unfair advantage to the latter. To judge from the extant evidence, the *equites* did not fight an entire duel on horseback, but would only begin the contest in such a fashion, armed with a lance. At a certain point, assuming they had not already been thrown or knocked off their horses, the *equites* would dismount and decide the issue with swords. The standard defensive armament of the *equites* was a brimmed helmet and round shield.[51]

In the case of *provocatores* ('challengers'), it is not readily apparent why they only fought against others of their own ilk in the arena. In many respects, the equipment borne by the *provocatores* was similar to that of the 'Samnites': a relatively ornate helmet, a greave on the left leg, and a large oblong shield. The most distinctive piece of equipment worn by the *provocator*, one that distinguished him from all other types of gladiator, was a metal breastplate secured by leather straps. Perhaps the best depiction of *provocatores* in Roman art is to be found on the previously-discussed tomb relief found just outside of Rome, and dating to the late first century BC.[52]

The gladiator types discussed above, as alluded to previously, were certainly not the only variants to appear in the arena. They were, however, the most popular. Other classes of combatant are known, but given their relatively infrequent appearances in the *munera* (at least as compared to gladiators like *retiarii*), they are not well attested in the relevant ancient sources. As a result, it is often quite difficult to reconstruct with accuracy their armament and fighting styles. One such category, for example, was the *essedarius* ('chariot fighter'), which appears to have emerged at roughly the same time as the *retiarius*, in the mid-first century AD. Unfortunately, however, we possess absolutely no examples of gladiator art from antiquity that unequivocally depict *essedarii*. As a result, a number of questions must remain concerning their tactics in the arena: did they, for example, fight the entirety of their bouts from their chariots, or did they, like the *equites*, dismount to conclude the duel?[53]

Two of the more interesting minor categories of gladiators were the *dimachaeri* ('two-handed fighters') and *scissores* ('splitters'). As the name suggests, the first of these performers fought without a shield, and instead bore a weapon in each hand. Lacking a shield, the *dimachaerus*, presumably, had to rely a little more on his speed and dexterity in combat to avoid the blows of his adversaries. Given the extremely limited evidence for this particular type of performer, it has recently been suggested that, rather than representing a distinct type of gladiator, the term *dimachaerus* merely referred to another type of gladiator, like a *secutor* for example, who would sometimes, for the sake of variety and increased spectator interest, wield blades in both hands rather than a sword and shield.[54]

Fortunately, we possess more definitive pictorial evidence for the *scissor*. In terms of his defensive armament, he was quite similar to the *secutor*. The weaponry of the *scissor*, however, was certainly among the most singular found within the gladiatorial ranks. The limited evidence for this particular performer suggests that he fought with a conventional sword in one hand, but bore a semicircular crescent blade, attached to a metal forearm covering, on his other arm. His name, perhaps, came from the sizeable slashing wounds that could be inflicted by such a wide blade.[55]

The different gladiatorial disciplines, as we shall discuss in more detail in our next chapter, required specific training: under ordinary circumstances, a given gladiator would be assigned a specific fighting-style early in his career, based upon his perceived strengths and weaknesses, and be placed under the tutelage of a trainer in that particular discipline. The majority of attested arena combatants specialized in a single fighting style for their entire careers, but a few fought in more than one discipline, an accomplishment noted in the epigraphic record of their achievements as further proof of their fighting prowess. Two gladiatorial inscriptions from northern Italy, for example, commemorate performers who fought respectively as a *murmillo* and *hoplomachus*, and *murmillo* and *provocator*. The three types of gladiator mentioned in these inscriptions, as noted previously, used similar equipment, which certainly makes the concept of a single performer fighting in more than one of these disciplines not at all implausible.[56]

An even more unusual case, evidently, was that of an arena combatant who switched from gladiatorial combat to the *venationes*, or vice versa. Nonetheless, at least one such example is known from antiquity. An epitaph from Nicaea, namely, records a certain Chrysomallus (?): '... *retiarius*, he was a hunter before ...' As in the case of the two inscriptions just cited, a switch between *venator* and *retiarius*, in terms of equipment and fighting tactics, is by no means unthinkable: both performers were relatively lightly-armed, and relied much more on their speed and agility to survive in the arena rather than any defensive armament. It should also be noted that the deceased switching from the beast hunting to the gladiatorial ranks does not necessarily mean that there was a hierarchy between the two disciplines, and that the transition was therefore viewed as a promotion. We have already seen that, in certain areas of the Empire at least, the *venationes* were evidently more popular than the gladiatorial *munera*.[57]

As stated previously, the equipment of the *venator* in the arena was decidedly limited. On occasion, beast hunters are depicted in relatively heavy armour, somewhat similar to the equipment worn by contemporary gladiators. Perhaps the best visual example of the use of such armament among *venatores* is found on a late first century BC relief from Rome. The scene depicts five beast hunters in combat with a variety of animals, including a lion and bear. The short swords and rectangular shields borne by many of the human combatants appear quite similar to those used by *murmillones* in the arena, while the round shield carried by the fallen *venator* in the bottom left corner of the scene is reminiscent of the equipment of the *hoplomachi*. One suggestion concerning the relatively unorthodox armour worn by the beast hunters in this particular scene is that at this comparatively early date, there was not yet a clear distinction between *venatores* and gladiators in terms of the armour they wore. Another consideration, particularly in the case of later depictions of armoured beast hunters, is that they may well have wished to wear extra protection when fighting particularly dangerous animals like bears and lions.[58]

Much more commonly, to judge from the extant artistic evidence, *venatores* wore next to no armour, relying instead upon their speed and mobility to evade the attacks of the animals they were pitted against. In many depictions, they are shown wearing only leggings, tunics, and/or a leather covering over their abdomens. The standard weapon employed by beast hunters was a long hunting-spear (*venabulum*), often equipped with a perpendicular bar behind the head of the spear to prevent it becoming stuck in one of the animals. A typical beast hunter, with his tunic, waistband, leggings, and spear is depicted on a second century relief from northern Italy. In his right hand, however, he also holds a whip, which was another weapon periodically employed by *venatores* in the arena.[59]

Like gladiators, beast hunters may have periodically altered their standard equipment, using such weapons as clubs, daggers, and whips to add variety and interest to their performances. The most unusual alternate weapons employed by them, however, were boxing-straps (*caestus*), similar to those employed by *pancratiasts* in Greek combat sports. As attested in a few ancient sources, the animals most commonly fought by *venatores* employing such implements were bears. On the face of it, of course, this would seem to be a horrible mismatch in favour of the bear. Such an impression, however, appears to be misleading: Pliny the Elder, writing in the later first century, claimed, in fact, that beast hunters could often kill the bears they were pitted against with a single punch. Presumably, the way this was achieved was by placing lead strips under the straps, a tactic also familiar to Greek *pancratiasts*. Such a dangerous event, with such a surprising outcome, if the bear was indeed incapacitated with a single punch, was undoubtedly very popular among audience members wishing for as novel a spectacle as possible.[60]

As we have just seen, many items of arena apparel appear to have originally been inspired by equipment used in other professions or occupations, such as the military. It is important to note, however, that the equipment used by arena performers, regardless of their particular specialization, was generally much more ostentatious than any counterparts found outside the arena. Gladiatorial accoutrements, for example, could include armour decorated with gold filigree or gems, as well as helmets topped by ostrich or peacock plumes. The lavishness of such apparel, of course, added to the positive impression of a given spectacle upon the audience, and was certainly another one of the ways in which an enterprising *editor* could demonstrate his munificence. Even condemned criminals could be specially equipped for the occasion: Pliny the Elder records with disgust that Julius Caesar, in the *munera* he staged as *aedile* in 65 BC, established the precedent of having *noxii* outfitted with silver equipment to fight against wild beasts in the arena.[61]

Perhaps the best, and most idiosyncratic examples of arena apparel are the helmets worn by many different types of gladiators, of which a number of examples were found in Pompeii. Originally, gladiatorial helmets were quite similar to their military counterparts, but by the early Empire, they had evolved into their own distinct style, with broad rims, elaborate visors and, often, embossed metal reliefs and/or feathers on the crest of the helmet used as decoration. It has been suggested that the visors added to gladiatorial helms during the reign of Augustus were intended to make the now faceless gladiator appear even more intimidating. It may also be, of course, that the individual identity of gladiators was considered of little importance because of their negligible social status.[62]

To this point, we have discussed some of the most prevalent attitudes of Romans towards arena spectacles, as well as the most common types of combatants participating in the *munera*. Before leaving the topic of 'performer and spectator', however, we shall discuss in more detail the events of a typical spectacle, a discussion which will not only illustrate further some of the themes and topics mentioned earlier in the chapter, but will also illustrate what a complex undertaking the staging of a *munus* was. This, in turn, will lead into our subsequent examination of the all-important organizational infrastructure necessary for the success of such an event.

The ceremonies and events associated with a typical day's *munus* did not merely begin with the first combat of the morning in the arena, but were instead initiated with a ritual known as the *cena libera* (free/public dinner) staged a night or two beforehand. On this occasion, the gladiators and other performers participating in the upcoming spectacle would partake of a banquet set up in a public area like the town forum. This would allow interested members of the community to get a relatively close look at the participants in a given *munus*, in particular any celebrity performers, even before they stepped into the arena. The closest, albeit imperfect, modern parallels to this custom would be the open practices sometimes scheduled by various sports teams, as well as the media scrums set up before various events like boxing.[63]

On the day of the spectacle proper, the festivities would begin with a procession of the *editor* and his performers, accompanied by attendants and musicians. The latter would not only play during this procession (*pompa*), but also during the subsequent bouts on the arena floor, as shown in a number of extant depictions of the *munera*. One is reminded of the modern day organists who play during ice hockey games and other contests in order to drum up spectator interest in the proceedings. A second preliminary spectacle before the actual combats was the *prolusio/proludium* ('prelude'). This warm-up segment of the *munus* often involved, in general, a non-lethal exhibition of martial skills, usually achieved with the use of blunted weapons. On occasion, however, particularly in the case of spectacles that included a *venatio*, the *prolusio* might also feature a procession of some of the exotic animals slated to fight in the arena, or a non-lethal (to the *venatores* at least) preliminary combat involving relatively harmless animals like rabbits and deer. A final important component of these preliminary proceedings was the so-called *probatio armorum* ('test of arms'), in which the *editor* would inspect the weapons to be used in the actual *munus*, confirming their lethality to the assembled spectators.[64]

With such opening festivities concluded, and with the audience's anticipation for the carnage whetted (hopefully!) to a fever pitch, the time had come for the day's main attraction, the genuine struggle between performers on the arena floor. Heralds and attendants bearing placards would inform spectators on the pertinent details of the bouts being contested before them, in particular the names and fighting record of the combatants. Such information, of course, was essential for the many members of the audience betting on the proceedings.

Under the developed programme of a typical *munus*, as stated previously, the first full fledged combat events of the day would be the *venationes*. These beast hunts, however, could take a variety of forms, including, most notably, *venatores* pitted against various animals, or the latter pitted against each other. In some cases, the choice of animals pitted against each other was meant to reflect real or imagined confrontations in the wild: on occasion, for example, crocodiles would fight against hippopotami, or rhinoceroses against elephants, two particular pairings reflecting the common (and mistaken) belief that these animals were mortal enemies in the natural world.[65]

Sometimes, the animals paired off in such a fashion were understandably hesitant to fight each other. Under such circumstances, the spectacle organizers could pursue a variety of means to force combat. One popular method was to link the animals together by a length of chain. Wild beasts, as to be expected, would not tolerate such a situation for long, and would soon attack each other in order to try to escape their enforced proximity. One of the best depictions of such a practice comes from the aforementioned Zliten mosaic: a bear and bull, linked by a long chain, are depicted in the midst of combat, while a scantily clad figure below extends what appears to be a long hook towards the chain. The identity or function of this figure is not clear, but one possibility is that he is an arena attendant who, having led the bear and bull out onto the arena floor by their chain, is depicted at the moment he withdraws his hook, allowing the animals to fight in earnest.

On occasion, in perhaps an even more dangerous pursuit, arena attendants would simply goad reluctant animals into fighting by poking them with sticks or firebrands. One of the most vivid depictions of this exercise comes from Martial's epigrams celebrating the first appearance of a two-horned rhinoceros in the Colosseum, an animal, which, at least initially, was hesitant to display its fighting prowess:

> While the trembling trainers were goading the rhinoceros and the great beast's anger was long a-gathering, men were giving up hope of the combats of promised warfare; but at length the fury we earlier knew returned ...[66]

One can well imagine the terrified attendants running for their very lives as the rhinoceros snapped into action!

As already mentioned, the animal events of a given *munus* did not always involve combat or death: on occasion, an *editor* would stage a display meant to illustrate the intelligence, rather than the fighting prowess, of the creature in question. Although such nonviolent displays appear to have been less common under the Empire than during the Republic, they are attested as late as the fourth century AD. Particularly popular in the imperial spectacles of Rome itself, to judge from the available evidence, were displays of elephants performing various alleged feats like tightrope-walking or synchronized dancing. One reason elephants appear to have been particularly common participants in such events, quite apart from the general affection in which many Romans appear to have held these highly intelligent animals, was their regal connotations. Many Roman emperors, in emulation of Alexander the Great and later Hellenistic rulers, associated themselves with these animals (e.g. by having themselves depicted on their coinage being driven in elephant-drawn chariots). It may have been considered unseemly, therefore, for elephants to be slaughtered in the arena like more mundane animals. A similar reason may also be behind the occasional appearance of lions, animals with their own regal connotations, in nonviolent displays under the Empire: the most famous example would be the lion trained to let hares in and out of his mouth unharmed, as recorded in the poetry of Martial.[67]

After the morning animal events, the midday pause would ensue, during which any condemned *noxii* the *editor* of the spectacle had been able to procure would be executed. On such occasions, the heralds would proclaim to the assembled audience the crimes for which the condemned were being punished: the deterrent effect of such executions would presumably be diminished somewhat if the spectators had no notion what specific crimes could merit such a grisly punishment. The midday pause also provided an opportunity for the attendants to prepare the arena for the gladiatorial combats of the afternoon. Among the mundane tasks that could be performed at this time, for example, was raking up the blood that had accumulated on the arena floor during the morning events, as well as any subsequent executions.

Although gladiators, as we have seen, could periodically fight in mass combats, the standard form of gladiatorial contest was a one-on-one duel. These combats were officiated by two referees known as the *summa rudis* ('first stick') and *secunda rudis* ('second stick'), named for the long sticks they wielded, with which they kept the gladiators in line. Such officials are commonly depicted in scenes of gladiatorial *munera*. Gladiators were expected to fight by a common set of rules, and the *summae* and *secundae rudes* stood by to punish any breach of conduct. Unfortunately, many ancient writers do not appear to have been overly interested in the niceties of gladiatorial combat, and as a result, we do not possess a great deal of information on the specific rules to be observed during a bout.[68]

In general, however, there were three possible outcomes to a gladiatorial combat. By far the most common was *missio* ('reprieve'), in which the defeated gladiator, presuming he fought well and did not earn the audience's displeasure, could be dismissed from the arena to fight again another day. As seen in a number of ancient depictions, a losing gladiator usually sought such a reprieve by lowering his weapons and raising his finger to the referee (i.e. the *summa rudis*), after which the latter would stop the fight and await the verdict of the crowd and *editor*. The referees apparently could also stop a combat at their own discretion, at least on occasion. A far less common type of combat, or combat outcome, was *sine missione* ('without reprieve'). In this more dangerous type of contest, the combat usually continued until one gladiator was incapacitated and unable to continue, either through serious injury or from dying at the hands of his opponent. Finally, a third attested outcome was *stantes missi* ('they [the gladiators] were sent away standing'). Under these circumstances, the combatants fought to a draw, and both were granted a reprieve after the combat was halted.[69]

The apparent prevalence of *missiones* ('reprieves') in gladiatorial combat suggests, as mentioned previously, that such duels did not lead to fatalities as often as commonly assumed. Apart from these formal rules, another factor that may have limited gladiatorial deaths (at least to a degree) was an informal code of conduct. A number of extant inscriptions indicate that gladiators who followed this code only sought to injure their opponents enough to secure victory, and in no way sought to kill them. One of the more interesting allusions to this code is found in the epitaph of a gladiator by the name of Diodoros:

> 'Here I lie victorious, Diodoros the wretched. After felling my opponent Demetrios, I did not kill him immediately. But murderous Fate and the cunning treachery of the *summa rudis* killed me, and leaving the light I have gone to Hades ...'

The text of the inscription suggests that Diodoros, as per the 'gladiators' code', let up on his attack against Demetrios during their bout, believing that he had done enough to secure victory. The dastardly *summa rudis*, however, (at least from Diodoros' perspective) did not stop the duel, but allowed it to continue. It was in the second phase of the contest that Demetrios, who evidently was not seriously wounded, slew Diodoros outright, and in so doing, violated the code.[70]

Of course, despite conventions such as *missio* that prolonged the average gladiator's lifespan in the arena, those combatants who fought poorly could still ultimately be condemned to death. When one gladiator had achieved the upper hand over his opponent, and the referee had stopped the contest to await the verdict of the *editor* and spectators, the losing gladiator would kneel on the arena floor, while his victorious opponent stood behind him with his sword pressed against the base of his neck. Depending upon the verdict, the latter would either sheathe his sword, or plunge it into his opponent's neck, severing his spinal column. It was now that the defeated gladiator could display the courage and contempt for death so admired by Seneca and other Roman writers. In fact, it was expected that, should the moment come, a true gladiator would not bewail his fate, but would calmly allow himself to be dispatched by his opponent.

After a given bout had concluded, the victorious gladiator, or *venator* for that matter, would receive his reward from the *editor* of the spectacle. In the late Republic and early Empire, victors would normally receive a sum of money, as well as the more symbolic prize of a palm branch. Those who fought particularly well could earn the especially prestigious reward of a laurel wreath (*corona*), or even monetarily valuable items like silver plate. In the later Empire, however, the *coronae* appear to have supplanted palm branches as a general symbol of victory, and ceased only to be given out to those who had especially distinguished themselves in the arena. Gladiatorial commemorations, be they artistic or epigraphic, often made reference to such palm branches and laurel wreaths as a useful shorthand to indicate the amount of success a given performer had enjoyed in the arena. A good example of the latter practice is the following epitaph of a gladiator from the mid-first century found in Spain: 'The *essedarius* Ingenuus, from the *ludus Gallicus* ['Gallic school'], a German by birth, lived twenty-five years and won twelve palms ...'[71]

One final aspect of arena spectacles that should be addressed in this chapter is their continuing religious overtones. Although, as we have seen, gladiatorial *munera* had moved beyond their funereal origins by the end of the Republic, enough of a religious veneer remained that the Christian critic Tertullian, writing at the beginning of the third century, could level the following broadside at such events:

> '...what am I to say about that dreadful place, the amphitheatre? Even perjury could not face it. For it is dedicated to more names, and more awful names, than the Capitol itself; it is the temple of all demons. There are as many unclean spirits gathered there as it can seat men.'[72]

One manifestation of such religious connotations is found in the terminology of the arena and its architecture. The two main gates leading onto the arena floor, for example, were known as the *porta Sanivivaria* ('Gate of Life') and the *porta Libitinensis* ('Gate of Death'). The former was the portal through which performers initially entered the arena, as well as through which those who survived their bouts were able to leave. The latter took its name from Libitina, the Roman goddess who oversaw funerals. It does not require much reasoning to deduce which performers exited the arena through this gate! The corpses of performers killed in combat were taken to the *spoliarum*, a chamber where their equipment would be stripped off prior to burial after passing through the *porta Libitinensis*.[73]

According to Tertullian, the pagan religious overtones of the arena were further betrayed by the costumes worn by many of the arena attendants during a given *munus*. At least some, for example, dressed as the Roman god Mercury, whose traditional duties included escorting the dead to the underworld. One of their tasks in the arena, according to Tertullian, was to poke prone gladiators to make sure they were dead. Other attendants, either dressed as the Roman god of the underworld, Pluto, or as his Etruscan equivalent, Charon, were specifically assigned the task of dragging dead performers out of the arena with a hook. It should be noted, of course, that Tertullian is the sole ancient author to mention these costumed attendants, and they are not depicted in the extant artistic evidence from the ancient world. It has also been noted by scholars that the ignominious treatment of being dragged out of the arena with a hook was reserved for the *noxii*, not the regular gladiators or *venatores*. Nonetheless, it appears unlikely that Tertullian completely fabricated these aspects of a *munus*, since his contemporaries could have easily refuted such an invention.[74]

We have examined up to this point the evolution of arena spectacles, as well as their importance within Roman society, which ranged from their perceived entertainment value to the deeper social and propaganda functions ingrained within them. We have also had occasion to survey the wide variety of performers and events that could form part of a given *munus*. Next, we shall turn our attention to the considerable infrastructure behind the staging of such events. As will become evident, an enormous amount of preparatory organization had to be carried out before the participants in a spectacle even set foot upon the arena floor.

*Chapter Five*

# The Infrastructure of the Arena

As alluded to periodically in our previous discussion, all *munera*, whether they were the massive imperial spectacles of Rome, or the countless, much more modest events staged every year throughout Roman territory, required a considerable degree of planning and organization beforehand. As we shall see, the preparation of a successful *munus* required a veritable army of officials and support personnel, whose responsibilities ranged from training gladiators and other performers to ensuring an adequate supply of healthy animals for a given *venatio*. One advantage possessed by the emperors in Rome was having the ready resources of the Roman army at hand to help pursue such objectives. Although such behind-the-scenes activities did not garner the attention of the spectacles themselves on the part of ancient writers, enough evidence remains to illustrate the tremendous investment in terms of both money and manpower which was necessary for the staging of *munera* across Roman territory over the course of several centuries.

One indispensable group in the preparation of an arena spectacle that we have already mentioned was the *familia*, a group of trained performers headed by a chief trainer/manager known as a *lanista*. Such groups, as we have seen, began to emerge in the later Republic as the gladiatorial *munera* became more and more popular. The tens of thousands of prisoners-of-war captured by Roman armies during the last two centuries of the Republic provided, of course, a more than ample pool of potential recruits for these *familiae*.

When an *editor* wished to stage a spectacle, he would normally procure the services of a *lanista* and his *familia*. The price the spectacle organizer had to pay, of course, depended upon a number of variables, most notably the number of performers he wished to include in his event. Another very important variable was the number of performers killed in the *munus*. Under ordinary circumstances, it appears, the *editor* was merely renting the services of a given *familia*, and the price charged by the *lanista* came with the nominal understanding that all of his performers would be returned unharmed after the spectacle (or at least not seriously injured). The spectacle organizer, then, had to pay extra compensation for any performers who were incapacitated or killed during his spectacle, an amount that might reach as much as fifty times what he had originally paid for the person in question![1]

With the spread of *munera* across the Empire came the concomitant proliferation of private *familiae*. We have already noted that priests of the imperial cult in various cities and towns throughout Roman territory purchased a number of these groups to expedite the staging of their spectacles. To judge from the extant evidence, these *familiae* were not all of a single, uniform type, but could vary in composition. While some groups, like the previously discussed *familia* from Hierapolis, could include both gladiators and *venatores*, others included only one category of performer. An inscription from Corsica dating to the late first or early second century, for example, makes mention of a *familia venatoria*, a local group evidently involved solely with the production of beast hunts.[2]

A number of other inscriptions make reference to the training system within such groups, in particular the *gladiatoriae familiae*. As mentioned previously, a prospective arena performer would normally be assigned to a specific fighting discipline soon after joining a given *familia*, and would thereby pass under the instruction of a specialist in that particular style. Numerous inscriptions found throughout Roman territory attest to *doctores* ('trainers') of the *secutores*, *murmillones*, *hoplomachi*, and other disciplines, all of whom had probably gained their expertise through fighting as gladiators themselves.[3]

The training regimen gladiators underwent, not surprisingly, was similar in many respects to that found in the Roman army. A novice gladiator (*tiro*), like an army recruit, would not begin his training by sparring against fellow recruits, a practice which at this stage might have resulted in serious injury, but would instead practice his weapon strokes initially against a wooden stake (*palus*). The ranking system of gladiators, in turn, took its name from these stakes. Each combatant was ranked within his discipline as 'first stake', 'second stake', 'third stake', and so on, depending upon his proficiency in the arena: the lower the number, the higher the skill level. The number of *palus* ranks within a typical *familia* likely numbered four or five, although as many as eight have been attested in the ancient sources. Not surprisingly, many extant gladiatorial epitaphs make note of the *palus* ranking which the deceased had achieved during his career in the arena: a third century inscription honouring a certain Peregrinus, for example, not only denotes him as a *murmillo*, but also specifies that he had achieved the rank of *primus palus*. Ordinarily, gladiators of an equal rank would be pitted against each other in the arena (e.g. a first-rank *retiarius* against a first-rank *secutor*), so as to make their contest as evenly-matched as possible, but as we have already seen, novices could be pitted against veterans, sometimes with surprising results![4]

Our best evidence for the facilities used by *familiae* in the smaller towns and cities of the Empire comes, not surprisingly, from Pompeii. The earliest known gladiatorial barracks at Pompeii was originally a private residence converted to house arena performers sometime between the reigns of Augustus and Claudius (14–41 AD). The large open courtyard of the house, along with the numerous small rooms flanking it on three sides, made it an ideal venue for gladiators to both train and live in. It appears that, at any given time, approximately twenty were resident in the house. Our main evidence for their presence in this building is the abundance of preserved graffiti left behind by the gladiators, which indicates that a variety of different gladiators, such as 'Thracians', *murmillones*, and *retiarii*, all stayed here.[5]

In 62 AD, because of the earthquake that damaged much of Pompeii in that year, the gladiators were forced to move to a new, and better-known facility, the *quadriporticus* (colonnaded square) behind the city's theatre. The extant evidence indicates that the rooms surrounding the square on all four sides were converted to a variety of purposes after 62 AD, including quarters, a kitchen, and a communal dining room. The larger size of this square meant, of course, that substantially more gladiators could be housed here than in the previous barracks in Pompeii. Among the most interesting archaeological finds in the *quadriporticus* were many examples of gladiatorial armament, as well as the previously discussed skeleton of a young noblewoman (see p. 107). Another skeletal find, that of a newborn infant, may suggest that at least some gladiators in Pompeii lived in the barracks with their families, assuming, of course, that the unfortunate infant was not simply left in the *quadriporticus* to die at the time of Vesuvius' eruption in 79 AD. The accumulated evidence from Pompeii, if it can be taken as at all representative of larger trends across the Empire, suggests that, while larger cities may have possessed purpose-built facilities for gladiators and other arena performers, their accommodations and training venues in smaller centres were much more *ad hoc* in nature.[6]

Alongside the private groups of gladiators and other arena performers scattered across the Roman Empire in towns like Pompeii were the state-owned *familiae*. One of the primary inspirations for the latter organizations were the gladiatorial cohorts which had been created in the late Republic under the auspices of prominent political leaders like Julius Caesar, who wished to have a supply of gladiators and other arena performers ready at hand for their *munera*. The practice of Roman leaders setting up their own private groups of arena performers continued into the imperial period. The emperor Nero, for example, created a new school of imperial gladiators known as the *Neroniani*, which supplemented the *Iuliani*, the *familia* originally instituted by Julius Caesar at Capua that had ultimately come under the control of Augustus and his successors.[7]

Just as the production of *munera* in Rome had been brought under much tighter control by the imperial bureaucracy, so too was the supervision of such imperial *familiae* carefully regulated during the imperial period. A number of inscriptions, in fact, attest to the regional procurators charged with overseeing state-owned *familiae* in different regions or cities of the Empire. To judge from the other important posts held by attested procurators of various *familiae*, this particular responsibility was considered to be of great importance, and was only bestowed upon equestrian officials of proven competence. A good example of such a procurator is Publius Cominius Clemens, whose career is recorded for posterity on a late second century inscription discovered near Venice. In addition to his post as procurator of a gladiatorial *familia* in northern Italy, Clemens is also recorded as having held, at one time or another, other important responsibilities, including command over the fleets stationed at Ravenna and Misenum, as well as the post of imperial procurator in two different provinces.[8]

Closely associated with the state-owned *familiae* under the Empire were the various imperial *ludi* (training schools), as well as their associated personnel.

The largest and most famous of these schools, not surprisingly, were located in Rome itself. Pride of place went to the *Ludus Magnus* ('Great School'), which was the main gladiatorial training facility in the city. Other gladiatorial barracks in the city included the *Ludus Gallicus*, evidently so-named because it had originally been built for the training of 'Gallic' gladiators, and the *Ludus Dacicus* ('Dacian School'). The origin of the latter school's name is even less clear than that of the *Ludus Gallicus*, but one plausible suggestion is that it was originally built in the late first or early second century AD to house and train the thousands of Dacian prisoners captured during Domitian's and Trajan's campaigns. Rounding out the prominent training schools in Rome was the *Ludus Matutinus* ('Morning School') for *venatores*, so named because, as we have seen, the beast hunts were traditionally staged in the morning. It is estimated that these *ludi* in Rome could have housed some 2,000 gladiators and *venatores* in total at any given time.[9]

It is not exactly clear when these state-owned training schools came into operation, but it may have been under the Flavian emperors, in the later first century AD. Clearly, the imperial bureaucracy associated with the *munera* had begun to evolve before that date: Suetonius, for example, mentions an unfortunate *curator munerum ac venatioum* ('manager of the gladiatorial games and beast hunts') who was beaten to death at the orders of Caligula. This emperor is also credited with building the first training school for arena performers in Rome, which may have formed the precedent for later facilities in the city. The earliest, specific references to the administrators of both the *Ludus Magnus* and *Ludus Matutinus*, however, date to the reign of Trajan.[10]

Given the accumulated evidence, a Flavian date for the imperial training facilities in Rome does not appear at all unreasonable. It was under this dynasty, of course, that the Colosseum was constructed, and it is certainly feasible that many associated structures like the *Ludus Magnus* were also built at this time, to ensure that there were enough trained performers ready at hand to participate in the lavish imperial spectacles made possible by this new facility. The Flavian period also saw an increasing bureaucratization of the *munera*, with the creation of new administrative posts like the *procurator a muneribus* ('manager of the *munera*'), whose responsibility was to oversee the organization of imperial spectacles. Conceivably the procurators put in charge of the various training schools could have been part of this administrative reorganization as well.[11]

All of the training schools, and in particular the *Ludus Magnus* and *Ludus Matutinus*, were, not surprisingly, located in close proximity to the Colosseum. Unfortunately, however, very little is known of the design and layout of these training schools, with the exception of the *Ludus Magnus*. The focal point of the latter structure was a large practice arena (63m by 42m in size), similar in layout to that of the Colosseum, and about three-quarters the size of the latter. The seating around the arena of the *Ludus Magnus* appears to have held up to 3,000 spectators. This venue, of course, not only allowed gladiators to train in conditions as close to those of the Colosseum as possible, but also allowed some Romans, presumably members of the elite, to get a sneak peak at them before the *munus* proper took place. A final important design feature of the *Ludus Magnus* was the tunnel connecting it to the Colosseum basement, which allowed gladiators to travel quickly and quietly to the amphitheatre on the day of their performance without being waylaid by overzealous pedestrians.[12]

The *Ludus Matutinus*, although only about half the size of the *Ludus Magnus*, appears to have been closely based in design upon the latter structure. Like the *Ludus Magnus*, for example, the *Ludus Matutinus* featured a practice arena for the performers housed within its walls. It is possible that a tunnel also connected the latter building to the Colosseum basement for the safe movement of both *venatores* and animals. Although the evidence is certainly not conclusive, it has been suggested that a passage branching off to the south from the tunnel connecting the *Ludus Magnus* and Colosseum originally led to the *Ludus Matutinus*. Such an arrangement certainly would have made sense, since the last thing spectacle organizers wanted was for members of their audience to be mauled on the streets by wild animals on their way to the arena![13]

As might be expected, given the close relationship between gladiatorial spectacles and the beast hunts under the Empire, the same person, at least on occasion, could hold the procuratorship of both the *Ludus Magnus* and the *Ludus Matutinus*. A late second century inscription from Palestrina, for example, records that a certain Titus Flavius Germanus, among many other important posts, was procurator of both *ludi* at successive points in his career. Similarly, another fragmentary inscription from Sicily, dating to the late second or third century AD, records an unnamed individual as having not only been in charge of the *Ludus Magnus* and *Ludus Matutinus* during his career, but also having been at one time *procurator* of the gladiatorial *familiae* in Sicily, Aemilia (north-eastern Italy) and Dalmatia (the present-day Croatian coast).[14]

As in the case of the previously discussed procurators of the imperial *familiae*, the procuratorship of the training schools, to judge from the extant epigraphic evidence, was only entrusted to equestrian officials of proven competence. Many of the attested officials, particularly in the case of the *Ludus Magnus*, had held previous military postings, which undoubtedly would have proven useful in their supervision of hundreds of armed arena combatants in the heart of Rome. The procuratorship of the *Ludus Magnus*, however, was a more prestigious post than that of the *Ludus Matutinus*, with holders of the former position earning an annual salary of 200,000 sesterces, considerably higher than the sum paid out to *procuratores Ludi Matutini*. The salary paid to the procurator of the *Ludus Magnus*, in fact, made him one of the highest-paid members of the imperial bureaucracy in Rome.[15]

Such officials, of course, are not the only personnel of the state-owned *ludi* attested by the epigraphic evidence. Numerous imperial freedmen worked under the auspices of the procurators, in a variety of capacities, to ensure the smooth functioning of their respective facilities. Among the personnel attested by extant inscriptions, for example, are a *dispensator Ludi Magni* ('steward of the *Ludus Magnus*'), a *commentariensis Ludi Matutini*, who evidently served as administrative secretary to the *procurator* of the 'Morning School', and even a *cursor Ludi Magni* ('messenger of the *Ludus Magnus*'). One of the more important attested officials, arguably, was the *praepositus armentario Ludi Magni*, who was in charge of the weapons armory (*armentarium*) attached to the training school. Not surprisingly, *medici* ('doctors') are also known to have been in residence at both the *Ludus Magnus* and *Ludus Matutinus*.[16]

Those *editores* who wished to stage a *venatio* as part of their *munus*, be they municipal officials or the emperors themselves, were faced with one particular challenge: namely, ensuring the successful capture and live transport of various wild animals to their ultimate destinations. Certainly, as we have already seen, it was common for at least some of the beasts imported for a given spectacle to die in transit before even reaching the towns or cities in which they were slated to appear. Another potential difficulty, which we shall have occasion to address, was keeping those animals who did successfully arrive at their destinations alive and in good health until the day of their spectacle.

Despite the challenges of the animal trade, however, a number of civilian entrepreneurs are known to have made their livings from this profession. We have already encountered a certain Patiscus who, as the correspondence of Cicero indicates, evidently supplied various exotic animals to wealthy and powerful clients in Rome during the late Republic. Such private entrepreneurs involved in the animal trade continued to exist even centuries later, as subsequent correspondence from the fourth and early fifth centuries confirms. In a series of letters from the mid-fourth century concerning his attempts to round up animals for upcoming spectacles in the eastern city of Antioch, the noted rhetorician and political figure, Libanius, twice mentions a certain Polycarp who, like Patiscus, evidently had under his employ a group of hunters who captured and shipped exotic beasts for wealthy clients. A few decades after Libanius' correspondence, the Roman aristocrat Symmachus wrote another series of letters detailing his own attempts to procure animals for future spectator events in Rome. Like his predecessors, Symmachus also made use of private personnel to oversee the capture and shipment of beasts to Rome; one seeming difference in the case of Symmachus' preparations, however, is that he also sent many members of his household staff to assist in the procurement of animals as well.[17]

Another apparent constant in the organization of animal spectacles over the centuries was that those involved in such an endeavour sought to make use of powerful political contacts to expedite the process as much as possible, just as Caelius pestered Cicero to find him some leopards while the latter was governor of Cilicia. Among the political notables solicited by Libanius centuries later in an attempt to procure animals and performers for upcoming spectacles in Antioch were the vicars of Asia (the regional governors of Roman provinces in what is now western Turkey), as well as the current governors of Bithynia and Phoenicia. Similarly, in his own attempts to facilitate the production of animal events in Rome, Symmachus pestered such notables as the praetorian prefect of Italy, the governor of Africa, and even the powerful general Stilicho, who at the time was arguably the most powerful man in the western Empire.[18]

Another interesting constant in many of these letters, regardless of whether they date to the late Republic or Empire, is the arguments used to try to persuade various correspondents to agree to what must have been expensive and time-consuming requests. As we have already seen in our survey of late Republican *munera*, for example (see p. 14), Caelius emphasized the alleged damage to Cicero's reputation that would result if he failed to procure any leopards for Caelius' spectacle in Rome.[19]

Centuries later, Libanius' letter to the governor of Phoenicia, Andronicus, similarly stresses the loss of personal and political standing that would theoretically ensue should the governor not honour Libanius' request:

'Well, perfection in the beast-shows depends mainly upon you [Andronicus]. Phoenicia produces expert huntsmen, and if you are willing, we shall employ them; if not, we will be deficient in this respect, and people will reproach not us, for our disappointment, but the one who pays no regard to his friends, for no one is unaware of the fact that we are inviting people from there or of the person to whom we direct our request.'[20]

One complicating factor in the preparation of animal spectacles that earlier *editores* like Caelius did not have to deal with, but is readily apparent in the later correspondence of Libanius and Symmachus, was potential interference on the part of the emperor and his officials. In our earlier survey of spectacles staged outside Rome, we already encountered some examples of local *editores* being granted imperial permission to stage particularly extravagant *munera* (at least by local standards). The letters of Symmachus and Libanius, however, clearly show that such imperial permission became even more important in the late Empire, particularly as the supply of exotic animals available for various spectacles became ever more reduced.

In the letter just quoted, for example, Libanius was asking Andronicus to overlook the fact that the current emperor, Constantius II, had already requested the huntsmen and animals in question for one of his own spectacles. In a subsequent letter, Libanius pleaded with yet another high official to work around the emperor's demand for animals, all so that Libanius' cousin would have enough beasts for his own event. Similarly, Symmachus had to do his own cajoling of the emperor and his representatives when arranging another series of spectacles a few decades later in Rome. One particular challenge was securing a supply of lions. As we shall see in our next chapter, lions were placed under an imperial monopoly in the late Empire, apparently because of their reduced population in Roman territory. As a result, Symmachus had to write more than one letter requesting an imperial indulgence for the inclusion of such animals in his son's *munera*.[21]

Much of our written evidence for the civilians actually involved in the capture and transport of beasts for the *munera* consists of allusions to men like Patiscus in the correspondence of Cicero, Libanius, and Symmachus. Much more testimony is available, as will be seen, for the involvement of Roman military personnel in the animal trade. Nonetheless, in addition to the evidence already cited, there is some limited epigraphic testimony pertaining to civilians who made a living supplying the *venationes*. Two early third-century inscriptions from the area of modern day Salzburg, for example, suggest that members of the household staff of a certain Lollius Honoratus were involved in animal capture, possibly, at least in part, for local spectacles. A certain Profuturus is identified as a *vestigiator* (tracker of wild animals), while one of Honoratus' slaves is denoted as a *cinctor*, a term meaning one who set traps or snares.[22]

Other epigraphic evidence from modern day Austria, in particular the associated reliefs depicting hunters in pursuit of such animals as bears, deer, and even a lion, also suggest that the prominent family of the Albii were involved in a similar occupation. One of these inscriptions, a dedication made to the health of one of the Albii by a local governor in the early third century, may have been commissioned because the former earned the governor's solicitude by previously supplying the animals for one of his spectacles. It is no surprise, of course, that various entrepreneurs like the Albii could make a lucrative living from the animal trade in a wildlife-rich area like Austria. It is reasonable to assume that civilians could have been involved in such an occupation in some of the other less-settled frontier regions of the Empire, although much of the specific evidence for their activities appears to have vanished in the intervening centuries.[23]

Far more literary and epigraphic evidence survives in relation to the Roman army's role in capturing animals for the *venationes*. The two principal reasons for this appear to be, first of all, that the various personnel of the military were very fastidious in recording their activities for posterity, and secondly, that the *munera* with which the Roman army was involved were larger and more important spectacles, more likely to be commemorated in the epigraphic record. In particular, Roman troops, as we shall see, were an indispensable source of labour with which the emperor and his officials could collect animals from across Roman territory for a given event. In a happy coincidence, most Roman troops settled on the less populated frontiers of the Empire, where wild animals were relatively abundant.

Although most of the extant evidence for Roman military involvement in the animal trade comes from various inscriptions, a number of literary references also attest to the practice of hunting in the Roman army. A third century encyclopedic work known as the *Cestes*, for example, actually recommends capturing animals in the wild as a useful military exercise, and includes instructions for capturing lions in particular. Similarly, Vegetius, in his treatise on the Roman military written in the late fourth century, states that stag and boar hunters make ideal recruits for the army. It should be noted, of course, that not every mention of hunting in such sources is necessarily related to capturing animals for Roman spectacles: at least some of the game captured or killed by Roman troops could have been used for other purposes, such as a supplement to the regular soldiers' diet. Nonetheless, it appears unlikely that soldiers involved in as mundane a task as killing animals for the dinner table would have their achievements commemorated for posterity so often in the extant epigraphic record.[24]

One of the best illustrations of the Roman army's role in capturing animals for the arena comes from an inscription datable to 147 AD found on the Danube frontier in modern day Bulgaria:

'Tiberius Claudius Ulpianus, tribune of the First Cilician Cohort, with
vexillations of the First Legion Italica, the Eleventh Legion Claudia,
and the Flavian fleet of Moesia, because of the successful capture of

bears and bisons ordered by the legate Claudius Saturninus for the imperial *venatio*, dedicated an altar to Diana …'[25]

The background to this particular dedication is that Saturninus, the current governor of the Roman province of Moesia, ordered troops from different military units under his command, including two separate legions, as well as the local fleet on the Danube, to capture and transport various wild beasts for an upcoming imperial spectacle. The most likely candidate for the *venatio* in question is the previously-mentioned lavish event which the current emperor, Antoninus Pius, staged to celebrate the 900th anniversary of the city of Rome in 148 or 149, an event which was noted for the wide variety of animals which participated in it. The European bisons – now extinct – mentioned in the inscription were likely a particular target for the troops involved in capturing animals, to add extra variety to the Emperor's event. This particular inscription, in fact, marks the first time this species is mentioned in extant Latin epigraphy, suggesting that it had appeared in few, if any, previous spectacles. Although not attested in the extant epigraphic record, it is likely, given the circumstances, that governors of other provinces (at least those with a sizeable population of wild animals) were likewise instructed by the imperial bureaucracy to round up as many local beasts as possible for Pius' *venatio*.[26]

One drawback of the inscription just cited is that it does not give us any details relating to the capture of the bears and bisons for the event in question. Apart from recorded Roman military expeditions into central Africa and their possible connection to the exhibition of such animals as Domitian's rhinoceros, which we have already had occasion to address, very few specific animal capturing expeditions are recorded in the extant sources. Among the possible reasons for this comparative silence is that such activities were considered part of a Roman soldier's regular duties, and normally took place relatively close to the fort(s) in which the participating soldiers were stationed: only those expeditions that were unusually large, or took place over an extended area may have been deemed worthy of commemoration for posterity.

One such expedition appears to be recorded on a fragmentary late second century inscription found in modern day Algeria. Like the previously discussed text from Bulgaria, the Algerian inscription mentions multiple military units: in this case, units normally stationed some 400kms to the east, in the Roman province of Numidia. One of the major questions pertaining to this inscription, therefore, is what these troops were doing so far from their regular base of operations. Two conclusions may be drawn from the preserved portion of the text. First, the mission they were on was considered important enough that the governor of Numidia himself rewarded their commander, a centurion by the name of Catulus, with a promotion. Secondly, the mission had something to do with lions over a forty-day period, as explicitly stated in one of the fragments of the inscription: '... *laeones [in] diebus XL ...*' The most likely conjecture, based upon this evidence, is that the soldiers were hunting or capturing lions during this period, in an area on the fringes of the Empire evidently considered to be relatively rich in wildlife.[27]

The mission in question, assuming our interpretation is correct, bears a number of similarities to another animal capturing expedition undertaken on the northern frontier of the Empire, near modern day Cologne. The latter undertaking is recorded in a late first or early second century inscription, which commemorates the achievements of the centurion Restitutus in capturing fifty bears over a six-month period. In both instances, the number of troops involved appears to have been relatively modest, to judge from the units specifically mentioned in both texts. Centurions like Catulus or Restitutus, junior commanders within the Roman military, would have been ideally suited to lead such small-scale expeditions. A final similarity is that both missions were evidently to be completed within a set period, be it forty or fifty days: presumably, Catulus' and Regulus' commanders did not want them taken away for too long from their other military duties.[28]

From the available evidence, we are comparatively well informed on the types of specialist soldiers who might have participated in missions like those of Catulus and Regulus. A number of sources, for example, specifically mention *venatores immunes* in the Roman army, who were specialist hunters granted an exemption (*immunitas*) from some of the more mundane military duties in return for their hunting expertise. Other attested *immunes* within the Roman army included weapons-smiths, bookkeepers, and even trumpet players. Among the known military hunters are two soldiers, Julius Longinus and Flavius Valerius, from the same camp in modern-day Bulgaria where the previously discussed inscription concerning preparations for an imperial *venatio* was found. Since the inscription denoting them as *venatores immunes* was commissioned only eight years after the earlier text, it is entirely possible, of course, that Longinus and Valerius were actually involved in the preparations in 147 AD for the upcoming spectacle in Rome.[29]

Some soldiers evidently possessed even more specialized hunting skills. The *vestigiatores* who were active in the civilian sphere, for example, could also be found in the Roman military. Such trackers appear to be alluded to in the aforementioned *Cestes* of Julius Africanus. In his section on the proper techniques of lion capture for the military, the author advises that, as a first step, the trackers specializing in large felines should locate the animal's lair. A second century pottery sherd from the site of the Roman fort at present day Zugmantel in Germany, inscribed with the word *vesstigiatorum* [sic] ('of the trackers') suggests the presence there of such specialists. In addition, a fragmentary first or second century letter from Roman Egypt, containing the term *vestigiator* transliterated from Latin into Greek, also indicates that such specialists were active in that particular corner of the Empire. The fact that the letter makes use of the transliterated Latin term, rather than simply using the Greek word for 'tracker', suggests the word denoted an official title within the local Roman military.[30]

A number of surviving inscriptions from the Roman provinces along the Rhine frontier also attest to the existence of specialist *ursarii* ('bear hunters') within the Roman army. Examples include a third century dedication to the forest god Silvanus from an *ursarius* of the 30th Legion stationed in Lower Germany, as well as another, similar dedication made to both Silvanus and Diana by unnamed *ursarii* in the province of Raetia (roughly modern day Switzerland). The Rhine frontier, to judge from such evidence, as well as the previously mentioned inscription from Cologne detailing a bear-capturing expedition, was comparatively abundant in such animals in antiquity.[31]

Specialist lion hunters also seem to have existed within the military on Rome's eastern frontier. Our best evidence for such troops comes from the site of Dura-Europos on the upper Euphrates, situated in a region that appears to have been relatively abundant in wildlife during the period under discussion. Several of the soldiers listed in surviving troop rosters from Dura-Europos, namely, have the notation *ad leones* ('to/for the lions') added next to their names. This rather curious notation suggests that the troops in question were involved in hunting/capturing lions or, perhaps, looking after such animals in captivity before they were shipped west – as we shall see shortly, some Roman units, in addition to their hunting activities, appear to have maintained their own *vivaria* (animal enclosures). One alternative suggestion to explain the presence of the 'lion soldiers' at Dura Europos is that, rather than being involved with the preparation for *venationes*, they were instead assigned to kill lions for officers within their unit like the *signiferi* (standard-bearers), who are known to have worn lion skins as part of their uniforms. One problem with this suggestion, however, is that the number of attested 'lion soldiers' appears too large for merely satisfying uniform needs. In 222, for example, there were as many soldiers assigned *ad leones* in the Dura Europos cohort as there were *signiferi*.[32]

The hunters involved in the preparations for various spectacles, be they soldiers or civilians, used the same techniques to capture and transport their quarry. Much of our evidence for these techniques comes from surviving artistic evidence, in particular mosaics from Roman North Africa, where many of the exotic animals for the *venationes* were captured. A number of such works, for example, illustrate the use of nets to surround and entrap a wide variety of beasts. The most informative artwork in depicting exotic animal capture and transport, however, the so-called 'Great Hunt' mosaic, is found not in North Africa, but at the site of a Roman villa near Piazza Armerina in Sicily. The sheer size of the mosaic (some 70m in length), as well as its central position within the villa complex, suggests that the unknown owner of the estate was intimately involved with the activities depicted in the mosaic, perhaps as a senior official in the imperial bureaucracy.[33]

The mosaic in question takes as its theme the capture of exotic animals from throughout the known world as a demonstration of Roman hegemony, a claim made clear by the personifications of India and Africa at either end of the mosaic. There are certainly some fantastic or unrealistic elements in the scene, such as the gryphon included as one of the allusions to India, whence the creature supposedly originated, or the single hunter shown carrying an ostrich all by himself, something physically impossible in real life. Nonetheless, in its depiction of the capture and transport of various animals, including lions, tigers, gazelles, elephants, and boars, the mosaic does provide a relatively realistic portrayal of at least some contemporary practices. One such practice illustrated in the mosaic is the collaboration of both civilian and military hunters in the capture and transport of beasts. Although we have discussed civilian and military hunters separately in this chapter, in reality the two groups must have frequently worked together, particularly when it came to gathering animals for large-scale *venationes* like those put on by the emperors in Rome. Also worthy of note are the animal cages depicted on both an oxcart and ship in the mosaic, very similar to the containers shown elsewhere in Roman art.[34]

Of the two methods of transport depicted in the Piazza Armerina mosaic, seaborne and overland, the Romans preferred to use the former as much as possible. Sea travel was much faster than land transport in antiquity, and correspondingly cheaper. One must keep in mind, in the case of any live animal shipment, that the beasts in question had to be fed during their journey, and depending upon the size and number of animals on a particular vessel or overland caravan, the costs of feeding them could become exorbitant. A single elephant, for example, requires at least twenty-seven kilograms of food and fifty litres of water per day.[35]

Such was the demand for exotic animals at the height of the Roman Empire that at least some shipping companies appear to have specialized in this lucrative cargo. Our best evidence for such business ventures comes from the so-called Square of the Corporations at Ostia, which was the main port of Rome. The floor mosaics surrounding this square were often decorated with scenes pertaining to the shipping interests of the businesses that commissioned them, and such evidence suggests that at least three of these corporations were involved in the animal trade. Not surprisingly, all three of the offices in question appear to have been set up by shipping concerns based in North Africa which, as we have already seen, was one of the most important sources for exotic animals used in Roman spectacles. Two of the mosaics, including one specifically identified as representing the shippers of Sabratha (in modern day Libya), are simply decorated with animals like elephants, stags, and boars, which suggests, perhaps, that the animal trade was the primary commercial interest of the companies involved. The third mosaic, commissioned by shippers based in Sullectum (modern day Tunisia) is not as explicit in terms of its connection to the exotic animal trade: it depicts two merchant vessels arriving at the port of Ostia. The top of an animal cage, however, can be seen in one of the vessels, suggesting that wild animals were indeed among the commodities shipped out of Sullectum.[36]

Despite the Roman preference for the maritime transport of animals, the vast majority would be transported overland for at least part of their journey, unless hunters were fortunate enough to capture a given animal in close proximity to a port city. We have less information on the logistics of overland animal shipment than on maritime transport during the Roman period, but one particular text gives us at least some idea of the challenges the former could represent. The text in question is an edict issued by the joint emperors Theodosius II and Honorius in 417 AD:

> 'Through the lamentation of the office staff of the Governor of Euphrates, We learn that those persons who by the ducal office staff are assigned to the task of transporting wild beasts remain, instead of seven or eight days, three or four months in the city of Hieropolis, contrary to the general rule of delegations, and in addition to the expenses for such a long period they also demand cages, which no custom permits to be furnished. We therefore direct that if any beasts are sent by the duke of the border to the imperial court, they shall not be retained longer than seven days within any municipality. The dukes and their office staffs shall know that if anything contrary hereto is done, they must pay five pounds of gold each to the account of the fisc.'[37]

The city of Hieropolis, with its strategic position between the upper Euphrates and the Mediterranean coast, was one of the major way-stations for animals and other goods being shipped from Rome's eastern frontier to points further west. As the edict suggests, in the late Empire at least, military personnel under the command of the provincial *duces* (generals) were responsible for supervising the transport of animals for imperial spectacles, and evidently had the authority to demand provisions and the like from the municipal councils of cities like Hieropolis which lay on their route. Importantly, however, these personnel were not to overstay their welcome, since supplying a group of animals and their handlers for even a few days could prove to be onerous for municipal officials. The crux of the complaint that gave rise to this edict, of course, was that some personnel involved in the animal trade were abusing their privileges, and forcing the city of Hieropolis to cater to their needs for months, rather than days at a time. To judge from the size of the threatened fines at the end of the edict, such an abuse of power was not limited to Hieropolis alone.[38]

Among the most critical components of the *venationes*' infrastructure were the animal enclosures (*vivaria*) found in military establishments and cities throughout Roman territory. Beasts destined for the arena would have to be safely contained and looked after at various points, whether in way-stations like Hieropolis, or in their destination cities awaiting the day of a spectacle. Not surprisingly, a number of such facilities appear to have been located in close proximity to Roman frontier forts: the soldiers stationed at these sites were evidently responsible for not only capturing animals, but also looking after them before they began their journeys to their ultimate destination. The Roman troops stationed at Cologne, for example, who were involved in capturing bears for the spectacles, also maintained just such a structure, to judge from an inscription recording that a centurion stationed there '… *vivarium saepsit*' ['fenced in an enclosure']. Cologne would have been an ideal gathering point for animals captured on the Rhine frontier, especially after it became headquarters of the Rhine fleet (the *classis Germanica*) in the late first century.[39]

The Praetorian Guard also maintained its own *vivarium* in the heart of Rome. We have already seen that the emperors, at least on occasion, entrusted these elite troops with various animal capturing responsibilities. Their spectacle-related duties also extended to the care and upkeep of various animals after their capture, as illustrated by the relevant epigraphic evidence. A third century inscription, for example, explicitly identifies some members of the Praetorian Guard as *venatores immunes cum custode vivari* ('specialist hunters with jurisdiction over the enclosure'). In addition, the *medici veterinarii* ('veterinary doctors') attested as belonging to the Praetorian Guard may have looked after the more exotic beasts in this enclosure in addition to the cavalry horses possessed by the unit.[40]

Not surprisingly, the imperial bureaucracy also maintained a number of other *vivaria* in and around Rome to ensure the smooth production of the various large-scale *venationes* attested in the sources. One of the best known is an enclosure described by the sixth-century historian Procopius as being located just outside the city walls beside the Porta Praenestina, one of the main gates on the eastern side of Rome. Although no physical evidence survives of this structure, the fact that locals referred to an area south of this gate as the *vivarium* for centuries thereafter, and that ancient wall-paintings depicting a variety of exotic animals, including lions, elephants, and a giraffe were discovered in the same area during the Renaissance, strongly suggests the accuracy of Procopius' testimony. Certainly, the Via Praenestina leading from the gate to the heart of the city would have provided relatively direct and easy access for animals brought to the Colosseum and/or the *Ludus Matutinus*.[41]

More evidence exists, however, for the enclosure (or enclosures) located at Laurentum, some 24kms south of Rome. The natural advantages of the site evidently made it an ideal location for such facilities. First, Laurentum was relatively close to the port of Ostia, and animals offloaded there, particularly those that had to wait for an extended period of time before appearing in a spectacle, could be easily transferred to Laurentum and kept there without endangering the populace of Rome. Secondly, the area possessed an ample supply of fresh water for the animals. The advantages of Laurentum in this regard were evidently recognized at an early date: the late Republican aristocrat Quintus Hortensius, for example, is known to have possessed a large animal enclosure at this site.[42]

One particular group of exotic animals that appears to have been kept long-term at Laurentum was the imperial elephant herd. A freedman *procurator Laurento ad elephantos* ['manager of the elephants at Laurentum'] is attested as early as the mid-first century, and the elephant *vivarium* implied by this title seems to have continued in existence well into the following century at least. The poet Juvenal, writing early in the second century, appears to refer to this same enclosure in the following extract from his work:

... here there are none, not even for cash. Such a beast doesn't breed in Latium or anywhere in our climate. It's grazing in Rutulian forests and the land of Turnus, for sure, but brought from the dark nation, a herd that belongs to Caesar. They are not prepared to be the slave of any private individual ...'[43]

It is also likely that the elephants hastily assembled by the emperor Didius Julianus in a vain attempt to defend Rome against the forces of Septimius Severus in 193 were levied from Laurentum.[44]

Other freedmen officials attested in the epigraphic evidence may also have overseen various animals sequestered at Laurentum. The first, who was active in the later first century, is described on his tombstone as *praepositus camellorum* ['supervisor of the camels']. Two other officials, both active about a century later, are described on their respective tombstones as *praepositus herbariarum* ['supervisor of the herbivores'] and *adiutor ad feras* ['assistant overseeing the wild beasts']. The second of these epitaphs implies, of course, that there was at least one other official above the *adiutor* in the hierarchy of the *vivarium*. Another, more general conclusion to be drawn from all of these inscriptions is that animals of different types or categories, each with their own assigned supervisory staff, were divided up among the imperial enclosures. This only makes sense, of course, since it is not difficult to imagine the chaos that would result if *ferae* like lions were not kept segregated from herbivores like antelopes![45]

Unfortunately, little detailed information has been preserved concerning the care and training of such animals in Roman enclosures. We know, for example, very little about the support staff working under such officials as the *procurator ad elephantos*. It is evident, however, that the Romans often imported foreign trainers to work with various exotic animals and prepare them for the din of the arena, in the belief, certainly valid in many instances, that personnel native to the same regions as their animal charges would make better trainers. Augustus, to name just one example, imported native tribesmen from Upper Egypt, along with several crocodiles, for one of his spectacles in Rome. Such a practice, of course, was not confined to ancient times: when British authorities brought the first hippo seen in Europe since the fall of Rome to London in the mid-nineteenth century, they were also careful to bring along an expert Egyptian trainer.[46]

One of the major challenges faced by those staging various animal spectacles, as alluded to previously, was keeping their beasts well fed and in fighting trim until the day of their appearance in the arena. Apuleius describes the misfortune befalling even the most conscientious of *editores* in his *Metamorphoses*:

'But such grand and splendid preparations for the public's pleasure [on the part of the *editor* Demochares] did not escape the baleful eyes of Envy. The bears, exhausted by their lengthy captivity, emaciated from the burning summer heat, and listless from their sedentary inactivity, were attacked by a sudden epidemic and had their numbers reduced almost to nothing. You could see the animal wreckage of their moribund carcasses lying scattered in most of the streets.'[47]

The *Metamorphoses*, it should be noted, is a work of fiction; nonetheless, Apuleius appears to be describing a scenario familiar to his contemporaries in the second century AD. Certainly, Symmachus, writing well over a century later, described similar problems with the ill health of the animals he had procured for various spectacles. Of sixteen horses he sent to Rome for one such event, for example, the majority either died en route or perished in the city before they were exhibited to the public.[48]

One particular challenge was keeping carnivorous animals properly fed. A single leopard, by way of example, requires 4lbs of meat per day. While herbivores could be fed with local crops, or with some of the vast quantities of grain regularly shipped to Rome and other large cities of the Empire, there were not as many readily apparent means to keep animals like lions from starving to death in captivity. One solution, certainly, was using cattle or other livestock to feed carnivores in their enclosures. Such a method, however, could become expensive. Indeed, Caligula is said to have fed condemned criminals to wild animals as a cost-saving measure. Another inexpensive source of meat, in particular for scavengers like lions, may have been the carcasses of wild beasts already slaughtered in the arena. There is not much evidence for this mundane practice, but the historian Ammianus Marcellinus is perhaps alluding to it when he compares the frenzy of Gallic troops to that of caged animals driven mad by the scent of carrion.[49]

Another related cost-saving measure pursued by the Romans, albeit with limited success, was the attempt to breed certain exotic animals in captivity. Such an attempt, if successful, would defray the considerable costs associated with capturing various beasts in the wild and transporting them long distances across Roman territory. To judge from the extant evidence, the Romans appear to have enjoyed a fair amount of success in breeding certain beasts like ostriches and African wild rams – animals that could acclimate to the Italian conditions with relative ease. Other animals, however, appear to have been far less fecund in captivity. Although the ancient sources record two spectacles that featured, respectively, twelve elephants and a rhinoceros born in Italy, these appear to have been isolated instances, and any breeding programme involving such animals certainly appears to have enjoyed limited success.[50]

Despite such challenges, and despite what we as a modern society might think of the types of spectacle so popular in ancient Rome, the achievement of the Romans in creating and maintaining the necessary infrastructure for both gladiatorial and animal events over hundreds of years is nonetheless impressive. Eventually, however, even the considerable resources of the Roman state, which at one time must have appeared inexhaustible, proved unable to maintain this apparatus. As the territory and wealth of Rome shrank in the later Empire, so too did the scale of her *munera*, until they disappeared entirely; it is this decline to which we shall now turn our attention.

*Chapter Six*

# The Demise of the Roman Arena

The final major topic to address in our survey of Roman arena spectacles is the complex of factors leading to their eventual disappearance; ultimately, such events failed to survive the state that created them. Although gladiatorial *munera* and the *venationes* were closely associated as arena events over the course of centuries, the factors leading to their respective demises were not identical. It is widely assumed that the growing influence of Christianity within the Roman state led directly to the end of the *munera*, and gladiatorial combats in particular, but as we shall see, the developments giving rise to the disappearance of both gladiatorial combat and the beast hunts as a formal institution were more varied than commonly assumed. We shall also examine how, particularly in the case of the *venationes*, traces of such events persisted in former Roman territories long after the fall of the Empire, which is not at all surprising when one considers how long arena spectacles had been a staple of public entertainment throughout much of Europe, North Africa, and the Near East.

Unfortunately, in tracing the history of Roman *munera* in the later Empire, the historian faces a number of disadvantages. Foremost, although epigraphic testimony is still extant for some of these later spectacles, literary texts are not nearly as abundant. Our fullest source for the reigns of emperors after the first century, in terms of its chronological scope, is the aforementioned *Scriptores Historiae Augustae* (SHA), a collection of imperial biographies extending from the reign of Hadrian (117–38) through to that of Carinus (283–85). As already mentioned, however, the SHA is full of not only inaccuracies, but also outright fabrications.

By way of example, the SHA claims that the future emperor Gordian I staged lavish monthly spectacles in Rome during his term as *aedile* under Septimius Severus, featuring no less than 150 pairs of gladiators at a time as well as, on various occasions, one hundred lions and 1,000 bears. There are, however, a number of reasons to doubt the veracity of this account, quite apart from the fact that no other extant literary sources mention these events. First of all, given the previously discussed imperial monopoly on the production of *munera* in Rome, it appears unlikely that Gordian as *aedile* would have been given permission to produce such a comparatively lavish series of spectacles which, through comparison with those put on by the Emperor himself, could have detracted from the prestige attached to the latter. Secondly, given what we know of the supply of arena performers in the later Empire, a topic that we shall presently discuss in more detail, it also appears doubtful that a mere *aedile* like Gordian would have had so many gladiators and animals at his disposal.[1]

For the first part of the period covered by the SHA, we are fortunate to have the histories of Dio and Herodian with which to corroborate the former's testimony, but after the accession of Gordian III in 238, we no longer have anything comparable with which to verify, or correct, the information contained in the SHA. We must therefore be particularly careful in accepting at face value the accounts of Gordian III and his successors contained within the SHA. One redeeming feature, however, is that the scale of the events described within the SHA was presumably not so outlandish as to be completely unbelievable to its contemporary readership. We can still use the SHA with caution, then, to illustrate some of the general trends of the arena spectacles of the later Empire down to the fourth century.[2]

The man who ultimately emerged victorious in the civil war that erupted soon after the assassination of Commodus was the then governor of Pannonia, Septimius Severus, who established a new imperial dynasty that lasted until 235 AD. Fortunately, we are comparatively well informed as to the *munera* staged by Severus and his immediate successors. The most notable spectacle of his reign was undoubtedly the elaborate *venatio* over the course of seven days which Severus staged in the Circus Maximus as part of the festivities surrounding his tenth anniversary in power in 202 AD, an event commemorated not only by contemporary witnesses like Dio, but on contemporary coinage as well. On this occasion, the animals involved in the *venatio* did not enter the circus by any conventional means, but instead were conveyed inside an elaborate ship model which, according to Dio, could hold up to 400 beasts at one time. At a prearranged signal, the ship collapsed, whereupon a horde of animals, including lions, bears, ostriches, and wild asses poured out onto the arena floor. Dio states that 700 animals were killed in the course of this spectacle, one hundred for each of the seven days of festivities staged by Severus. Other notable features of these celebrations, according to the same author, included a combat involving the sixty wild boars of Severus' praetorian prefect, Plautian, as well as the slaughter of an elephant and a corocotta. The fact that Dio draws special attention to a single slaughtered elephant suggests that the participation of such animals in contemporary spectacles was normally limited to nonviolent events.[3]

Severus' son, Caracalla, who ascended the throne in 211 AD, was especially devoted to the spectacles, as testified to by a number of ancient sources. Dio states that Caracalla delighted in seeing the blood of gladiators on the arena floor and, like his predecessor Commodus, periodically fought as a gladiator himself. More specifically, he relates the story of an unfortunate gladiator by the name of Bato, who was forced to fight three men in one day, and subsequently was given a lavish funeral by Caracalla after perishing in the third bout. Dio, certainly no fan of this particular emperor, no doubt included this particular anecdote in his history as one of many illustrations of Caracalla's cruel and erratic nature.[4]

The Emperor's passion for spectacle and violence, however, was certainly not limited to gladiatorial combat. Caracalla not only drove chariots in public, but also, according to a number of ancient sources, slew multitudes of wild animals during his reign. Caracalla was so especially proud of having slain a lion that he thereafter likened himself to Hercules, just as his predecessor Commodus had done. Undoubtedly, Caracalla slew many such exotic animals in the wild when the chance arose, such as during his campaign against Parthia at the end of his reign, but others appear to have been slain in public, like the one hundred wild boars on one occasion specifically noted by Dio.[5]

The same author also notes that Caracalla, in addition to slaying numerous beasts, also kept many, especially lions, as pets in the imperial palace. One particular favorite of the Emperor, according to Dio, was a lion by the name of Rapier, which appears to have followed Caracalla docilely wherever he went. In fact, one of the alleged clear omens of the Emperor's assassination in 217 occurred shortly beforehand when Rapier unexpectedly bit Caracalla and tore his clothing.[6]

Although contemporaries like Dio may have deemed certain actions of Caracalla unworthy of an emperor, the objectionable behaviour of this particular ruler was soon to be surpassed by the infamous emperor Elagabalus (218–22), who seized power less than a year after his relative Caracalla's assassination. In studying the reign of Elagabalus, it is often difficult to separate fact from fiction as regards the depraved acts ascribed to him by sources like the SHA, but the emperor's passion for spectacle is nonetheless clear in such accounts. The latter source, for example, credits Elagabalus with being the first emperor in some time to stage a *naumachia* in Rome, one evidently staged in a ditch or canal surrounding the Circus Maximus. The SHA also adds that the canal was filled with wine rather than water on this occasion, a detail which, if true, illustrates the extravagance (and wastefulness!) of Elagabalus.[7]

Other extravagant spectacles of the Emperor specifically recorded by the ancient sources occurred as part of the lavish festivities surrounding Elagabalus' marriage to Cornelia Paula in 220. Dio gives no details of the number of gladiators slain on this occasion, but does record that the animals slain during the celebratory *venatio* included an elephant and fifty-one tigers. According to the author, this was the largest number of tigers ever slaughtered on a single occasion in the arena.[8] If this claim is accurate, it would certainly underline the impression, as one might expect, that Elagabalus spared no expense for the celebration of his nuptials.

Despite the fact that the Colosseum was ravaged by fire in 217, just before Elagabalus' reign, and was unusable for several years thereafter, the Emperor was nonetheless able to stage events such as these in alternate venues like the Circus Maximus. In fact, according to the SHA, such was the Emperor's passion for bloodshed that he would often watch gladiatorial combats or boxing matches before one of his extravagant banquets, and have his couch positioned in such a way that he had a clear view of criminals torn apart by wild beasts while he enjoyed his repast.[9]

One particular venue in which Elagabalus could stage some of these more intimate spectacles was the so-called Amphitheatrum Castrense, part of a lavish new imperial palace complex (the Sessorium) built during his reign. Broadly speaking, the Amphitheatrum Castrense was a miniature Colosseum, seating at most 7000 spectators. In terms of the evolution of imperial spectacles, this particular arena is symptomatic of the development that saw later Roman rulers commonly stage more intimate events for themselves and a select group of guests, in effect monopolizing the current supply of both wild beasts and gladiators for their own private enjoyment.[10] As we shall subsequently discuss, this development may well have reflected not only the decreasing supply of such performers in the later Empire, but also contemporary changes in the manner of imperial governance.

Like his predecessor Caracalla, Elagabalus not only drove chariots in public (pulled by a variety of exotic animals), but also kept numerous domesticated animals on the grounds of the imperial palace for his own amusement, including an assortment of Egyptian animals. Tame lions, in particular, were a staple of the imperial palace under both emperors. One particular prank Elagabalus allegedly liked to play was to have such animals, as well as bears and leopards, silently let into the bed chambers of his unsuspecting guests while they were sleeping: upon waking and seeing these unwelcome interlopers, of course, the guests would receive a nasty shock. Sadly, not everyone found this joke as funny as the Emperor, in particular those guests said to have died of fright at the sight of a lion or other carnivore in their bed chambers.[11]

Unfortunately, mention of specific gladiatorial events or beast hunts become more sporadic in the available literary sources following the assassination of Elagabalus in 222 AD. Mention is made of the gladiators involved in the riots that broke out in Rome in 238, for example, or those who participated in the emperor Aurelian's triumphal procession in 273, but as compared to the late Republic or early Empire, we know comparatively little about the specific events in which such performers might have participated. The SHA, for example, relates that Aurelian staged *venationes*, gladiatorial contests, and a *naumachia* in the days following his triumphal procession, but provides absolutely no details about these events.[12]

One reason for this lack of detailed information, as mentioned previously, is the relative scarcity of extant historical sources for the later Empire. Another reason, however, appears to be that, following the assassination of Elagabalus' successor, Severus Alexander, in 235, the Empire was plunged into a state of comparative chaos lasting almost five decades. The rulers of this period often did not have the time or the resources to stage as frequently the type of spectacles in which they might otherwise have indulged.

Nonetheless, the extant sources do provide us with some information on at least a few of the more noteworthy spectacles of the period. One such event (or group of events) was the Secular Games (*Ludi Saeculares*) staged by the emperor Philip the Arab to celebrate the millennial anniversary of the city of Rome in 248. As might be expected, Philip appears to have spared no expense when it came to such a momentous occasion. According to the SHA:

'There were thirty-two elephants at Rome in the time of Gordian [Gordian III, Philip's predecessor] ... ten elk, ten tigers, sixty tame lions, thirty tame leopards, ten *belbi* or hyenas, 1,000 pairs of imperial gladiators, six hippopotami, one rhinoceros, ten wild lions, ten giraffes, twenty wild asses, forty wild horses, and various other animals of this nature without number. All of these Philip presented or slew at the secular games.'[13]

Some corroboration for the SHA's account, at least in terms of the variety of animals presented to the Roman populace by Philip, may be gleaned from contemporary currency: namely, a number of coins minted in 248 depict Philip, his wife, or his son on the obverse, and various animals on the reverse, including a lion, hippopotamus and elk. The accompanying legend, *SAECULARES AUGG* ('Secular Games of the Emperors [Philip and his son]) leaves no doubt that this issue of coinage was meant to commemorate the variety of animals which Philip presented to the Roman people as part of the *munera* staged to help celebrate Rome's anniversary.

The SHA also provides a relatively detailed account of the massive spectacles allegedly staged by the emperor Probus as part of his triumphal celebration in 281. According to this source, one such event was staged in the Circus Maximus, whose track had been decorated with transplanted trees to make it look like a forest. This naturalistic illusion was further enhanced by the multitude of herbivores released into the Circus, including 1,000 wild boars, 1,000 stags, and 1,000 ostriches. Interestingly, the animals were not slaughtered: instead, the spectators were allowed to go onto the track and seize whatever animals they wished (or could!) for themselves. We have already seen that the giving of various prizes at Roman spectacles was not at all uncommon, but if the SHA is to be believed, this particular spectacle of Probus achieved new heights of generosity, as well as audience participation![14]

The other spectacles staged by Probus for his triumph appear to have been much more conventional. A *venatio* in the Colosseum featured a hundred maned lions, 200 leopards from Syria and Libya, a hundred lionesses, and 300 bears: despite the relatively large number of animals collected for this event, however, their slaughter allegedly '... made a spectacle more vast than enjoyable'. Finally, Probus is also said to have staged a combat featuring 300 pairs of gladiators, many of whom had been captured as prisoners of war in the Emperor's recent campaigns.[15]

The account of Probus' *munus* found in the SHA is one of the last references to a specific gladiatorial combat to be found in the extant ancient sources. The SHA's account of the various spectacles staged by Probus' successor Carus (282–283), for example, makes no mention of gladiators. As we move into the fourth century and beyond, in fact, relevant references in the sources often seem to revolve around various animal spectacles, or a given emperor's fondness for hunting and/or exotic animals.[16]

A good example of the latter theme is found in various accounts of the emperor Valentinian I (364–75 CE) and his sons. According to the contemporary historian Ammianus Marcellinus, Valentinian was such a fan of the *venationes* that he actually kept two 'star performers' in his residence for a time to ensure that they were in fighting trim for upcoming events:

> '... having two savage, man-eating she-bears, one called Goldflake and the other Innocence, he [Valentinian] looked after them with such extreme care that he placed their cages near his own bedroom, and appointed trustworthy keepers, who were to take particular care that the beasts' lamentable savageness should not by any chance be destroyed. Finally, after he had seen the burial of many corpses of those whom Innocence had torn to pieces, he allowed her to return to the forest unhurt, as a good and faithful servant, in the hope that she would have cubs like herself ...'[17]

Valentinian's eldest son, Gratian (367–83), is said to have hunted wild animals in various enclosures (*vivaria*), and to have staged private *venationes* for himself and select groups of guests in order to further satisfy his love of hunting. Gratian's younger sibling, Valentinian II (375–92) evidently shared his brother's passion for hunting and the *venationes*, and only gave up such pursuits when criticized for this unhealthy obsession by Ambrose of Milan.[18]

Having identified some of the apparent trends in late imperial spectacles, we can turn to a discussion of the possible reasons for these developments. We cannot discount the personal preference of various emperors when it came to the arena: Commodus, for example, was a much more passionate devotee of gladiatorial *munera* than his father Marcus Aurelius. Nonetheless, there appear to be a number of much more general factors present in the later Empire that may have contributed to such phenomena as the increasing number of private gladiatorial and animal contests staged by various emperors in late antiquity, as well as the private exotic animal collections possessed by many of these same rulers.

We have already noted that the private animal enclosures possessed by Roman aristocrats in the later Republic appear to have been built at least partly in emulation of the royal animal preserves encountered by Roman troops in the Hellenistic East during the same period. The association of hunting prowess with royal virtue in Hellenistic ideology (itself derived from earlier Near Eastern propaganda) may also explain, to a degree, the fondness for hunting demonstrated by philhellene emperors like Nero and Marcus Aurelius. Similarly, the ideological influence of Rome's later eastern rival, Sassanid Persia, appears to have influenced the perceived relationship between imperial majesty and the collection and/or hunting of exotic animals in contemporary Rome.

Following the establishment of the Sassanid state in 224 AD, its rulers proclaimed that they were entitled to all of the territory once possessed by the Persian Empire of old (that which had been conquered by Alexander the Great in the fourth century BC), including territories like Egypt and Syria which were under Roman jurisdiction: the latter, understandably, did not agree with this territorial claim. As a result, the Roman-Sassanid frontier zone was the site of frequent warfare between the two states over the succeeding centuries, and the frequent incursions of Roman troops into Sassanid-held territory allowed an increasing Roman familiarity with Sassanid customs and ideology. To judge from ancient accounts of Julian the Apostate's ill-fated invasion of Sassanid Persia in 363, for example, the Roman soldiers participating in this campaign were particularly impressed with the royal hunting facilities they encountered during their march into Sassanid territory.[19]

One apparent effect of this cross-cultural exchange was an increased fondness for hunting on the part of the Roman elite, visible in mosaics and other artwork from the later Empire. More particularly, later Roman emperors like Valentinian, in addition to hunting, maintained their own collections of exotic fauna, evidently, like their Sassanid counterparts, believing such activities demonstrated their worthiness to rule. During the same period, as already noted in passing, Roman emperors appear to have frequently staged private spectacles for the enjoyment of themselves and a select group of guests, as opposed to the massive public events characteristic of the early Empire. While much of this apparent shift may well be due to a dwindling supply of the requisite performers, a topic to which we shall return shortly, another factor may have been the much more autocratic nature of the Roman state in late antiquity, an autocracy which had more in common with Sassanid kingship than the Principate of Augustus.

The Roman Empire's movement towards a more authoritarian style of governance was precipitated by the period of the so-called 'soldier-emperors' between 235 and 284. This was a time of various crises for the state, not the least of which was the frequent and often successful attacks against the Roman frontiers launched not only by the Sassanid Persians, but by powerful Germanic tribal coalitions as well. During this period, as the term 'soldier-emperor' suggests, most of the Roman rulers, rather than belonging to the senatorial elite as had been the previous custom, were instead raised from the ranks of the army to deal with the various external threats against the Roman state, as well as the myriad other problems Rome faced at that time. Unfortunately, many of the short-lived emperors of this period were unsuccessful in their efforts, as imperial assassinations and civil wars between rival army commanders vying for the throne were also common phenomena during the heyday of the soldier-emperors. Not surprisingly, as the Roman army and its commanders achieved more and more political importance, the power of the Senate correspondingly diminished.

The culmination of this change towards a more authoritarian style of governance in Rome was reached with the reign of Diocletian (284–305), who emerged from the chaos of the soldier-emperor period to return some much-needed stability to the Roman state. One of the hallmarks of this renewed stability, however, was a pronounced elevation in status of the Roman emperor: the more exalted a figure the ruler was, the less likely (at least in theory!) the possibility that one of his subjects would dare to even think of assassinating him. Gone was the collaborative spirit of Augustus' Principate, wherein the emperor was ostensibly 'first among equals' when it came to his colleagues in the Senate, and was expected to treat them with due deference. Instead, under Diocletian's new system of rule, the emperor was clearly elevated above all his subjects, even members of the senatorial elite. Among the many manifestations of this change in policy were the emperor's relative seclusion from his subjects, and the practice of *adoratio*, whereby those subjects fortunate enough to receive an audience with the emperor were forced to prostrate themselves in his presence. [20]

Many of these hallmarks of authoritarian government appear to have been borrowed from the Sassanid Persians to the east, where they had long been a staple of rule. Given the Roman willingness to borrow from their eastern neighbours at this time, it is not surprising that other aspects of Sassanid royal culture, like a fondness for hunting and the collecting of exotic animals, appear to have become more prevalent in the Roman Empire as well. It is also not surprising, given the relative scarcity of arena performers in the later Empire, as well as the changed nature of governance, that rulers of the period often appear to have staged more intimate spectacles for a select group of guests, rather than much larger events in venues like the Colosseum, where they would be forced to interact with the populace.[21]

Despite the ongoing popularity of Roman spectacles in late antiquity, however, whether staged in large arenas or in more intimate venues, they ultimately disappeared as a form of public entertainment. As we shall see, a variety of factors ultimately led to the demise of both gladiatorial combat and the animal spectacles. It should also be noted that while theses two types of events had been closely associated for centuries, their respective downfalls did not follow the same trajectory: in fact, the *venationes* ultimately lasted for over a century after the last recorded gladiatorial combat in Rome.

The most common reason brought forward for the demise of gladiatorial *munera* in Rome, of course, is the formal conversion of the Empire to Christianity, beginning with the emperor Constantine (306–37). Simply put, the new Christian ideals that became dominant in the state were incompatible with the concept of men fighting to the death, or being thrown to wild beasts, as a form of public entertainment.

It should be noted, however, that various Christian writers had attacked Roman spectacles on the grounds of their immorality long before Constantine took the throne. One of the most thorough denunciations of Roman entertainments, in fact, is found within the polemic *De Spectaculis* ('On the Spectacles') written by Tertullian at the turn of the third century AD. After attacking the spectacles, as well as the Roman theatre, for their pagan associations and, in his eyes, consequent idolatry, Tertullian goes on to criticize the moral turpitude and inconsistency of those who take pleasure in such events:

'… he who shudders at the body of a man who died by nature's law, the common death of all, will, in the amphitheatre gaze down with most tolerant eyes on the bodies of men mangled, torn in pieces, defiled with their own blood…he who comes to the spectacle to signify his approval of murder being punished will have a reluctant gladiator hounded on with lash and rod to do murder…the man who calls for the lion as the punishment for some notorious murderer will call for the rod of discharge for a savage gladiator and give him the cap of liberty …'[22]

Such denunciations, however, do not appear to have had much of an effect upon the Christian population of the Roman Empire, at least initially. Most continued to attend the spectacles just as eagerly as their pagan counterparts did. In addition, wealthy Christians, on occasion, even staged such events in their own communities. Nonetheless, various Christian writers continued to denounce the spectacles for centuries after the death of Tertullian, using many of the same arguments he had earlier employed.[23]

Apart from gladiatorial combat, another specific target of Christian critics in terms of arena spectacles was the slaughter of condemned criminals by wild beasts (*damnatio ad bestias*). Such a form of execution, although not exclusively reserved for Christians, was nonetheless commonly employed against them, as can be seen in many martyrdom accounts surviving from late antiquity. Even today, of course, the phrase 'throwing the Christians to the lions' (or its like) is still common parlance. Salvian's comments on the arena, written in the fifth century, can be seen as typical of the disgust *damnatio ad bestias* could provoke in many Christians:

> '... the greatest pleasure is to have men die, or, what is worse and more cruel than death, to have them torn to pieces, to have the bellies of wild beasts gorged with human flesh; to have men eaten, to the great joy of the bystanders and the delight of onlookers, so that the victims seem devoured almost as much by the audience as by the teeth of beasts.'[24]

The eastern emperor Anastasius attempted to ban this particular form of execution at the end of the fifth century, but despite his efforts, *damnatio ad bestias* continued to be employed sporadically against unlucky victims at least as late as the early seventh century.[25]

Similarly, imperial legislation directed against gladiators and gladiatorial combat in general did not lead to an immediate cessation of such events. Statutes directed against the gladiatorial *munera* began to appear as early as the reign of Constantine: in 325, in fact, only a year after he had secured control of the entire Empire, the Emperor issued a rescript forbidding gladiators. Such legislation, however, did not put an end to gladiatorial spectacles, as subsequent imperial statutes directed against the practice make clear. Constantine's alleged distaste for the arena, for example, did not deter him from condemning captured Franks to the beasts on two separate occasions during his reign, or condemning other criminals to fight as gladiators. Similarly, the Calendar of Philocalus clearly indicates that as late as 354, ten days in December, coinciding with the festival of the Saturnalia, were still reserved for gladiatorial contests in Rome. Just as the conversion of the Roman state to Christianity did not occur in one fell swoop, so gladiatorial combat disappeared only gradually from the Empire.[26]

A number of scholars in the past have suggested, based upon the testimony of the ecclesiastical historian Theodoret, that the gladiatorial *munera* were finally abolished during the reign of Honorius (395–423). According to

Theodoret's account, this measure was precipitated by the actions of the monk Telemachus, who descended to the arena floor in an attempt to stop a gladiatorial *munus* in 404. The spectators, enraged at this interruption, stoned Telemachus to death, whereupon Honorius, disgusted at the murder of so pious a man, forthwith banned the gladiatorial spectacles. Upon closer examination of the available evidence, however, it appears unlikely that this ban was universal, or more than temporary in its duration. There is, for example, some evidence to suggest that at least one gladiatorial combat was staged in Rome as late as the mid-430s. Nonetheless, if such a spectacle was indeed staged at this comparatively late date, it appears to have been the last of its kind; by 439, the year the imperial court moved to Ravenna, gladiatorial *munera* were no longer being produced in Rome.[27]

Many scholars have rightly pointed out that economic and political factors, in addition to the oft-cited Christian criticism of the arena, may have played an important role in the gradual disappearance of gladiatorial *munera*. In areas of the western Empire like Gaul and Britain, in fact, such spectacles had already begun to disappear in the third century, long before Constantine took the throne. One factor in their disappearance was the ever growing cost of gladiators, which made it more and more difficult for local magistrates to stage the *munera*. We have already discussed the efforts of previous emperors like Marcus Aurelius and Commodus to limit the costs of gladiators, to ease the financial burden of producing spectacles, but such efforts do not appear to have been overly successful.[28]

Exacerbating such problems was the aforementioned crisis that struck the Empire in the third century. The economic dislocation caused by the frequent attacks across the frontiers led to skyrocketing inflation across the Empire, which made expensive commodities like gladiators even more difficult to obtain for all but the wealthiest of Roman citizens. In addition, the physical damage done to a number of cities in the northwestern Empire during this period by various Germanic tribes, which in some cases included amphitheatres and other entertainment venues, made the staging of arena spectacles even more difficult, and consequently even more sporadic. By the fifth century, gladiatorial events could still be produced in a wealthy city like Rome, but elsewhere in the Empire, they appear to have become a thing of the past.[29]

As regards Roman animal spectacles, economic factors appear to have played an even more decisive role in their eventual disappearance than in the case of gladiatorial *munera*. This is not to say, however, that the *venationes* did not periodically come under the same kind of criticism from Christian writers to which gladiatorial games were subjected. John Chrysostom's comments on the *venationes*, written in the late fourth century, can be viewed as typical of such criticism:

> 'Why need I speak of the sort of charm which is found...in the contests of the wild beasts? For ... [they] ... train the populace to acquire a merciless and savage and inhuman kind of temper, and practise them in seeing men torn in pieces, and blood flowing, and the ferocity of wild beasts confounding all things.'[30]

It should be noted that in many cases, including the passage just cited, the particular target of Christian critics appears to be *damnatio ad bestias*, as opposed to the animal spectacles in general.[31]

In general, Christian criticism of the *venationes* does not appear to have been as strong as that directed against gladiatorial *munera*. One reason for this apparent discrepancy may be related to the prevailing Christian attitude towards wild beasts. A number of passages in the Bible associating various animals, like snakes and lions, with Satan understandably led many Christians to associate wild beasts with danger and evil. In addition, as supported by the Book of Genesis, Christians (like many of their pagan counterparts) felt they had the right to use animals in whatever way they thought best, which theoretically included using them in the arena. In any event, many Christians appear to have found the slaughter of animals in the amphitheatre far less objectionable than the slaughter of their fellow man.[32]

In fact, as gladiatorial games came to be staged less and less frequently in the late Empire, animal spectacles actually grew in popularity, evidently taking over much of the acclaim that had previously been reserved for the former events.[33] Ample evidence of this development can be seen, for instance, in Libanius' description of contemporary *venationes* in Antioch:

'In the case of other entertainments, people stroll along to them at daybreak, but for the beast fights, they suffer under the night sky and think the stone benches softer than their beds, and the spectators' eyes anticipate the beast fighters in action!'[34]

Such a situation is certainly reminiscent of fans in the present day who camp out for tickets to upcoming rock concerts and the like, or in order to get the best seat possible!

Certainly, even those Christian writers who advocated for the end of other arena spectacles could view the *venationes* as a perfectly viable substitute. In this context, the comments of Prudentius, dating to the early fifth century, are instructive:

'Let no man fall at Rome that his suffering may give pleasure, nor [Vestal] Virgins delight their eyes with slaughter upon slaughter. Let the ill-famed arena be content now with wild beasts only, and no more make a sport of murder with blood-stained weapons.'[35]

Societal pressure, then, does not appear to have caused the demise of wild animal spectacles in Rome; rather, it was the worsening of the supply of animals that led to their disappearance. As in the case of the gladiatorial *munera*, problems with supply appear to have begun in earnest in the troubled third century. The complicated system that had ensured the shipment of untold numbers of animals to amphitheatres across the Empire came under severe strain because of the frequent warfare of the period, both foreign and domestic, and as a result, even the emperors in Rome had fewer exotic beasts at their disposal. In addition, of course, the cost of such animals, like other commodities in the third century, skyrocketed.

One of the clearest indications of the inflated prices for animals comes from the so-called *Edict on Maximum Prices*, a decree issued by the emperor Diocletian in 301 in an attempt to control commodity prices and thereby halt inflation. The document lists, among other commodities, the maximum prices for a number of exotic animals. A first-grade African lion, for example, is priced at 150,000 *denarii* (60 *solidi*), while a second-grade lion costs 125,000 *denarii* (50 *solidi*). By way of comparison, one should note that the approximate price of a cow in the eastern Empire at this time was approximately 10,000 *denarii* (4 *solidi*).[36]

Given these exorbitant prices, little wonder then that magistrates staging *venationes* often could not afford to purchase all of the requisite animals, and were forced to beg their political associates or wealthy relatives for assistance. A clear example of such a situation can be found in the correspondence of Libanius: in 356/57, in fact, he wrote a series of letters to his associates in order to try and round up as many animals as possible for his cousin's upcoming spectacle in Antioch. The financial situation in the city ultimately became so dire that in 409 the imperial treasury granted the councillors of Antioch 600 *solidi* to help defray the costs of such spectacles. It is important to note, however, that this sum (discounting inflation in the century since Diocletian issued his price edict) would only pay for ten first-grade lions![37]

Another factor in the worsening supply of exotic animals in the later Empire is the effect centuries of Roman animal capture and slaughter had upon various wild animal populations. One problem in assessing this factor, however, is that much of our available evidence is anecdotal, and we have no way to assess accurately the negative effect of Roman activities upon the different animal populations commonly used in their spectacles. Another complication lies in the fact that, in certain cases, declines in local animal populations could have been caused by other factors, like the clearance of arable land for agriculture. Nonetheless, the available evidence does suggest, for example, that species like lions, elephants, and hippopotami in North Africa were under duress, at least partly as a result of the Roman *venationes*, by the later Empire. Such a circumstance, of course, would be hardly surprising, since this region had been one of most important sources of exotic animals for Roman *editores* since such spectacles began.[38]

Evidence for the worsening supply of animals is found in accounts of various animal spectacles in the later Empire. If we closely examine the SHA's account of the events staged by Philip the Arab in the mid-third century to celebrate the Secular Games, as well as Rome's millenial anniversary, we see that the Emperor is said to have exhibited various exotic animals including: thirty-two elephants, sixty lions, thirty leopards, ten giraffes, and a rhinoceros, as well as '…various other animals without number'. One interesting aspect of this passage is that the numbers given for specific animal species (e.g. sixty lions) appears to be rather low, especially for such a grand celebration as that occasioned by the millennial anniversary of Rome. Compare this figure with the hundreds or even thousands of animals said to have been included in various spectacles of the early Empire.[39]

Other evidence for a worsening supply of animals involves the type of spectacles staged in the later Empire. As we have seen, nonviolent animal displays had periodically been staged in the late Republic and early Empire, but they appear to have become particularly prevalent in late antiquity, perhaps because *editores* were placing more of a premium upon the lives of the costly animals they had been able to obtain for their events. A few such displays were allegedly staged during the reign of Carus (282–83), when he not only presented a number of bears presenting a mime, but also an event involving a *toechobates* (wall-climber). The purpose of the latter event was that the wall-climber would entertain the crowd by climbing a wall and, in doing so, elude the attacks of a bear on the arena floor below him. The salient feature of both of these events, of course, is that the animal participants were evidently in no danger whatsoever.[40]

Much of our evidence for the nonviolent animal spectacles of late antiquity comes from the sixth century, in the form of ivory consular diptychs produced in the eastern Empire to commemorate various events, as well as the correspondence of Cassiodorus in Italy.[41] By this time, the Western Roman Empire had fallen (an event traditionally dated to 476), and Italy had ultimately come under the control of the Ostrogothic king, Theoderic (471–526). Despite the change in government, however, the Ostrogothic administration still preserved numerous aspects of the previous Roman government, including the periodic staging of animal spectacles. Cassiodorus, who served Theoderic's government in various capacities, was well-positioned to preserve for posterity various aspects of contemporary politics and society, including the *venationes*.[42]

One letter preserved in Cassiodorus' correspondence was written by Theoderic himself to the *consul* Maximus in 523. Within this text, the king makes clear that contemporary animal spectacles posed far more of a risk to their human performers than their animal participants – it was the attempted evasion of animal attacks that entertained the crowd in such instances, not the slaughter of the animals involved:

'... what gift should be spent on the huntsman who strives by his death to please the spectators? ... trapped by an unhappy destiny, he hastens to please a people who hope that he will not escape. A hateful performance, a wretched struggle, to fight with wild beasts which he knows that he will find the stronger. His only confidence lies in his tricks, his one hope in deception.'[43]

Elsewhere in the same letter, Theoderic goes into detail describing the types of events in which these performers were forced to participate. One such relatively simple albeit dangerous display involved them pole-vaulting over onrushing animals, a feat that presumably did not always turn out as intended! Prudentius, writing over a century earlier, confirms that this particular type of spectacle was already popular among contemporary audiences by the late fourth century: '... rash figures spring with flying leap over wild beasts and sport amid the risks of death.'[44]

Another event that, although not unheard of in the early Empire, evidently attained much greater popularity in late antiquity, featured a device known as a *cochlea*. This mechanism consisted of two or more wooden panels fastened to a wooden pole, which was designed to rotate on the arena floor. One of the most vivid descriptions of the *cochlea* in action is found in the aforementioned letter from Theoderic to Maximus:

'... one man trusts in angled screens, fitted in a rotating four-part apparatus. He escapes by not retreating; he retreats by keeping close; he pursues his pursuer, bringing himself close up with his knees, to escape the mouths of the bears. Draped on his stomach over a slender spar, he [?] lures on the deadly beast, and can find no way of surviving without peril.'[45]

The exact meaning of this passage is unclear, but what Theoderic is most likely describing is a situation wherein a performer has draped himself over the bars on top of the wooden panels, and has pulled his legs up and out of reach of the bears below. The reference to '...no way of surviving without peril ...' presumably refers to the bears keeping the panels constantly in motion by swatting at them in an attempt to reach their quarry above: if they were to cease their attacks, the *cochlea* would come to a standstill, putting the performer in even greater danger.

Fortunately, as mentioned earlier, a series of late antique diptychs provide important visual evidence on the use of the *cochlea* as well as other devices in contemporary spectacles. A particularly good example is provided by the lower half of one of the diptych panels commissioned to commemorate the games staged in Constantinople by the *consul* Areobindus in 506. In the top left corner of the arena scene, a performer is depicted hiding behind one of the panels of a *cochlea*, while an enraged bear pushes against it. To the right, another performer is shown at the apex of his vault over another onrushing bear. The right side of the arena scene, meanwhile, depicts performers emerging from two *portae posticae*, which were gates or doors set into the podium wall of the arena. Performers chased by animals could take refuge in the niches behind these doors, and venture forth once more onto the arena floor once the threat had passed.[46]

Two further contraptions used in animal events of the period are shown on the lower left and middle of the panel. In the bottom left corner, two performers are depicted attempting to evade a bear on what appears to be a railed bridge-like structure. Such artificial bridges or 'pulpits' were periodically used as early as the first century BC to add excitement and variety to a given spectacle, but were particularly well suited for the animal displays of late antiquity which, as we have already seen, commonly featured human performers attempting to evade various wild animals. In the scene depicted on the Areobindus diptych, one performer appears to have made it to safety on the bridge, while his less fortunate colleague is about to be bitten by a bear below.[47]

The final contraption depicted in the bottom centre of the diptych panel is arguably the most elaborate of the devices employed in animal spectacles of the period. Two performers are shown suspended above the arena floor in what appear to be large baskets, while yet another bear lunges at them. Each of the baskets is attached to a large central pole by smaller posts. In this particular instance, the baskets could apparently be pivoted back and forth around the axis of the central pole by the swats of the animal below: just as in the case of the *cochlea*, continued motion helped ensure the performers' safety. In another variant of this device known from artistic evidence, the baskets or platforms were actually attached by rope pulleys to the central pole, which allowed the performers to raise them up or down in order to provoke and then escape the attacks of animals on the arena floor.[48]

One final way in which the emperors themselves, or those producing spectacles on behalf of the emperor, attempted to deal with the diminished numbers of exotic animals was through imperial monopolies: those outside the imperial circle who wished to use the animals in question for their own spectacles had first to seek permission from the emperor or his officials. An imperial monopoly on lions certainly existed in the late Empire, although it is not clear when it came into effect. Since lions, as we have seen, are still listed as a saleable commodity in the *Edict on Maximum Prices*, it may be that this particular monopoly came into effect after 301. Elephants, too, were brought under strict imperial control by the mid-third century: in this instance, permission had to be sought to even hunt these animals, much less use them in an upcoming spectacle. Other exotic animals, like leopards, may also have been brought under an imperial monopoly as their available numbers diminished, but unfortunately, we possess no conclusive evidence on this point.[49]

Despite the evident challenges in staging *venationes*, such events continued to be staged, at least on an intermittent basis, for over a century after gladiatorial spectacles had disappeared. Concessions were made to Christian sensibilities, such as the law of 469 that forbade the staging of beast hunts on a Sunday, but these do not appear to have hindered their production to any great degree. As we have already seen, *venationes* actually survived the fall of the Western Roman Empire, and continued to be staged in Rome as late as the reign of the Ostrogothic king Theoderic. The last recorded *venatio* in Constantinople was produced in 537, during the reign of the emperor Justinian. In summary, it appears to have been the increasing logistical and economic difficulties of staging such events that led to their demise, rather than a change in societal tastes or values.[50]

It is important to note, in this regard, the fate of the *venationes* in Roman North Africa. As we have already noted, beast hunts were very popular spectator events in this region under Roman rule, and just as in Italy, they continued to be staged even after the Western Roman Empire lost control of its African provinces. In 429, the Vandals, one of the main Germanic tribes migrating into Roman territory at this time, had crossed the Straits of Gibraltar from Spain and begun their conquest of Roman North Africa, a campaign culminating in the capture of Carthage a decade later. One of the many effects of this conquest was that Rome was now cut off from one of her main sources of exotic animals, which, of course, made the staging of *venationes* that much more difficult. The Vandals, however, like the Ostrogoths in Italy, continued to stage beast hunts in North Africa as their Roman predecessors had done, as amply attested by both literary and artistic evidence. Like other aspects of the Roman state and society, the *venationes* and their legacy ultimately survived the fall of the culture that had created them.

# Conclusion

The foregoing survey of Roman arena spectacles has amply illustrated their central importance in Roman society. Far from simply being sadistic displays of brutality, the gladiatorial *munera* and beast hunts, as we have seen, fulfilled a number of important roles apart from that of mere entertainment. One of the best indicators of their perceived importance, of course, is the fact that they continued to be staged over the course of several centuries, in the midst of myriad political and social changes in the Roman state, and in the case of the *venationes*, actually outlasted for a time the state that had created them.

Another clear indicator of the spectacles' importance within Roman society was, of course, the vast resources devoted over the course of centuries to their continued production. In the Republican period, as we have seen, the arrangements behind various *munera*, such as the collection of the requisite gladiators, was somewhat *ad hoc* in nature, facilitated in part by the dramatic Roman conquests and territorial expansion of the period. This gave various *editores* access to an ample supply of both prisoners-of-war and exotic animals to fight in the arena. As time went on, however, such arrangements became ever more formalized, culminating in the state-owned *familiae* of the imperial period, as well as the army of officials who oversaw every aspect of the spectacles' production. Perhaps the most impressive aspect of this infrastructure, one which this book has sought to emphasize, was the Roman logistical achievement in capturing and transporting untold numbers of animals over hundreds of years for *venationes* staged across the Empire.

The reason why the Romans were willing to devote so many resources to the production of arena spectacles was, of course, the central position they held in Roman social and political life. Indeed, the *munera* in many respects served as a microcosm of the Roman world, and a celebration of Roman values and traditions. One of the commonly cited benefits of gladiatorial spectacles, for example, was the role they played in reminding the assembled audiences of the martial values and *virtus* which had enabled Rome to conquer such a massive empire. It was a reminder that was perhaps even more important under the Empire, when decisive military victories ultimately occurred much less frequently than they had during the last centuries of the Republic. The various ethnic types of gladiators, such as 'Samnites' and 'Thracians', which were especially common in earlier *munera*, served as an even more pointed reminder of specific wars and campaigns in Rome's illustrious military past.

The *munera*, however, did not simply serve to sate the Romans' nostalgia for past military triumphs. One of the most important aspects of such events was to reaffirm important aspects of contemporary Roman society. The very seating arrangement found in venues like the Colosseum, in which the proximity of spectators to the arena floor was determined by the rank and privilege which they enjoyed within the state, served as a clear illustration of the distinct segregation within Roman society. The relative powerlessness of slaves as well as many women, for example, which in many respects consigned them to the fringes of Roman social and political life, was reflected in the seats they were assigned in the upper tiers of various amphitheatres, as far distant from the arena floor, and the Roman elite seated directly above it, as possible.

Another very important social role of the *munera* was to serve as a venue for capital punishment, and in so doing reassure the assembled spectators of the efficacy of Roman justice. As we have seen, the public execution of criminals guilty of serious offences like arson were included in Roman arena spectacles from a relatively early date, and continued to be a staple of such events for centuries thereafter. Such executions not only reassured the audience that law and order was being maintained, but also, through the truly demeaning and humiliating way in which many condemned criminals were killed, sought to ensure that there would be no outpouring of sympathy for the condemned, thereby further reinforcing social solidarity and the rule of law within the state.

Closely linked to the social role of the arena was its political importance. The public execution of criminals in the arena, for example, was just one of the ways in which Roman emperors sought to demonstrate not only the effectiveness of Roman law, but also the effectiveness of their own rule, to their assembled subjects. Even more importantly, the arena was one of the few venues in the Rome where members of the populace, regardless of their wealth or social status, could interact with the prominent political leaders who had sponsored a given *munus*, and feel that their voice was being heard. Most commonly, this collective expression consisted of voting on whether or not a defeated gladiator should be spared, but spectators could also use the arena as a venue in which they could express their displeasure with a given leader and/or his policies. This became even more important under the autocracy of the Empire, when the voting assemblies of the Republic had long since fallen by the wayside. Certainly, those emperors who ignored such mass expressions of discontent did so at their own risk.

Although the spectacles of the arena served a variety of roles specific to Roman state and society, in other respects they addressed broader concerns and possessed characteristics that would be familiar in other cultures, including our own. Perhaps the best example of the latter is the celebrity status successful gladiators, *venatores*, and even certain arena animals could achieve. Although fighting in the arena was legally considered among the basest professions in Roman society, particularly proficient combatants could gain a popularity akin to modern day rock stars or famous athletes. The desire for such acclaim, as we have seen, could even prompt an emperor like Commodus to descend into the arena himself.

Unsurprisingly, the Roman arena spectacle which addressed a variety of broader cross-cultural concerns, the *venatio*, arguably enjoyed the most significant legacy following the collapse of the Roman Empire. Although the form of the *venatio* was uniquely Roman, owing certain elements to contemporary gladiatorial spectacles, many of its underlying messages certainly were not. The Romans, for example, did not invent the concept of using staged animal hunts to demonstrate mastery over nature, or the extent of a particular ruler's wealth and territory. Such propaganda aims continued to hold a certain fascination long after the fall of Rome, which helps to explain why certain spectacles and events reminiscent of the *venationes* continued to appear in various states for centuries thereafter.

A number of European monarchs of the medieval and early modern periods, for example, staged their own spectacles inspired, at least to a degree, by the Roman beast hunts. To name two such instances: the Holy Roman Emperor Frederick II, an avid collector of exotic animals, periodically staged combats between a number of them for his subjects in Palermo; while at a later date, the Portuguese king, Manuel I unsuccessfully attempted to stage a combat between an elephant and a rhinoceros, inspired by the mention of similar contests in Roman texts.[1]

The collection and display of exotic animals, even in the modern period, continued to be an element of imperial propaganda. In the mid-nineteenth century, namely, at the height of the British Empire, an entire army division was entrusted with the task of bringing a hippopotamus from Egypt to London, incidentally the first such animal shipped from Africa to Europe since the fall of the Roman Empire. Such an assignment, as we have seen, would have been perfectly familiar to the Roman troops stationed along the frontiers of their empire, who played such an indispensable role in supplying the imperial *munera* of Rome over the course of centuries.[2]

# Notes

Unless otherwise noted, all translations of Greek and Latin sources in this work are taken from the Loeb Classical Library.

## Chapter One

1. Nicolaus of Damascus, *Athletics*, 4.153: Wiedemann (1995), p. 30.
2. Livy 9.40.17: Silius Italicus 11.51: Wiedemann (1995), pp. 30–31: Dodge (2011), pp. 27–29.
3. Dodge (2011), pp. 28–29. Consuls from the Junii family are known to have earlier campaigned in both northern Italy and Campania. It is, however, impossible to determine with certainty whether the family's past history in one of these areas influenced the decision of the later Junii to stage the first gladiatorial contest in 264 BCE: see Kyle (1998), p. 46, 65, n. 70.
4. Wiedemann (1995), p. 6: Dodge (2011) p. 29.
5. Ville (1981), pp. 43–44: Terence, *Hecyra*, Prologue 31.
6. Dodge (2011), p. 29.
7. Toynbee (1996), p. 16: Anderson (1985), pp. 78–79. The earlier pharaohs, it should be noted, had established their own royal game preserves in Egypt centuries before Alexander conquered it.
8. Bertrandy (1987) 213.
9. Jennison (1937), p. 135.
10. Rice (1983) *passim*: Shelton (2007), pp. 112–16.
11. Pliny, *Natural History*, 8.6: Seneca, *On the Brevity of Life*, 13.3.
12. Livy 39.22.2.
13. Cassiodorus, *Variae*, 5.42.2–4: Barnish (1992), p. 91.
14. Isocrates, *Antidosis*, 213.
15. Anderson (1985), pp. 84–85.
16. Futrell (1997), pp. 15–16: Weege (1909), p. 135.
17. Kyle (1998), pp. 42–43. It should be noted for future reference that the same term in Latin (*ludus*) could refer both to a religious festival (e.g. the *Ludi Florales*) and, later, a gladiatorial training school.
18. Kyle (1998), pp. 47–49.
19. Livy 40.44.8–12.
20. Pliny, 8.24: Beacham (1999), p. 12: Bertrandy (1987), p. 212.

21. Ville (1981) 94–95, 97–99: Shelton (1999) 233–34: Deniaux (2000) 1302. Other magistrates, such as praetors and consuls, are also periodically recorded as having staged *munera* in Rome, but such events were far less common than the events staged by *aediles*.
22. Plautus, *Poenulus*, 1011–12: Livy 44.18.8: Aurelius Victor, *On Illustrious Men*, 66. 1–2: Ville (1981), p. 57.
23. Plutarch, *Life of Sulla*, 5.
24. Livy, *Periochae*, 51.22–24: Valerius Maximus 2.7.13–14: Edmondson (1999), p-. 78–80.
25. Pliny, *Natural History*, 8.7.20: Seneca, *On the Brevity of Life*, 13.6: Athenaeus 5.194C.
26. Welch (2009), p. 81–82.
27. Seneca, *Moral Epistles*, 70. For Seneca's view on the immoral behaviour of crowds, see *Moral Epistles*, 7.
28. Plutarch, *On the Cleverness of Animals*, 959C: Most (1992), p-. 403–05.
29. Pliny, 8.6.
30. Sallust, *Jugurthine War*, 26.
31. Plautus, *Poenulus*, 1011–12.
32. Livy 44.18.8: Jennison (1937), p. 45.
33. Deniaux (2000), p-. 1306–07.
34. Plutarch, *Life of Sulla*, 5: Deniaux (2000), p. 1300.
35. Pliny, *Natural History*, 8.7; 8.20: Seneca, *On the Brevity of Life*, 13.6: Athenaeus 5. 194C: Deniaux (2000), p. 1300; MacKinnon (2006), p. 143. When Sulla finally did achieve the praetorship in 93 BC, he staged a *venatio* for which he procured both lions and Mauretanian hunters from King Bocchus.
36. Cicero, *Letters to his Friends*, 8.8.10.
37. Cicero, *Letters to his Friends*, 8.9.3. The Latin term *pantherae* used in this letter, which technically could refer to a few different species of spotted feline, is commonly taken by scholars in this instance to denote leopards: see Jennison (1937), p. 137.
38. Cicero, *Letters to his Friends*, 2.11.2.
39. Cicero, *Letters to his Friends*, 2.11.2: *Letters to Atticus*, 5.21; 6.1.
40. Livy 28.21.2–3: Ville (1981), p. 47.
41. Ville (1981), p. 47.
42. Appian, *Civil Wars*, 116–20: Mackay (2009), p-. 203–05.
43. Welch (2009), p. 34–35.
44. Harris (1972), p. 185–86: Kyle (1998), p. 42–43: Coleman (1990), p. 52.
45. Plautus, *Persa*, 197–98. It is interesting to note that, at this relatively early date, the Romans did not yet have a specific term for ostriches. Here, Plautus uses the phrase *marinus passer* ('sea sparrow'), a euphemism which apparently arose because the Romans brought these birds across the Mediterranean from North Africa: see Arnott (2012), p. 229.

46. Welch (2009), p. 76–77.
47. Welch (2009), p. 59–65.
48. Welch (2009), p. 49–54.
49. Ville (1981), p. 49.
50. Livy 41.20.
51. Polybius 30.25–26. Polybius notes that 250 pairs of gladiators participated in Antiochus' festival. The text is not explicit, but it is certainly plausible that they were provided by gladiatorial *ludi* operating in Italy.
52. Cicero, *Against Vatinius*, 37; *For Sestius*, 133: Kaster (2006), p. 375.
53. Cicero, *For Sestius*, 135: Kaster (2006), p-. 376–77.
54. Pliny, *Natural History*, 8.7.20–21. It is certainly plausible that Scaurus, who had served as Pompey's quaestor from 65 to 59 BC, was able to use some of these same contacts to procure animals for his own spectacle in 56 BC.
55. It is not absolutely clear whether or not the rhinoceros in question was Asian or African: see Coleman (2006), p-. 102–03.
56. Merten (1991) 140–42: Ville (1981) 348, n. 10: Shelton (1999) 245–46, 249–50.
57. Cicero, *Letters to his Friends*, 7.1.3: Shelton (2004), p. 374–78. Pompey appears to have had a run of bad luck when it came to elephants. In 80 BC, as part of the triumphal celebrations for his recent victories in North Africa, Pompey had attempted to enter Rome on an elephant-drawn chariot. Much to his embarrassment, however, the elephant team was too large to fit through the gates of the city: see Pliny, *Natural History*, 8.2: Plutarch, *Life of Pompey*, 14.4.
58. Pliny, *Natural History*, 33.16.53: Kyle (2007), p. 287: Ville (1981), p. 60.
59. Kyle (2007), p. 287. As we have seen, the Senate had passed somewhat similar legislation over a century earlier, in the wake of Nobilior's *venatio*, to limit the political acclaim an individual magistrate could gain through the staging of animal spectacles.
60. Suetonius, *Life of Julius*, 75.3.
61. cf. Suetonius, *Life of Julius*, 11.1–2.
62. Dio 43.23.5: Suetonius, *Life of Caesar*, 39.1: Levick (1983), p-. 105–06.
63. Pliny, *Natural History*, 8.7: Suetonius, *Life of Caesar*, 39: Dionysius 3.68.1–4: Golvin (1988), p. 50: Platner and Ashby (1929), p. 115: Scobie (1988), p. 211. Evidently, Caesar's elephants were given more of a fighting chance on this occasion than Pompey's elephants in 55 BC, since we hear of no spectator displeasure associated with the later spectacle.
64. Welch (2009), p. 38–42.
65. Kyle (2007), p. 288: Coleman (1993), p. 50.
66. Pliny, *Natural History*, 8.70: Jennison (1937), p. 59.

## Chapter 2

1. Dio 43.22.4
2. Jennison (1937), p. 177.

3. Octavian, the political leader later known as Augustus, did not actually receive that title until 27 BC. For sake of convenience, however, I refer to him as Augustus throughout this work.
4. *Res Gestae*, 22.
5. Dio 54.1.3–4: Wiedemann (1995), p. 8, 48, n. 16: Galsterer (1981), p-. 415–16: Robinson (1994), p. 169. Imperial magistrates, such as the *aediles*, continued to periodically stage various *munera* (with imperial permission), particularly in the early Empire when Republican traditions were still familiar to many citizens.
6. Scobie (1988), p. 195: Ville (1981), p-. 123–26: Wiedemann (1995), p-. 11–12.
7. Ville (1981), p-. 126–27.
8. Strabo 6.273: Coleman (1990), p-. 53–54.
9. Ville (1981), p. 99–100: 108–09. A similar spectacle, featuring both single and mass gladiatorial combat, was staged in honour of the deceased Agrippa in 7 BC: see Ville (1981), p. 103–04.
10. Jaczynowska (1978), p-. 48–53: Ville (1981), p-. 216–20, 269–70. As we shall later discuss, the participation of aristocratic *iuvenes* in such events was not limited to Rome alone, but is also attested in other cities of the Empire.
11. Suetonius, *Life of Augustus*, 43: Levick (1983), p-. 106–07.
12. Dio 51.23.1: Welch (2009), p. 108–26.
13. Suetonius, *Life of Nero*, 4.3: Ville (1981), p. 101.
14. Ville (1981), p. 110.
15. Ville (1981), p-. 110–11.
16. Suetonius, *Life of Augustus*, 43.11.
17. Ville (1981), p-. 104–05.
18. *Res Gestae*, 23: Coleman (1993), p-. 51–54. It should be noted that Augustan propaganda following the battle of Actium emphasized it as a victory over a foreign enemy, rather than a victory over a fellow Roman.
19. Levick (1983), pp. 107–08.
20. Allsen (2006), *passim*.
21. *Anthologia Graeca* 7.626: Allsen (2006), p. 169.
22. Suetonius, *Life of Tiberius*, 47.1: Ville (1981), p. 129.
23. Tacitus, *Annals*, 1.76: Dio 57.14.3: Levick (1983), passim: Coleman (2000), p. 497.
24. Tacitus, *Annals*, 4.62–63: Suetonius (*Life of Tiberius*, 40) claims that over 20,000 were killed at Fidenae. Dio [58.1.1] appears to be alluding to the same event when he states that Tiberius' decision to ban hunting spectacles in the capital led some unspecified entrepreneurs to exhibit such events in wooden theatres outside of the city which subsequently collapsed.
25. Dio 59.5.2.
26. Dio 59.2.6: Suetonius, *Life of Caligula*, 37.3.
27. Dio 59.10.5: Suetonius, *Life of Caligula*, 21: Ville (1981), p. 133.
28. Dio 59.14.1–4: Ville (1981), pp. 164–65.
29. Dio 59.7: Ville (1981), p. 130.

30. Dio 59.8.3: Suetonius, *Life of Caligula*, 27.2: Ville (1981) 130–31.
31. Dio 10.1–4: Suetonius, *Life of Caligula*, 27.9: Ville (1981), pp. 131–32. In the case of the latter equestrian condemned to the arena, Suetonius and Dio give differing accounts of what seems to be the same individual. Dio states that the individual in question, after having successfully fought as a gladiator, was hauled off and executed nonetheless, while Suetonius claims that he was forced to fight wild animals. As a result of loudly protesting his innocence, the condemned man was briefly removed from the arena and had his tongue cut out on Caligula's orders, before being returned to the arena floor.
32. Dio 59.13.8–9: Ville (1981), p. 132.
33. Suetonius, *Life of Caligula*, 26.5; 27.1.
34. Suetonius, *Life of Claudius*, 21.4: Ville (1981) 136.
35. Ville (1981), p. 134.
36. Suetonius, *Life of Claudius*, 24.2: Dio 60.5.6. Ville [(1981), p. 165] suggests that this measure was implemented both to spare the praetors from any financial difficulties which this obligation might cause, and to prevent any political one–upmanship between praetors staging the *munera*. At a much later date, these praetorian games were reestablished by Constantine: Jones (1992) 537; Ville (1981) 390–91.
37. Dio 60.13.1–4.
38. Suetonius, *Life of Claudius*, 21.3: Dio 60.7.4; 13.5.
39. Suetonius, *Life of Claudius*, 21.3–4: Dio 60.17.9: Ville (1981), p. 135.
40. Suetonius, *Life of Claudius*, 21.6: Coleman (1993), p. 49.
41. Tacitus, *Annals*, 12.56: Suetonius, *Life of Claudius*, 21.6: Dio 61.33.3–4: Coleman (1993), p. 56.
42. Ibid. A common misconception is that the proclamation of the condemned criminals to Claudius on this occasion was commonly repeated by gladiators to the assembled spectators at other *munera*. This is, however, the only recorded instance of this proclamation prior to a spectacle.
43. Tacitus, *Annals*, 13.5.1–2; 13.31.4–5: Ville (1981), pp. 166–68: Balsdon (1969), p. 304.
44. Dio 61.9.1.
45. Calpurnius Siculus, *Eclogues*, 7.
46. Dio 61.9.5: Suetonius, *Life of Nero*, 12.1: Ville (1981), pp. 138–39.
47. Calpurnius Siculus, *Eclogues*, 7.
48. Coleman (1993), pp. 56–58: Ville (1981), pp. 141–42.
49. Tacitus, *Annals*, 14.14; 15.32: Dio 62.17.2–5: Ville (1981), pp. 139–40.
50. Tacitus, *Annals*, 15.37: Dio 62.15: Coleman (1993), p. 51: Ville (1981), pp. 140–41.
51. Tacitus, *Annals*, 15. 38–44.
52. Ville (1981), p. 143.
53. *Anthologia Palatina* 11.184: Coleman (1990), pp. 60–61.
54. Dio 65.15.2.
55. Welch (2009), p. 147–61: Mann (2013), p. 67–68. The name 'Colosseum' was first used for the amphitheatre in the Middle Ages; in antiquity, it was known as

the Flavian Amphitheatre. For the sake of convenience, however, I will refer to it throughout by its better-known name.

56. Welch (2009), pp. 130–41: Hönle and Henze (1981), pp. 128–29: Bomgardner (2000), pp. 146–51.
57. Suetonius, *Life of Titus*, 7.3: Dio 66.25: cf. Martial, *On the Spectacles*, 6.
58. Coleman (1993), pp. 58–60.
59. Dio 66.25.2–3: Coleman (1993), pp. 60–62, 65.
60. Martial, *On the Spectacles*, 28: Coleman (1993), pp. 62–65.
61. Martial, *On the Spectacles*, 34: Coleman (1993), pp. 65–66.
62. Dio 66.25.3–4: Suetonius, *Life of Titus*, 7.3: Coleman (1993), pp. 65–66.
63. Coleman (1993), 67.
64. Wistrand (1992), pp. 20–21: Coleman (1993), pp. 68–74: Allsen (2006), pp. 147–48.
65. Martial, *On the Spectacles*, 10; 24–25: Although many of the poems in *On the Spectacles* commemorate the inaugural games of the Colosseum, it is unclear in other instances if particular events described by Martial were staged by Titus or by his brother and successor Domitian: see Coleman (2006), pp. xlv–lxiv.
66. Martial, *On the Spectacles*, 6.
67. Clement, *Letter to the Corinthians*, 1.5–6: Apuleius, *Metamorphoses*, 10.29.34: Coleman (1990), p. 64: Wiedemann (1995), pp. 88–89.
68. Shaw (1993), pp. 8–9; 16–19.
69. Livy 1.12: Martial 1.21; 8.30; 10.25: Ville (1981), p. 154. Ville suggests that this particular re-enactment may have been performed on multiple occasions, with more than one criminal, of course, playing the role of Scaevola.
70. Suetonius, *Life of Domitian*, 4.1.
71. Martial, *On the Spectacles*, 11: cf. *On the Spectacles*, 26; Martial 14.53. The date of this spectacle is not certain, but it appears to have been staged in 84 or 85: see Ville (1981), p. 149.
72. Desanges (1978), pp. 201–08: Coleman (2006), pp. liv–lvi.
73. Desanges (1978), pp. 323–25: Coleman (2006), pp. 268–69: Pliny, *Natural History*, 6.68; 6.188: Seneca, *Natural Questions*, 6.8, 3–4. Members of the Praetorian Guard are also said to have participated in an expedition during the reign of Septimius Severus (193–211) to capture zebras from unnamed islands in the Red Sea: see Dio 76.14.3.
74. Desanges (1978), pp. 210–13: Birley (1972), pp. 31–35.
75. Ptolemy 1.8.4; 4.8.2: Desanges (1978), pp. 197–201: Desanges (1964), pp. 713–14; 722–25.
76. Martial 1.14: Ville (1981), pp. 149–50: cf. Martial 1.6;22;48;51;60;104.
77. Suetonius, *Life of Domitian*, 4.1–2: Coleman (1993), pp. 54–55: Ville (1981), pp. 150–54.
78. Statius, *Silvae*, 1.6.53–61. Cf. Suetonius, *Life of Domitian*, 4.1: Dio 67.8.4: Ville (1981), pp. 150–54.
79. Juvenal, *Satires*, 6. 252–53.
80. Suetonius, *Life of Domitian*, 4.1. As previously noted, Claudius had made the quaestors responsible for producing ten days of *munera* every year by a law which

was passed in 47 AD. This obligation, however, had been subsequently removed from the quaestors by Nero.

81. Suetonius, *Life of Domitian*, 4.4: Ville (1981), p. 159.
82. Suetonius, *Life of Domitian*, 4; 10.1: Dio 67.4.4. We shall discuss the different types of gladiators in a subsequent chapter.
83. Dio 67.14.3: Suetonius, *Life of Domitian*, 19.
84. Dio 67.4.5: Suetonius, *Life of Domitian*, 23.1.
85. Dio 68.2.3. Nerva also ordered repairs to the Colosseum during his brief reign [CIL VI, 37137], which suggests that he had no objection to the spectacles per se, just the enormous cost of staging them too frequently as Domitian had done.
86. AE (1933), n. 30: Dio 68.10; 68.15: Merten (1991), p. 143. Later notable events staged by Trajan included the *munera* put on to celebrate the dedication of a lavish new bathing complex for the capital in 109: cf. Fora (1996), pp. 37–42, nos. 9–10.
87. CIL 14.4546: SHA, *Life of Hadrian*, 7.12; 19: Fora (1996), pp. 42–43, n. 11.
88. *Digest* 48.8.11.1–2: SHA, *Life of Hadrian*, 14.11; 17.12; 18.8–9: Wiedemann (1995), pp. 76–77. As Wiedemann states, one probable purpose of such legislation was to limit control over capital sentences to the emperor and his officials.
89. Dio 69.8; 69.10: SHA, *Life of Hadrian*, 20.12–13; 26.
90. Suetonius, *Life of Titus*, 7.3; *Life of Domitian*, 4.4; *Life of Caligula*, 26.5: Wistrand (1992), pp. 24–25.
91. SHA, *Life of Antoninus Pius*, 10.9.
92. CIL 6.33990: Sabbatini Tumolesi (1988), pp. 87–88: Merten (1991), p. 143: Aymard (1951), pp. 186–89: Jennison (1937), pp. 84–85.
93. SHA, *Life of Antoninus Pius*, 8.2; 12.3.
94. SHA, *Life of Marcus Aurelius*, 4.8; 8.12; 17.7: SHA, *Life of Lucius Verus*, 6.9–7.1; 10.8: Dio 72.28. Dio alleges that Marcus Aurelius was so averse to bloodshed that he made gladiators fight with blunt (and non-lethal) weapons during his reign. It is doubtful, however, that this was really done on a regular basis. One presumes that most Roman spectators would have found such displays quite boring in comparison to regular gladiatorial events.
95. CIL 2. 6278: SHA, *Life of Marcus Aurelius*, 27.6: Carter (2003), *passim*.
96. Carter (2003), pp. 85–87.
97. Dio 73.16.3.
98. Dio 73.17.3; 73.19.2: Herodian 1.15.8; p. 99, n. 3.
99. Dio 73.10; 73.18–19; 73.20.3: Herodian 1.15.1–6: SHA, *Life of Commodus*, 12.12: Ammianus Marcellinus 31.10.18–19.
100. Herodian 1.15.5: Dio 73.21.1–2.
101. Dio 73.22: Herodian 1.16–17.
102. Herodian 1.15.7.
103. Wiedemann (1995), p. 18, 49, n. 45.

## Chapter 3

1. Bomgardner (2000), p. 56. A second type of arena spectacle, the *munus assiforanum*, in which the *editor* attempted to make a profit by charging admission to the spectators, is also mentioned in the extant sources, although far less commonly than the regular *munera* staged by municipal officials and the like. Any gain to be made in terms of the latter events, of course, involved political popularity rather than financial profit.
2. Bomgardner (2000), pp. 208–10. It is notoriously difficult to convert ancient monetary amounts into modern currency, so the figures listed give no more than an approximate cost of the spectacles in question.
3. Ritti (1998), p. 448, 485–86: Coleman (2005), p. 2.
4. Roueché (1993), pp. 61–64: Coleman (2005), p. 4: Evangelisti (2011), pp. 32–34, n. 9.
5. CIL 14. 3663.
6. Pliny, *Letters*, 6.34.
7. *Anthologia Palatina*, 7.626: Rosenblum (1961), p. 147: Bomgardner (1992), pp. 162–64. Although the career of Luxorius took place after North Africa was lost to the Roman Empire, he was writing at a time when Roman-style spectacles were still being staged in the region by the subsequent Vandal administration.
8. Julian, *Epistles*, 28.
9. Spawforth (1994), pp. 211–28.
10. CIL IX.2237: Buonocore (1992), pp. 52–54, n. 28.
11. Robert (1971), pp. 81–82, n. 15; pp. 159–60, n. 133; p. 313: Buonocore (1992), pp. 81–83, n. 53.
12. Carter (2003), pp. 86–88.
13. Tacitus, *Annals*, 13.49.1.
14. By the later Empire, *noxii* became an even more valuable commodity, as gladiatorial contests became more and more expensive and infrequent. Legislation from the third century, in fact, specifically instructs provincial governors to reserve especially belligerent condemned criminals for the imperial spectacles in Rome: see MacMullen (1990), p. 206–07.
15. CIL X.6012: CIL XI.6357: Gregori (1989), pp. 34–35, n. 15: Robert (1971), p. 118, n. 63; pp. 274–75.
16. CIL 11.4580: Gregori (1989), pp. 52–53, n. 33. Examples of local notables holding a variety of political and religious offices within their respective communities are certainly not limited to Victorinus in Carsulae: for a very similar case, see e.g. CIL 11. 4371: Gregori (1989), pp. 51–52, n. 31.
17. CIL 12.533: Vismara (2000), pp. 51–52, n. 31: Courtney (1995), p. 327: Carabia (1985), p. 124–25.
18. Dunbabin (1978), pp. 71–72.
19. Tacitus, *Annals*, 14.17: Jacobelli (2003), p. 72, 106.
20. Dunbabin (1978), p. 66: Dunbabin (1999), pp. 119–21.
21. Wiedemann (1995), pp. 16–17.

22. Dunbabin (1978), pp. 67–68. Much of our present knowledge of the North African hunting-corporations is due to the pioneering work of the Tunisian scholar Azedine Beschaouch, who, over the course of decades, wrote a series of very important articles on the artistic and epigraphic evidence for these groups.
23. The translation is largely based on that of Wiedemann (1995), p. 17 and Veyne (1987), p. 111.
24. Beschaouch (1987), pp. 679–80.
25. Beschaouch (1966), pp. 156–57: Beschaouch (1979), p. 418: Salomonson (1960), pp. 27–28: Dunbabin (1978), p. 78.
26. Salomonson (1960), pp. 49–53: Dunbabin (1978), pp 78–83.
27. Dunbabin (1978), pp. 82–84.
28. Beschaouch (1966), pp. 151–57: Beschaouch (1977), *passim*: Beschaouch (2006), pp. 1405–10.
29. Kehoe (1988), pp. 151–52: Mattingly (1997), p. 130.
30. Beschaouch (1977), pp. 496–500: Dunbabin (1978), p. 74, 272; Pl. XXIV, n. 59: CIL 8.2392; 8.7049: Kehoe (1988), p. 201.
31. Libanius, *Orations*, 33, 21.
32. Oppian, *Halieutica*, 2. 350–54: Jennison (1937), pp. 154–56: Scobie (1988), pp. 209–10: Ville (1981), pp. 385–86: Loisel (1912), p. 118. Exhibitions in the fora of various towns and cities continued into the later Empire, although they were naturally overshadowed by the larger and more elaborate spectacles staged in the amphitheatres. It should also be noted, of course, that the latter structures found in smaller centres like Pompeii did not possess the amenities of larger edifices like the Colosseum: in lieu of animal cages and pens in an amphitheatre's basement, for example, the caged animals would usually be brought into an amphitheatre just before a given show was set to commence, and be released onto the arena floor through openings in the podium wall.
33. Gabucci (2001), pp. 42–45: Gebhard (1975), pp. 46–55.
34. Welch (2009), pp. 178–83: Capps Jr. (1949), pp. 65–67: Gebhard (1975), pp. 61–63: Bieber (1961), pp. 219–20.
35. Welch (1998), pp. 123–30, 137.

## Chapter 4

1. Ovid, *The Art of Love*, 1.135–70: Jacobelli (2003), p. 25: Mann (2013), p. 20.
2. Bomgardner (2000), pp. 17–18: Welch (2009), p. 159.
3. Plass (1995), pp. 25–28.
4. Thompson (2002), p. 31.
5. Augustine, *Confessions*, 6.8.
6. Wistrand (1992), pp. 11–19.
7. Seneca, *Moral Epistles*, 74.7: Herodian 5.6.9: Merten (1991), pp. 161–62: Kyle (1995), pp. 202–03.

8. Tertullian, *Apology*, 9.11: Kyle (1995), pp. 188–89, 199–200: MacKinnon (2006), pp. 154–56: De Grossi Mazzorin (1993), p. 309, 312–14.
9. Garnsey (1968), p. 157: Thompson (2002), pp. 36–37.
10. MacMullen (1990), pp. 205–06: Musurillo (2000), pp. 75–9.
11. Coleman (1990), p. 57: Robinson (1994), p. 168.
12. Carter (2003), pp. 86–8: Oliver and Palmer (1955), pp. 324–43: MacMullen (1990), pp. 206–07: Hopkins (1983), p. 10.
13. Juvenal, *Satires*, 3.36: cf. Wiedemann (1995), p. 95.
14. Kyle (1998), pp. 131–3: Wiedemann (1995), pp. 68–97.
15. Ville (1981), pp. 228–46: Wiedemann (1995), p. 106.
16. Wiedemann (1995), pp. 105–06. Private slave-owners are also known to have sold their own unruly slaves to be killed by the beasts in the arena, but like the private sale of slaves *ad ludos*, this practice was banned by imperial legislation in the second century. The fact, however, that the emperor Constantine issued a rescript against this practice in the early fourth century suggests that there were still some slave owners trying to have their slaves condemned *ad bestias* over a century later: see *Theodosian Code* 9.12.1; Wiedemann (1995), pp. 76–77. Given the evident popularity of public executions as an arena spectacle in the later Empire, it is not surprising that some overly greedy slave owners might be tempted to resort to such a practice.
17. E.g. Robert (1971), pp. 87–90, n. 25; 328: Wiedemann (1995), pp. 107–08.
18. Petronius, *Satyricon*, 117.5.
19. Potter (1996), pp. 130–31: Wiedemann (1995), pp. 28–9, 105: Dodge (2011), p. 30.
20. Cicero, *Against Vatinius*, 17.40; *Letters to Quintus*, 2.4.5; *For Sestius*, 84–85: Ville (1981), pp. 270–71, 292–93: Wiedemann (1995), p. 123.
21. Wiedemann (1995), p. 122.
22. CIL 5.563: Mahoney (2001), pp. 22–23, 68–69.
23. CIL 4. 1179: Jacobelli (2003), p. 47.
24. Jacobelli (2003), pp. 51–52.
25. Köhne and Ewigleben (2000), pp. 37–39.
26. Bomgardner (1984), p. 88: Tremel (2004), pp. 79–80, 224–29, nos. 96–97.
27. Tremel (2004), p. 80, 221, n. 93.
28. Martial, *On the Spectacles*, 23, 31: Coleman (2006), pp. 169–73, 218–34.
29. Martial, *On the Spectacles*, 32: Coleman (2006), pp. 235–43.
30. Martial, *On the Spectacles*, 17: Coleman (2006), pp. 140–47.
31. Rosenblum (1961), p. 151, n. 67.
32. Rosenblum (1961) pp. 151–53, n. 68.
33. Dio 72.29: Toynbee (1996), p. 31.
34. Martial, *Epigrams*, 13.98–100. Rigging an animal combat to (hopefully) ensure a given outcome is not unheard of in other cultures with a tradition of such events. Combats between tigers and elephants in southeast Asia, for example, were

routinely set up so that the elephant, emblematic of royal authority, would win the struggle: see Allsen (2006), pp. 157–58.

35. Statius, *Silvae*, 2.5.
36. Martial, *On the Spectacles*, 8: Coleman (2006) 78–81.
37. Coleman (2000), *passim*.
38. Dio 76.16.1: Coleman (2000), pp. 497–98.
39. Juvenal, *Satires*, 6. 107–12.
40. Köhne and Ewigleben (2000), p. 132.
41. Jacobelli (2003), p. 48–49.
42. Köhne and Ewigleben (2000), p. 133.
43. Köhne and Ewigleben (2000), p. 133.
44. Dio 59.2.6; 73.192: Suetonius, *Life of Caligula*, 37.3: Köhne and Ewigleben (2000), p. 128.
45. Livy 9.40: Dodge (2011), p. 31: Köhne and Ewigleben (2000), p. 37.
46. Dodge (2011), p. 31: Köhne and Ewigleben (2000), pp. 37, 51–52.
47. Dodge (2011), p. 31: Köhne and Ewigleben (2000), p. 37.
48. Köhne and Ewigleben (2000), pp. 48–55.
49. Köhne and Ewigleben (2000), pp. 51–57.
50. Köhne and Ewigleben (2000), pp. 59–63.
51. Köhne and Ewigleben (2000), p. 37: Dodge (2011), p. 33.
52. Köhne and Ewigleben (2000), pp. 57–58: Dodge (2011), 33.
53. Köhne and Ewigleben (2000), p. 63.
54. Köhne and Ewigleben (2000), p. 63: Junkelmann (2000), p. 127.
55. Junkelmann (2000), pp. 110–12.
56. Gregori (1989), pp. 59–62, nos. 41–42.
57. Robert (1971), pp. 132–33, n. 81.
58. Coarelli (2001), p. 161, 173.
59. Loisel (1912), pp. 130–31: Robert (1949), pp. 127–28: Robert (1971), p. 324: Gregori (1989), p. 73, n. 56.
60. Pliny, *Natural History*, 8.54: Robert (1971), pp. 90–92, 201, 205, 325: Lehmann (1990), p. 143.
61. Pliny the Elder, *Natural History*, 33.53: Wiedemann (1995), p. 14. One wonders if the *noxii* referred to by Pliny were not actually criminals condemned *ad bestias* (who appear to have been given no equipment whatsoever), but rather criminals condemned to the arena (*ad ludos*) who, as mentioned previously, were at least given a fighting chance of survival.
62. Köhne and Ewigleben (2000), pp. 35–45.
63. Köhne and Ewigleben (2000), pp. 64–65.
64. Symmachus, *Letters*, 2.77: Ville (1981), p. 408: Kockel (1983), pp. 75–85, pl. 20: Jacobelli (2003), p. 25.
65. Pliny, *Natural History*, 8.29: Keller (1913), Vol. 1, pp. 384–85; Vol. 2, p. 267: Coleman (2006), p. 103.

66. Martial, *On the Spectacles*, 26: Coleman (2006), pp. 186–94.
67. Pliny, *Natural History*, 8.2: Aelian, *On the Nature of Animals*, 2.11: Martial, *Epigrams*, 1.6; 1.14; 1.22; 1.44; 1.48; 1.51; 1.60; 1.104: Libanius, *Orations*, 46.14: SHA, *Life of Carus*, 19.2: Toynbee (2006), pp. 39–49; 57–58; 108: Coleman (2006), p. 156–57: Merten (1991), p. 167. Other animals which performed tricks in the arena, at least on occasion, included monkeys, bears, and dogs.
68. Carter (2006/07), pp. 102–04. The term *rudis* was also used to refer to the wooden sword used in gladiatorial training.
69. Carter (2006/07), pp. 102–06.
70. Robert (1971), pp. 130–31, n. 79: Carter (2006/07), pp. 106–12.
71. Gómez-Pantoja (2009), p. 92–94, n. 19: Wiedemann (1995), p. 122: Köhne and Ewigleben (2000), p. 69.
72. Tertullian, *On the Spectacles*, 12.
73. Bomgardner (2000), p. 46, 137.
74. Tertullian, *Ad Nationes*, 1.10. 47; *Apology*, 15.5: Köhne and Ewigleben (2000), p. 68.

### Chapter 5

1. Carter (2006/07), pp. 100–01.
2. Buonocore (1992), pp. 27–28, n. 4.
3. E.g. Gregori (1989), pp. 57–8, n. 37: Gómez-Pantoja (2009), pp. 91–92, n. 18: Sabbatini Tumolesi (1988), pp. 60–65, n. 54–61: Köhne and Ewigleben (2000), pp. 32–33.
4. Evangelisti (2011), p. 60, n. 29: Mann (2013), pp. 53–54: Köhne and Ewigleben (2000), p. 66.
5. Jacobelli (2003), pp. 65–66.
6. Jacobelli (2003), pp. 66–67.
7. Bomgardner (2000), p. 55, 238, n. 69.
8. CIL 5. 8659: Gregori (1989), pp. 20–21, n. 2: Wiedemann (1995), pp. 170–71.
9. Ville (1981), pp. 282–83: Dodge (2011), p. 36.
10. Suetonius, *Life of Caligula*, 27.4: Gabucci (2001), p. 54: Buonocore (1992), p. 28.
11. Sabbatini Tumolesi (1988), pp. 39–40, 127–28: Gabucci (2001), p. 54.
12. Dodge (2011), p. 36: Gabucci (2001), p. 134: Bomgardner (2000), p. 22.
13. Golvin (1988), p. 150, n. 435: Rea (2001), pp. 273–74.
14. Buonocore (1992), p. 26, n. 3: Fora (1996), pp. 30–32.
15. Fora (1996), pp. 33–34, n. 5: Sabbatini Tumolesi (1988), p. 128: Buonocore (1992), p. 26: Gabucci (2001), p. 54.
16. Sabbatini Tumolesi (1988), pp. 37–42, n. 28–35.
17. Libanius, *Letters*, 1399–1400: Symmachus, *Letters*, 4.7; 5.56; 5.82; 6.33; 7.48; 7.82; 7.97; 7.106.
18. Libanius, *Letters*, 217, 586–87, 599, 1118, 1131, 1399, 1400: Symmachus, *Letters*, 2.76; 4.7; 4.8; 4.12; 5.59; 5.62; 5.65: Beltrán Rizzo (2003), pp. 57–58.
19. Cicero, *Letters to his Friends*, 8.9.3.

20. Libanius, *Letters*, 217. Were the 'expert huntsmen' referred to by Libanius perhaps similar to groups like the *Telegenii* in North Africa?
21. Libanius, *Letters*, 217–18: Symmachus, *Letters*, 2.46; 7.122: Jennison (1937), p. 96. Symmachus was also forced to obtain imperial permission to use the Colosseum, and to flood it for some sort of aquatic spectacle, presumably involving the crocodiles which are also mentioned in his correspondence: see Symmachus, *Letters*, 4.8; 6.33; 6.43; 9.151: Jennison (1937), p. 97.
22. Egger (1967), pp. 19–24.
23. Egger (1966), pp. 615–23.
24. Julius Africanus, *Cestes*, 14: Vegetius, 1.7: Marrou (1978), pp. 273–74.
25. Velkov and Alexandrov (1988), p. 272.
26. Velkov and Alexandrov (1988), pp. 271–75.
27. CIL 8. 21567: Schulten (1925), p. 1497: Picard (1944), pp. 58–60: Von Petrokovits (1960), p. 241.
28. CIL 13. 12048: Devijver (1992), p. 143: Vismara (2000), pp. 83–84, n. 48.
29. CIL 3. 7449: Velkov and Alexandrov (1988), pp. 273–74: Watson (1993), pp. 75-77.
30. Julius Africanus, *Cestes*, 14: Marrou (1978), pp. 273–74: Egger (1967), p. 20: Kießling (1960), n. 9272: Davies (1989), pp. 155–56.
31. CIL 13. 5243; 8639: Vismara (2000), pp. 85–87, n. 50, 52. Since the latter inscription doesn't explicitly mention any military units, we cannot be absolutely certain that the *ursarii* mentioned in it were soldiers. It was found, however, in relatively close proximity to the site of a Roman fort, which in my opinion makes a military identification, as opposed to a civilian one, more likely.
32. Ammianus Marcellinus, 23.5.7: Welles (1959), p. 41: Rostovtzeff (1952), pp. 48–49: Davies (1989), pp. 44, 170.
33. Wilson (1983), pp. 24, 97–98.
34. Marrou (1978), pp. 281–84: Merten (1991), pp. 144–45.
35. Krebs (1965), pp. 96–97.
36. Bertrandy (1987), p. 228: Toynbee (1996), pp. 52–53: Becatti (1953), pp. 69–70, 76–77, nos. 95 and 109.
37. *Theodosian Code*, 15.11.2: Pharr (1969), p. 436.
38. Jennison (1937), p. 141, 152: Bomgardner (2000), p. 213: Millar (1993), p. 243.
39. CIL 13. 8174: Velkov and Alexandrov (1988), pp. 271–75: Davies (1989), p. 286, n. 43: Jennison (1937), p. 141: Ternes (1986), p. 235.
40. CIL 6. 130: For one of the Praetorian veterinarians, see e.g. ILS 9071.
41. Procopius, *Gothic War*, 1. 22–23: Jennison (1937), p. 175: Lanciani (1990), pp. 277–78. Unfortunately, none of the wall-paintings in question survive to the present day: all we possess are copies made after their discovery.
42. Varro, *On Agriculture*, 3.13: Bertrandy (1987), pp. 223–26: Loisel (1912), p. 102.
43. Juvenal, *Satires*, 12. 102–07.
44. CIL 6. 8583: Herodian 2.11.9: Sabbatini Tumolesi (1988), pp. 24–25, n. 8: Rudd (1991), p. 110.

45. AE (1971), n. 68: CIL 6. 10208; 10209: Sabbatini Tumolesi (1988), pp. 24–26, nos. 9–10: Fora (1996), p. 29: Bertrandy (1987), pp. 231–32.
46. Strabo 17.1.44: Blunt (1976), p. 108.
47. Apuleius, *Metamorphoses*, 4.14.
48. Symmachus, *Letters*, 2.76; 5.56; 6.43.
49. Suetonius, *Caligula*, 27.1: Ammianus Marcellinus 19.6.4: Allsen (2006), p. 93.
50. Aelian, *On the Nature of Animals*, 2.11: Pliny the Elder, *Natural History*, 8.29: Varro, *On Agriculture*, 3.12.1: Columella, *On Agriculture*, 7.2.4–5: Toynbee (1996), p. 47, 238: Jennison (1937), pp. 115–16.

**Chapter Six**

1. SHA, *Three Gordians*, 3.5–8.
2. Wiedemann (1995), p. 13.
3. Dio 77.1: Pighi (1965), p. 161: Toynbee (1996), p. 18: Coleman (1996), p. 54: Humphrey (1986), pp. 115–16. The collapsing ship *venatio* appears to have been staged in the Circus Maximus simply because the floor of the Colosseum was not large enough to accommodate this particular spectacle. Dio states that the corocatta (hyena?) brought to Rome for Severus' celebrations was the first such animal ever seen in the city, but as already noted, the SHA claims that one had already appeared in Rome during the reign of Antoninus Pius.
4. Dio 78.6.2; 78.17.4.
5. Dio 78.10: Herodian 4.11.9: SHA, *Life of Caracalla*, 5.9. Presumably, if and when Caracalla slew animals as part of a spectacle, he employed at least some of the same safety precautions earlier used by Commodus. According to Dio (79.7.2–3), the emperor's passion for lions in particular was such that he even kept a number of them as pets. Dio also records (79.21.3–5) that a certain noble by the name of Lucius Priscillianus partly owed his rise in power and prestige under Caracalla to the fact that he, like the emperor, killed various wild animals in public. Priscillianus' evident skill suggests that he did not take up combat with wild animals solely as a means to impress Caracalla, but was rather a genuine enthusiast of the sport.
6. Dio 79.7.2.
7. SHA, *Life of Elagabalus*, 23.1.
8. Dio 80.9.1–2. According to the same author (77.7.5), the previous record for the most tigers slain in a single *venatio* was ten, achieved during the reign of Caracalla.
9. SHA, *Life of Elagabalus*, 25: Gabucci (2001), 175–76. Elagabalus began the repair of the Colosseum during his reign, but this monumental project was not completed until the reign of Gordian III (238–44), over twenty years after the fire.
10. Bomgardner (2000), 200.
11. SHA, *Life of Elagabalus*, 21.1; 25.1; 28. 1–3.
12. Herodian 7.11: SHA, *Life of Aurelian*, 33; 34.6. Presumably, however, most of the gladiators and animals which participated in the procession also participated in the subsequent spectacles.

13. SHA, *The Three Gordians*, 33.1.
14. SHA, *Life of Probus*, 19.2–4.
15. SHA, *Life of Probus*, 19.5–8.
16. SHA, *Life of Carus*, 19.
17. Ammianus Marcellinus 29.3.9. Valentinian's unusual choice of pets would be in keeping with his savage temper and periodic cruelty as described elsewhere in Ammianus' work.
18. Sozomen 7.25.10–12: Ammianus Marcellinus 31.10.19: Philostorgios 11.1: Ambrose, *On the Death of Valentinian II*, 15: Jennison (1937) 136.
19. Ammianus Marcellinus 24.5.2: Zosimus 3.23: Allsen (2006) 37–38; 139: Lavin (1963) 276–77.
20. Allsen (2006) 40–41: Cameron (1993) 42: Jones (1992) 40; 126–27.
21. Sozomen's account of Gratian (7.25.10–12) indeed suggests that such private exhibitions were commonplace by the late fourth century.
22. Tertullian, *On the Spectacles*, 21.
23. Ville (1960) 294–96. We have already had occasion to mention the well-known anecdote of Augustine's friend Alypius, and the moral degradation he suffered as a result of the *munera*.
24. Salvian, *On the Governance of God*, 6.2.10: Kyle (1998) 185.
25. Roueché (1993) 77–78: Kyle (1998) 184–86: Epplett (2004) *passim*.
26. *Theodosian Code* 9.18.1; 15.12: *Panegyric of* Constantine 12.3: Pharr (1969) 436: Nixon and Rodgers (1994) 235: Bomgardner (2000) 206.
27. Theodoret, *Ecclesiastical History*, 5.26: Ville (1960) 326–31: Bomgardner (2000) 206–07; 257, n. 47: Wiedemann (1995) 158.
28. MacMullen (1990) 147.
29. Ville (1960) 333: Wiedemann (1995) 159. As Bomgardner [(2000) 206] notes, the fact that the bishop of Apamea in Syria, Marcellus, employed gladiators and other troops to attack pagan temples in the late fourth century clearly indicates that such performers still existed at that time in the eastern Empire. The fact that they were available to be hired as de facto mercenaries, however, may suggest that the gladiatorial *munera* themselves were no longer being actively staged in the region at that time.
30. John Chrysostom, *Homilies on First Corinthians*, 12.10: Chambers (1969) 69.
31. Kyle (1998) 184–86.
32. *Genesis* 1.26: Wiedemann (1995) 154–55: Dinzelbacher (2000) 266–67: Grant (1999) 6–7: Gilhus (2006) 169–70.
33. Ville (1960) 324–25.
34. Libanius, *Letters*, 1399: Bradbury (2004) 73–74.
35. Prudentius, *Against Symmachus*, 2.1126–29: Ville (1960) 295.
36. Sperber (1974) 105: Harl (1996) 149–54: Mattingly (1927) 227–28: Jones (1992) 1017–18. The *denarius* was the greatly debased silver coin of the period, while the *solidus* was a gold coin introduced by Diocletian as part of his currency reforms.

37. Libanius, *Letters*, 218, 544, 1399–1400: Liebeschuetz (1959) 122; (1972) 141–42, 157.
38. Ammianus Marcellinus 22.15.24: Shaw (1981) 387: MacKinnon (2006) 151–54: Hughes (1996) 106: Bertrandy (1987) 227: Scullard (1974) 233–35, 252.
39. SHA, *The Three Gordians*, 33.1. I consider the statement that Philip slew 'various animals without number' to be something of a passing comment just to emphasize to the reader how massive Philip's *venationes* really were (allegedly!). The higher number of animals and performers listed by the SHA for the spectacles of Aurelian and Probus later in the third century, if not entirely an invention of the author, may be explained by the fact that the Empire was on somewhat sounder footing at this time than it had been during the reign of Philip, and that both Probus and Aurelian had waged successful campaigns on the frontiers of the Empire which perhaps allowed them to bring back considerable numbers of prisoners and animals which could later be used in various spectacles.
40. SHA, *Life of Carus*, 19.2: Merten (1991) 169.
41. By the late Empire, arena spectacles, apart from those staged by the emperor himself, were most commonly staged as part of consular games: see Ward-Perkins (1984) 115–16.
42. It was not uncommon, particularly in late antiquity, for authors to use the term *venatio* to refer to any type of animal spectacle, whether or not the event in questions actually involved the killing of animals.
43. Cassiodorus, *Variae*, 5.42.1: Barnish (1992) 90.
44. Cassiodorus, *Variae*, 5.42.6: Prudentius, *On the Origin of Sin*, 369–70.
45. Cassiodorus, *Variae*, 5.42.7: Barnish (1992) 92: Merten (1991) 173.
46. Golvin (1988) 319–20.
47. CIL 10. 1074: Bachielli (1990) 769–72: Volbach (1976) 33–34, n. 11.
48. Volbach (1976) 33–34, n. 11; 35–36, n. 17. It should be noted that many depictions of animal spectacles from late antiquity, such as the Areobindus diptych, feature bears as the principal opponents of the human performers. This is not surprising, given the fact that exotic animals were no longer as readily available as they had once been, and bears were relatively common in Europe, the Near East, and North Africa, and therefore less expensive.
49. *Theodosian Code* 15.11.1: Aelian, *On the Nature of Animals*, 10.1: Jennison (1937) 141: Orth (1914) 563–64: Ville (1981) 351, n. 22. A letter written by Stilicho in 400 [*Letters*, 4.12] thanks the current emperor Honorius for providing leopards to his son's spectacle in Rome, which certainly suggests that these animals were currently under strict imperial control as well.
50. *Code of Justinian*, 3.12.9; *Novels* 105.2: Wiedemann (1995) 153–54, 157–58: Ville (1960) 318–19.

## Conclusion

1. Jiménéz Sánchez (2003) 112: Bedini (1997) 117–19. Not surprisingly, many scholars have argued that modern day bullfights are ultimately descended from the Roman *venationes*. This opinion, however, is not universally accepted, and it is beyond the scope of the present study to analyze this scholarly dispute in greater detail.

2. Friedländer (1968) Vol. 2; 65: Pearson (1973) 120–22: Weeber (1994) 28–29: Blunt (1976) 107–10.

# Bibliography

Allsen, T, *The Royal Hunt in Eurasian History* (Philadelphia, 2006).

Anderson, J K, *Hunting in the Ancient World* (Berkeley, 1985).

Arnott, WG, *Birds in the Ancient World from A to Z* (London, 2012).

Aymard, J, *Essai sur les chasses romaines des origines à la fin des Antonins.* (Paris, 1951).

Bachielli, L, 'I *pontarii*: una definizione per via iconografica', in *L'Africa romana* 7 (1990), pp. 769-72.

Balsdon, J P V D, *Life and Leisure in Ancient Rome* (London, 1969).

Barnish, S J B, trans, *Cassiodorus: Variae* (Liverpool, 1992).

Beacham, R C, *Spectacle Entertainments of Early Imperial Rome* (New Haven, 1999).

Becatti, G, *Scavi di Ostia. Vol. IV* (Rome, 1953).

Bedini, S A, *The Pope's Elephant* (New York, 1997).

Beltrán Rizo, E, 'Gloria et favor populi: los *ludi venatorii* en las *editions* de Q Fabio Memio Símaco', in *Ludica* 9 (2003), pp. 55–75.

Bertrandy, F, 'Remarques sur le commerce des betes sauvages entre l'Afrique du Nord et l'Italie', in *MEFRA* 99 (1987), pp. 211–41.

Beschaouch, A, 'La Mosaïque de Chasse a l'Amphithéâtre découverte a Smirat en Tunisie', in *CRAI* (1966), pp. 134–57.

Beschaouch, A, 'Nouvelles Recherches sur les Sodalités de l'Afrique Romaine', in *CRAI* (1977), pp. 486–503.

Beschaouch, A, 'Une Sodalité Africaine Méconnue: Les *Perexii*,' *CRAI* (1979), pp. 410–20.

Beschaouch, A, 'A propos de la mosaïque de Smirat', in *L'Africa romana* 4 (1987), pp. 677–80.

Beschaouch, A, 'Que savons-nous des Sodalités Africo-Romaines?', in *CRAI* (2006), pp. 1401–17.

Bieber, M, *The History of the Greek and Roman Theater* (Princeton, 1961).

Birley, A, *Septimius Severus: the African Emperor* (Garden City, N.Y., 1972)

Blunt, W, *The Ark in the Park* (London, 1976).

Bomgardner, D L, *An Analytical Study of North African Amphitheatres.* Ph.D. thesis: University of Michigan (Ann Arbor, 1984).

Bomgardner, D L, 'The Trade in Wild Animals for Roman Spectacles: A Green Perspective', in *Anthropozoologica* (1992), pp. 161–66.

Bomgardner, D L, *The Story of the Roman Amphitheatre* (London, 2000).

Bradbury, S., trans. *Selected Letters of Libanius from the Age of Constantius and Julian* (Liverpool, 2004).

Buonocore, M, *Epigrafia anfiteatrale dell'Occidente Romano III: Regiones Italiae II-V. Sicilia, Sardinia et Corsica* (Rome, 1992).

Cameron, A, *The Later Roman Empire* (London, 1993).

Capps Jr, E, 'Observations on the Painted *Venatio* of the Theatre at Corinth and on the Arrangments of the Arena', in *Hesperia Suppl.* 8 (1949), pp. 64–70.

Carabia, J, '*Felicissimus* ou la Perfection: L'epitaphe d'un jeune medecin d'Aix-en-Provence', in Mathe, R ed. *Etudes Antiques* (Limoges, 1985), pp. 111–31.

Carter, M, 'Gladiatorial Ranking and the 'SC de Pretiis Gladiatorum Minuendis' (CIL II 6278 = ILS 5163)', in *Phoenix* 57, No. 1/2 (2003), pp. 83–114.

Carter, M, 'Gladiatorial Combat: The Rules of Engagement', in *Classical Journal* 102, No. 2 (2006/07), pp. 97–114.

Chambers, T W, ed, *The Nicene and Post-Nicene Fathers. 1st Series. Vol. XII* (Grand Rapids, 1969).

Coarelli, F, 'L'armamento e le Classi dei Gladiatori', in La Regina, A., ed. *Sangue e Arena* (Rome, 2001), pp. 153–73.

Coleman, K M, 'Fatal Charades: Roman Executions Staged as Mythological Enactments', in *JRS* 80 (1990), pp. 44–73.

Coleman, K M, 'Launching into History: Aquatic Displays in the Early Empire', in *JRS* 83 (1993), pp. 48–74.

Coleman, K M, 'Ptolemy Philadelphus and the Roman Amphitheater', in W J Slater, ed. *Roman Theater and Society* (Ann Arbor, 1996), pp. 49–68.

Coleman, K M, '*Missio* at Halicarnassus', in *Harvard Studies in Classical Philology* 100 (2000), pp. 487–500.

Coleman, K M, *Bonds of Danger: Communal Life in the Gladiatorial Barracks of Ancient Rome* (Sydney, 2005).

Coleman, K M, *Martial: Liber Spectaculorum* (Oxford, 2006).

Courtney, E, *Musa Lapidaria: A Selection of Latin Verse Inscriptions* (Atlanta, 1995).

Davies, R, *Service in the Roman Army* (Edinburgh, 1989).

De Grossi Mazzorin, J, 'La Fauna Rinvenuta nell'Area della Meta Sudans nel Quadro Evolutivo degli Animali Domestici in Italia', in *Att del 1 Convegno Nazionale di Archeozoologia* (Rovigo, 1993), pp. 309–18.

Deniaux, E, 'L'importation d'animaux d'Afrique à l'époque républicaine et les relations de clientele', in *L'Africa romana* 13 (2000), pp. 1299–1307.

Desanges, J, 'Note sur la datation de l'expedition de Julius Maternus au pays d'*Agisymba*', in *Latomus* 23 (1964), pp. 713–25.

Desanges, J, *Recherches sur l'Activité des Méditerranéens aux Confins de l'Afrique* (Rome, 1978).

Devijver, H, 'Bears and Bisons…and the Roman Army', in *The Equestrian Officers of the Roman Imperial Army. Vol. 2* (Stuttgart, 1992), pp. 140–47.

Dinzelbacher, P, ed. *Mensch und Tier in der Geschichte Europas* (Stuttgart, 2000).

Dodge, H., *Spectacle in the Roman World* (London, 2011).

Dunbabin, K M D, *The Mosaics of Roman North Africa: Studies in Iconography and Patronage* (Oxford, 1978).

Dunbabin, K M D, *Mosaics of the Greek and Roman World* (Cambridge, 1999).

Edmondson, J C, 'The Cultural Politics of Public Spectacle in Rome and the Greek East, 167–166 BCE', in B Bergmann and C Kondoleon, eds. *The Art of Ancient Spectacle* (New Haven: 1999), pp. 77–95.

Egger, E, 'Bemerkungen zu einem Salzburger Mithräum', in *Wiener Studien* 79 (1966), pp. 613–23.

Egger, R, 'Aus römischen Grabinschriften', in *Sitzungsbericht der österreichischen Akademie der Wissenschaft* 252, No. 3 (1967), pp. 19–26.

Epplett, C, 'Anastasius and the *Venationes*', in *Nikephoros* (2004), pp. 221–30.

Evangelisti, S, *Epigrafia anfiteatrale dell'Occidente Romano VIII: Regio Italiae I, 1: Campania praeter Pompeios* (Rome, 2011).

Fora, M, *Epigrafia anfiteatrale dell'Occidente Romano IV: Regio Italiae I. Latium* (Rome, 1996).

Friedländer, L., *Roman Life and Manners under the Early Empire. Vol. 2* (New York, 1968).

Futrell, A, *Blood in the Arena: The Spectacle of Roman Power* (Austin, 1997).

Gabucci, A, ed. *The Colosseum* (Los Angeles, 2001).

Galsterer, H, 'Spiele und "Spiele": Die Organisation der *ludi Juvenales* in der Kaiserzeit', in *Athenaeum* 69 (1981), pp. 410–38.

Garnsey, P, 'Why Penalties Become Harsher: The Roman Case, Late Republic to Fourth Century Empire', in *Natural Law Forum* 13 (1968), pp. 141-62.

Gebhard, E, 'Protective Devices in Roman Theatres', in J. Wiseman, ed. *Studies in the Antiquities of Stobi. Vol. 2* (Belgrade, 1975), pp. 43–63.

Gilhus, I, *Animals, Gods and Humans: Changing attitudes to animals in Greek, Roman and early Christian ideas* (London, 2006).

Golvin, J.-C., *L'amphithéâtre romain: Essai sur la théorisation de sa forme et de ses functions* (Paris, 1988).

Gómez-Pantoja, J L, *Epigrafia Anfiteatrale dell'Occidente Romano VII: Baetica, Tarraconensis, Lusitania* (Rome, 2009).

Grant, R, *Early Christians and Animals* (London, 1999).

Gregori, G., *Epigrafia Anfiteatrale dell'Occidente Romano II: Regiones Italiae VI-XI* (Rome, 1989).

Harl, K, *Coinage in the Roman Economy* (Baltimore, 1996).

Harris, H A, *Sport in Greece and Rome* (London, 1972).

Hönle, A and Henze, A, *Römische Amphitheater und Stadien* (Feldmeilen, 1981).

Hopkins, K, *Death and Renewal* (Cambridge, 1983).

Hughes, J D, *Pan's Travail: Environmental Problems of the Ancient Greeks and Romans* (Baltimore, 1996).

Humphrey, J H, *Roman Circuses: Arenas for Chariot Racing* (Berkeley, 1986).

Jacobelli, L, *Gladiators at Pompeii* (Rome, 2003).

Jaczynowska, M, *Les Associations de la Jeunesse Romaine sous le Haut-Empire* (Wroclaw, 1978).

Jennison, G, *Animals for Show and Pleasure in Ancient Rome* (Manchester, 1937).

Jiménez Sánchez, J A, 'La crisis de las *venationes* clásicas. Desaparición o evolución de un espectáculo tradicional romano?', in *Ludica* 9 (2003), pp. 93-117.

Jones, A H M, *The Later Roman Empire* 2 vols. 3rd ed. (Baltimore, 1992).

Junkelmann, M, *Das Spiel mit dem Tod* (Mainz, 2000).

Kaster, RA, ed., *Cicero: Speech on Behalf of Publius Sestius* (Oxford, 2006).

Kehoe, D, *The Economics of Agriculture on Roman Imperial Estates in North Africa* (Göttingen, 1988).

Keller, O, *Die antike Tierwelt*. 2 vols. (Leipzig, 1913).

Kießling, E, *Sammelbuch griechischer Urkunden aus Ägypten. Vol. 6:2* (Wiesbaden, 1960).

Kockel, V, *Die Grabbauten vor dem Herkulaner Tor in Pompeji. Vol. I.* (Mainz, 1983).

Köhne, E, and C Ewigleben, *Gladiators and Caesars*, (Berkeley, 2000)

Krebs, W, 'Einige Transportprobleme der antiken Schiffahrt', in *Altertum* 11 (1965), pp. 86–101.

Kyle, D, 'Animal Spectacles in Ancient Rome: Meat and Meaning', in *Nikephoros* 7 (1995), pp. 181–205.

Kyle, D, *Spectacles of Death in Ancient Rome* (London, 1998).

Kyle, D, *Sport and Spectacle in the Ancient World* (Malden, Mass., 2007).

Lanciani, R, *Storia degli Scavi di Roma. Vol. II.* 2nd ed. (Rome, 1990).

Lavin, I, 'The Hunting Mosaics of Antioch and Their Sources', in *Dumbarton Oaks Papers* 17 (1963), pp. 179–286.

Lehmann, S, 'Ein spätantikes Relief mit Zirkusspielen aus Serdica in Thrakien', *BJ* 190 (1990), pp. 139–74.

Levick, B, 'The *Senatus Consultum* from Larinum', *JRS* 73 (1983), pp. 97–115.

Liebeschuetz, W, 'The Syriarch in the Fourth Century', in *Historia* 8 (1959), pp. 113–26.

Loisel, G, *Histoire des ménageries de l'Antiquité à nos jours* (Paris, 1912).

Mackay, C, *The Breakdown of the Roman Republic: From Oligarchy to Empire* (Cambridge, 2009).

MacKinnon, M, 'Supplying Exotic Animals for the Roman Amphitheatre Games: New Reconstructions combining Archaeological, Ancient Textual, Historical and Ethnographic Data', in *Mouseion* 6 (2006), pp. 137–61.

MacMullen, R, 'What Difference did Christianity Make?' in R MacMullen *Changes in the Roman Empire: Essays in the Ordinary* (Princeton, 1990), pp. 142–55.

Mahoney, A, *Roman Sports and Spectacles: A Sourcebook* (Newburyport, MA, 2001)

Mann, C, *Die Gladiatoren* (Munich, 2013).

Marrou, H I, 'Sur deux mosaïques de la villa romaine de Piazza Armerina', in H I Marrou *Christiana Tempora: mélanges d'histoire, d'archéologie, d'épigraphie et de patristique* (Rome, 1978), pp. 253–95.

Mattingly, D, 'Africa: a landscape of opportunity?', in D Mattingly, ed, *Dialogues in Roman Imperialism* (Portsmouth, R I, 1997), pp. 117–39.

Mattingly, H, *Roman Coins* (London, 1927).

Merten, E, 'Venationes in der Historia Augusta', in *Historia-Augusta Colloquium 1986–89* (Bonn, 1991), pp. 139–78.

Millar, F, *The Roman Near East* (Cambridge, Mass., 1993).

Most, G, '*Disiecta membra poetae*: The Rhetoric of Dismemberment in Neronian Poetry', in H Hexter and D Selden eds. *Innovations of Antiquity* (New York, 1992), pp. 391–419.

Musurillo, H, *Acts of the Christian Martyrs*. 2nd ed. (Oxford, 2000).

Nixon, CEV and BS Rodgers, *In Praise of Later Roman Emperors: The Panegyrici Latini* (Berkeley, 1994).

Oliver, J H, and REA Palmer, 'Minutes of an Act of the Roman Senate', in *Hesperia* 24 (1955), pp. 320–49.

Orth, F, 'Jagd', in *Real-Encyclopädie* Vol. IX, 1 (Stuttgart, 1914), pp. 558–604.

Pearson, J, *Arena: The Story of the Colosseum* (New York, 1973).

Pharr, C, trans. *The Theodosian Code and Novels and the Sirmondian Constitutions* (New York, 1969).

Picard, G C, *Castellum Dimmidi* (Paris, 1944).

Pighi, I, *De Ludis Saecularibus Populi Romani Quiritium* (Amsterdam, 1965).

Plass, P, *The Game of Death in Ancient Rome: arena sport and political suicide* (Madison, WI, 1995).

Platner, S, and T. Ashby, *A Topographical Dictionary of Ancient Rome* (London, 1929).

Potter, D, 'Performance, Power, and Justice in the High Empire', in W J, Slater, ed. *Roman Theater and Society* (Ann Arbor, 1996), pp. 129–60.

Rea, R, 'Gli animali per la *Venatio*: cattura, trasporto, custodia', in A La Regina, ed. *Sangue e Arena* (Rome, 2001), pp. 245–75.

Rice, E, *The Grand Procession of Ptolemy Philadelphus* (London, 1983).

Ritti, T, and S Yilmaz, (1998) 'Gladiatori e Venationes a Hierapolis di Frigia', in *Atti della Accademia Nazionale dei Lincei. Memorie. Classe di Scienze Morali, Historiche e Filogiche. Memorie* 10.4 (1998), pp. 439–543.

Robert, L, 'Monuments de Gladiateurs dans l'Orient Grec', in *Hellenica* 7 (1949), pp. 126–51.

Robert, L. *Les Gladiateurs dans l'Orient Grec*. 2nd ed. (Amsterdam, 1971).

Robinson, O F, *Ancient Rome: City Planning and Administration* (London, 1994).

Rosenblum, M, *Luxorius: A Latin Poet among the Vandals* (New York, 1961).

Rostovtzeff, M, *Excavations at Dura-Europos III: The Palace of the Dux Ripae and the Dolicheneum* (New Haven, 1952).

Roueché, C, *Performers and Partisans at Aphrodisias in the Roman and Late Roman Periods* (London, 1993).

Rudd, N., trans. and Barr, W, (1991) Juvenal: The Satires. Oxford.

Sabbatini Tumolesi, P, *Epigrafia anfiteatrale dell'Occidente Romano I: Roma* (Rome, 1988).

Salomonson, J W, 'The Fancy Dress Banquet', in *BABesch* 35 (1960), pp. 25–55.

Schulten, A, 'Legio III Augusta', in *Real-Encyclopädie* Vol. XII, 2 (Stuttgart, 1925), pp. 1493–1505.

Scobie, A, 'Spectator Security and Comfort at Gladiatorial Games', in *Nikephoros* (1988), pp. 191–243.

Scullard, H H, *The Elephant in the Greek and Roman World* (London, 1974).

Shaw, B D, (1981) 'Climate, environment, and history: the case of Roman North Africa', in T M L Wigley, M J Ingram, and G Farmer, eds. *Climate and History: Studies in past climates and their impact on Man* (Cambridge, 1981), pp. 379–403.

Shaw, B D, 'The Passion of Perpetua', in *Past & Present* 139 (1993), pp. 3–45.

Shelton, Jo-Ann, 'Elephants, Pompey, and the Reports of Popular Displeasure in 55 BC', in S N Byrne and E P Cuerva, eds. *Veritatis Amicitiaeque Causa: Essays in Honor of Anna Lydia Motto and John R Clark* (Wauconda, Ill., 1999), pp. 231–71.

Shelton, Jo-Ann, (2004) 'Dancing and Dying: The Display of Elephants in Ancient Roman Arenas', in M Joyal and R Egan, eds. *Daimonopylai* (Winnipeg, 2004), pp. 363–82.

Shelton, Jo-Ann, (2007) 'Beastly Spectacles in the Ancient Mediterranean World', in L Kalof, ed. *A Cultural History of Animals in Antiquity*. Vol. I (Oxford, 2007), pp. 97–126.

Spawforth, J S, 'Corinth, Argos, and the Imperial Cult: Pseudo-Julian, Letters 198', in *Hesperia* 63 (1994), pp. 211–32.

Sperber, D, *Roman Palestine 200–400: Money and Prices* (Ramat-Gan, Israel, 1974).

Ternes, C M, *Römisches Deutschland* (Stuttgart, 1986).

Thompson, L, 'The Martyrdom of Polycarp: Death in the Roman Games', in *The Journal of Religion* 82, 1 (2002), pp. 27–52.

Toynbee, J M C, *Animals in Roman Life and Art*. 2nd ed. (London, 1996).

Tremel, J, *Magica Agonistica: Fluchtafeln in antiken Sport* (Hildesheim, 2004).

Velkov, V, and G. Alexandrov "*Venatio* Caesariana': Eine neue Inschrift aus Montana (Moesia Inferior)', in *Chiron* 18 (1988), pp. 271–77.

Veyne, P, ed. *A History of Private Life. From Pagan Rome to Byzantium* (Cambridge, Mass., 1987).

Ville, G, 'Les Jeux de Gladiateurs dans l'Empire Chrétien', in *MEFRA* 72 (1960), pp. 273–335.

Ville, G, *La gladiature en Occident des origines à la mort de Domitian* (Rome, 1981).

Vismara, C, and M, Caldelli *Epigrafia Anfiteatrale dell'Occidente Romano V: Alpes Maritimae, Gallia Narbonensis, Tres Galliae, Germaniae, Britannia* (Rome, 2000).

Volbach, W F, *Elfenbeinarbeiten der Spätantike und der frühen Mittelalters.* (Mainz, 1976).

Von Petrikovits, H, 'Die Spezialgebäude römischer Legionslager', in *Das römische Rheinland: archäologische Forschungen seit 1945* (Cologne, 1960), pp. 229–52.

Ward-Perkins, B, *From Classical Antiquity to the Middle Ages: Urban Public Building in Northern and Central Italy AD 300–500* (Oxford, 1984).

Watson, G R, *The Roman Soldier*. 3rd ed. (Ithaca, N.Y., 1993).

Weeber, K-W, *Panem et Circenses* (Mainz, 1994).

Weege, F, 'Oskische Grabmalerei', in *JDAI* 24 (1909), pp. 99–162.

Welch, K, 'Greek stadia and Roman spectacles: Asia, Athens, and the tomb of Herodes Atticus', in *JRA* 11 (1998), pp. 117–45.

Welch, K, *The Roman Amphitheatre: From Its Origins to the Colosseum*. 2nd ed. (New York, 2009).

Welles, C B, et al., *The Excavations at Dura-Europos: Final Report V, Part I.* (New Haven, 1959).

Wiedemann, T, *Emperors and Gladiators*. 2nd ed. (New York, 1995).

Wilson, R J, *Piazza Armerina* (London, 1983).

Wistrand, M, *Entertainment and Violence in Ancient Rome: The attitudes of Roman writers of the first century A.D.* (Gothenburg, 1992).

# Index